JENNY sparks™

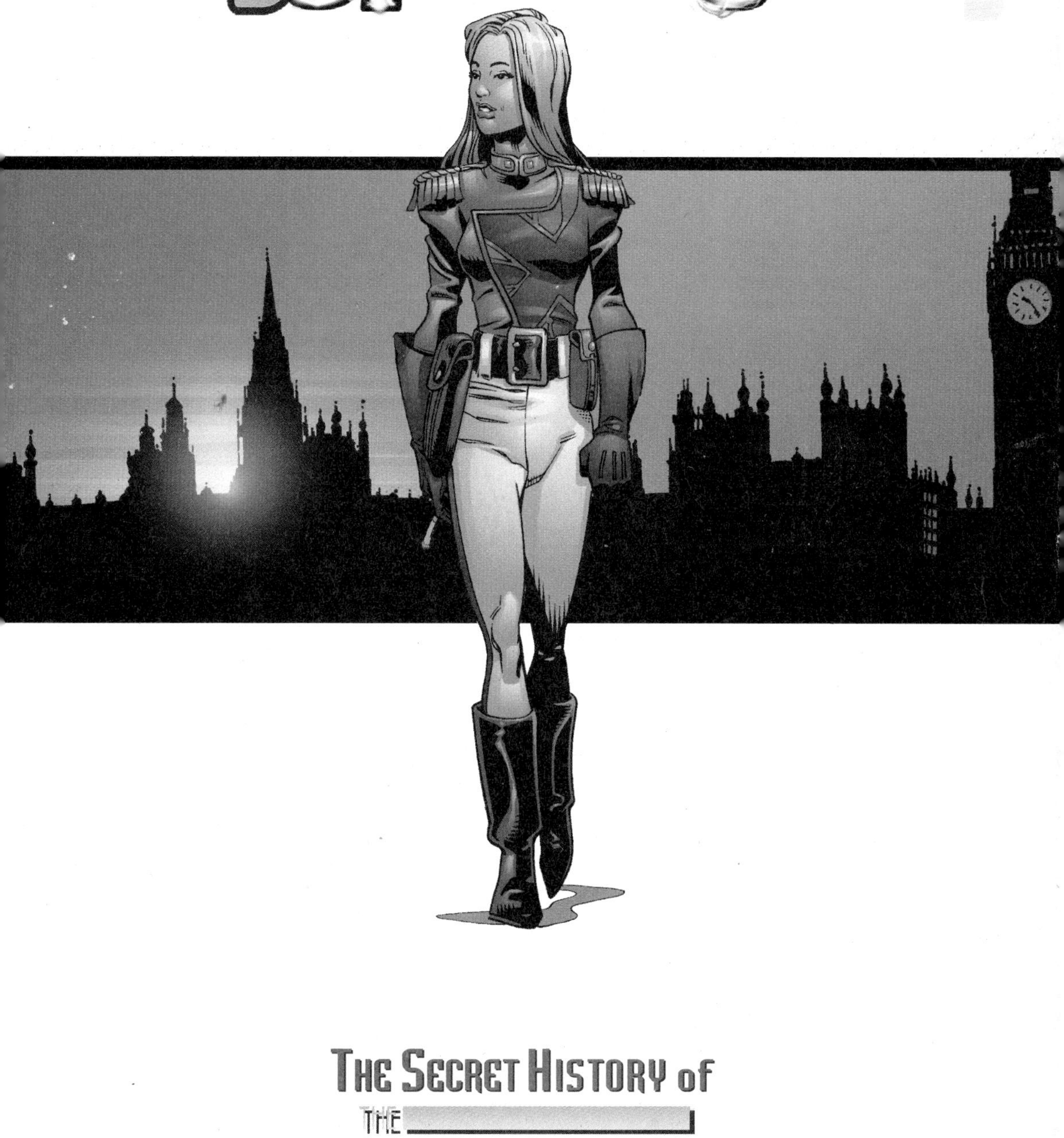

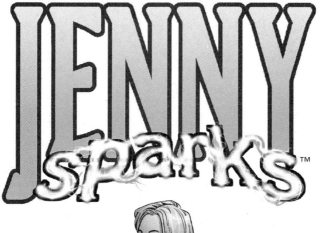

The Secret History of The Authority™

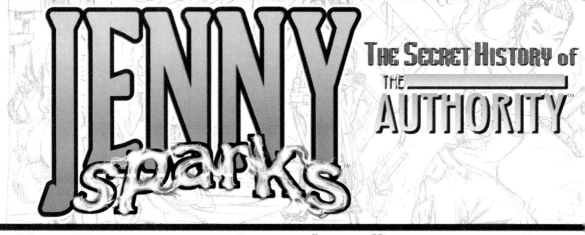

JENNY sparks

THE SECRET HISTORY of THE AUTHORITY

MARK MILLAR
WRITER

JOHN McCREA
PENCILER

JAMES HODGKINS
INKER

IAN HANNIN
COLORIST

BILL O'NEIL
LETTERER

JOHN LAYMAN
EDITOR

AMBER BENNETT & DAVID BARON
BOOK DESIGN

JOHN McCREA & DAVID BARON
COVER & COVER COLORS

THE AUTHORITY CREATED BY WARREN ELLIS AND BRYAN HITCH

JENNY SPARKS: THE SECRET HISTORY OF THE AUTHORITY.
Published by WildStorm Productions, an imprint of DC Comics. Editorial
offices 7910 Ivanhoe Ave #438 La Jolla, CA 92037. Cover and
compilation copyright © 2001 WildStorm Productions. All Rights
Reserved. Originally published in single magazine form as
JENNY SPARKS: THE SECRET HISTORY OF THE AUTHORITY 1-5.
Copyright © 2000, 2001 WildStorm Productions. All rights reserved.
All chracters, their distinctive likenesses and related indicia featured in
this publication are trademarks of DC Comics. The stories, characters,
and incidents featured in this publication are entirely fictional.
Printed in Canada.
ISBN: 1-56389-769-5
DC Comics. A division of Warner Bros. - An AOL Time Warner Company

CENTURY

An introduction
by
Warren Ellis

When Tom Raney and Randy Elliott drew Jenny Sparks for the first time, she was exactly what STORMWATCH and the 20th Century needed: cranky, wreathed in a cloud of pollutants, running headlong from 1900. When Bryan Hitch and Paul Neary drew her for her last year, she was what the millennium-turn and THE AUTHORITY needed: glamorous, wry, looking back with hard-won irony. When John McCrea drew her for this book, she was exactly what was required: clever, knowing, youthful but never really young.

I'm here because I created Jenny Sparks, and gave her her mad dash through the century. And I killed her, too. Because the great heroes of fable had deaths as well as lives. Robin Hood fires his last arrow to mark his gravesite. Cuchulain's guts are thrown upon the ground. Arthur is carried off to Avalon. Jenny Sparks electrocutes God seconds before the turn of the popular millennium and so ceases to be. Okay, it doesn't have quite the simplicity and epic romance of the others, but I'm the bloody writer and I'll execute God if I want.

I created Jenny Sparks and I was pretty much the only one to write her during her three years or so of existence as a character. Mark Millar -or "Greta," as they know him on the transsexual donkey show circuit- decided that he wanted to cover the other ninety-odd years of her life as counterpoint to THE AUTHORITY, which he was now writing. Having given up those characters to the creative community, I waited with fascination to see what he'd do. Mark is one of the smartest writers I know, and also the most unpredictable. In person, I'd trust him about as far as I could throw him -about fifteen feet- but as a writer I'll go anywhere he goes. Creatively, the man is berserk in a compelling, Rasputin-like way - you know what he's doing is Wrong and Sick but you just have to look.

Read the damn thing. He doesn't disappoint. It wasn't what I expected. Which is just what I wanted.

Jenny Sparks is dead, but, like any women you miss, it's nice to see her come out for one last dance.

Warren Ellis
Southend
March 2001

Chapter One
Doctor's Orders

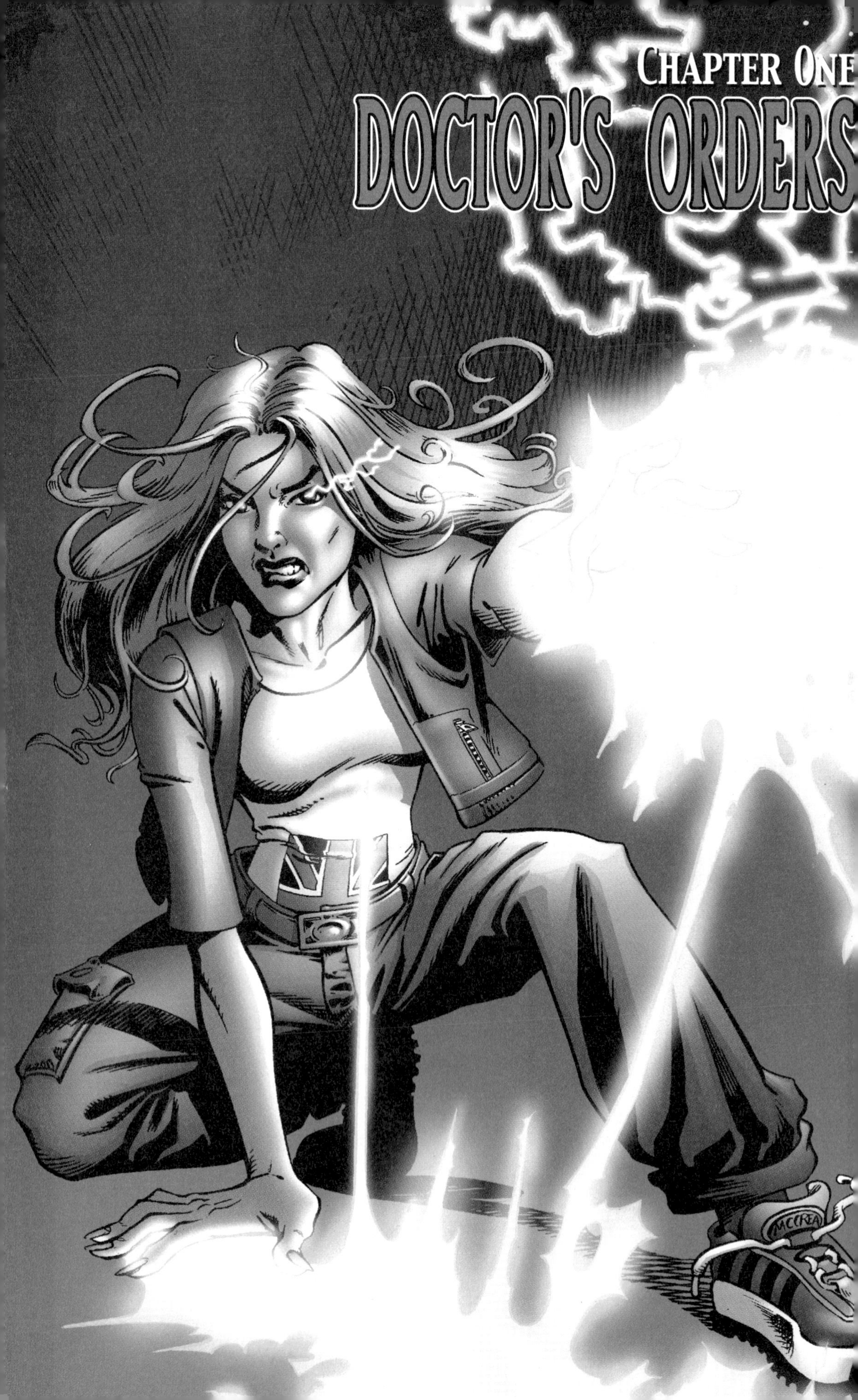
MCCREA

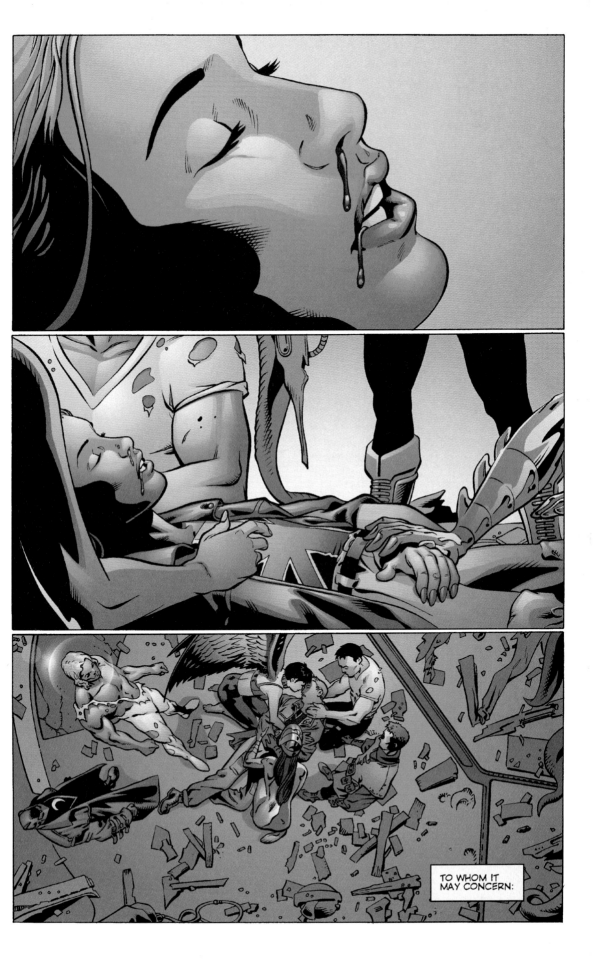

TO WHOM IT
MAY CONCERN:

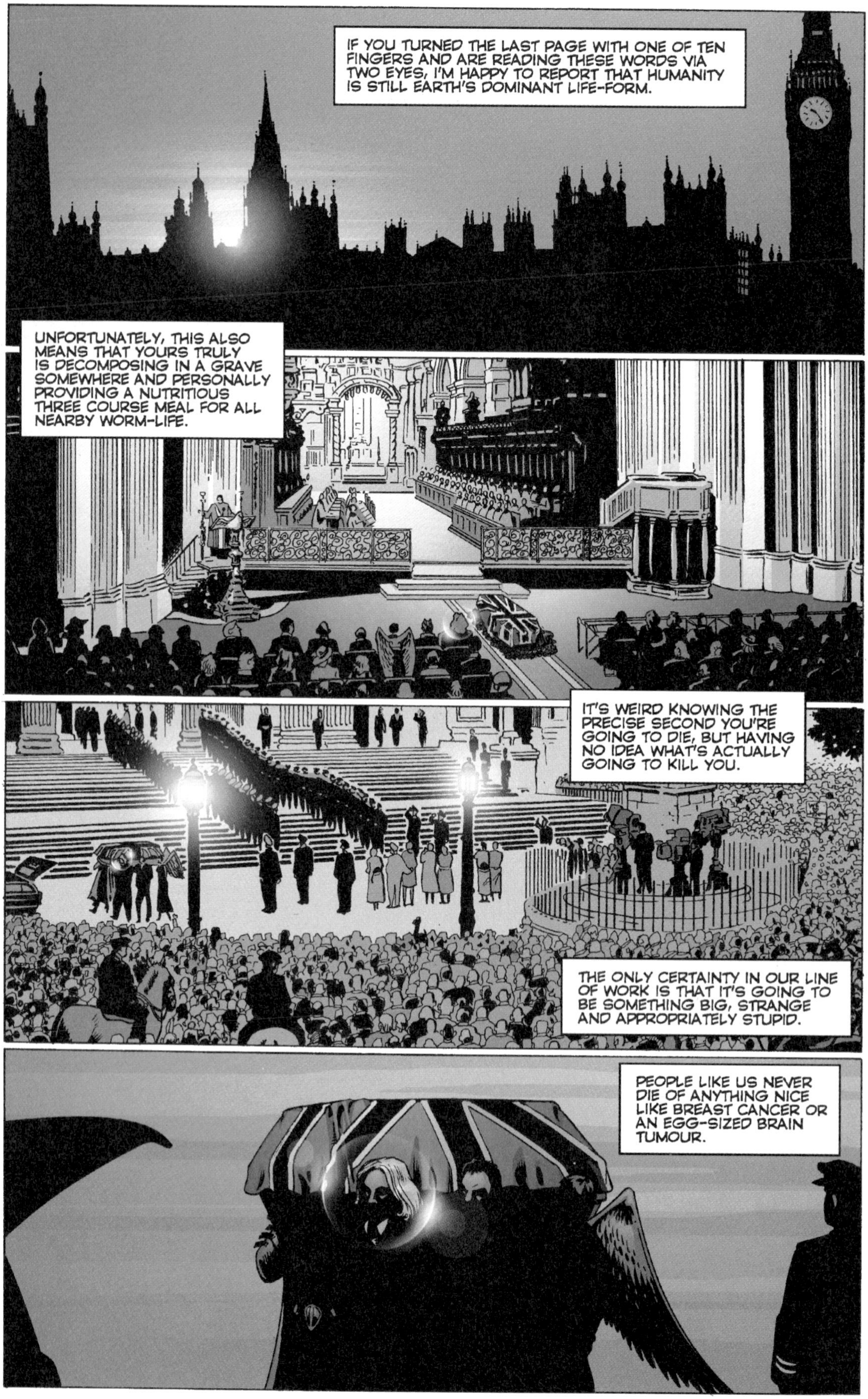
IF YOU TURNED THE LAST PAGE WITH ONE OF TEN FINGERS AND ARE READING THESE WORDS VIA TWO EYES, I'M HAPPY TO REPORT THAT HUMANITY IS STILL EARTH'S DOMINANT LIFE-FORM.
UNFORTUNATELY, THIS ALSO MEANS THAT YOURS TRULY IS DECOMPOSING IN A GRAVE SOMEWHERE AND PERSONALLY PROVIDING A NUTRITIOUS THREE COURSE MEAL FOR ALL NEARBY WORM-LIFE.
IT'S WEIRD KNOWING THE PRECISE SECOND YOU'RE GOING TO DIE, BUT HAVING NO IDEA WHAT'S ACTUALLY GOING TO KILL YOU.
THE ONLY CERTAINTY IN OUR LINE OF WORK IS THAT IT'S GOING TO BE SOMETHING BIG, STRANGE AND APPROPRIATELY STUPID.
PEOPLE LIKE US NEVER DIE OF ANYTHING NICE LIKE BREAST CANCER OR AN EGG-SIZED BRAIN TUMOUR.

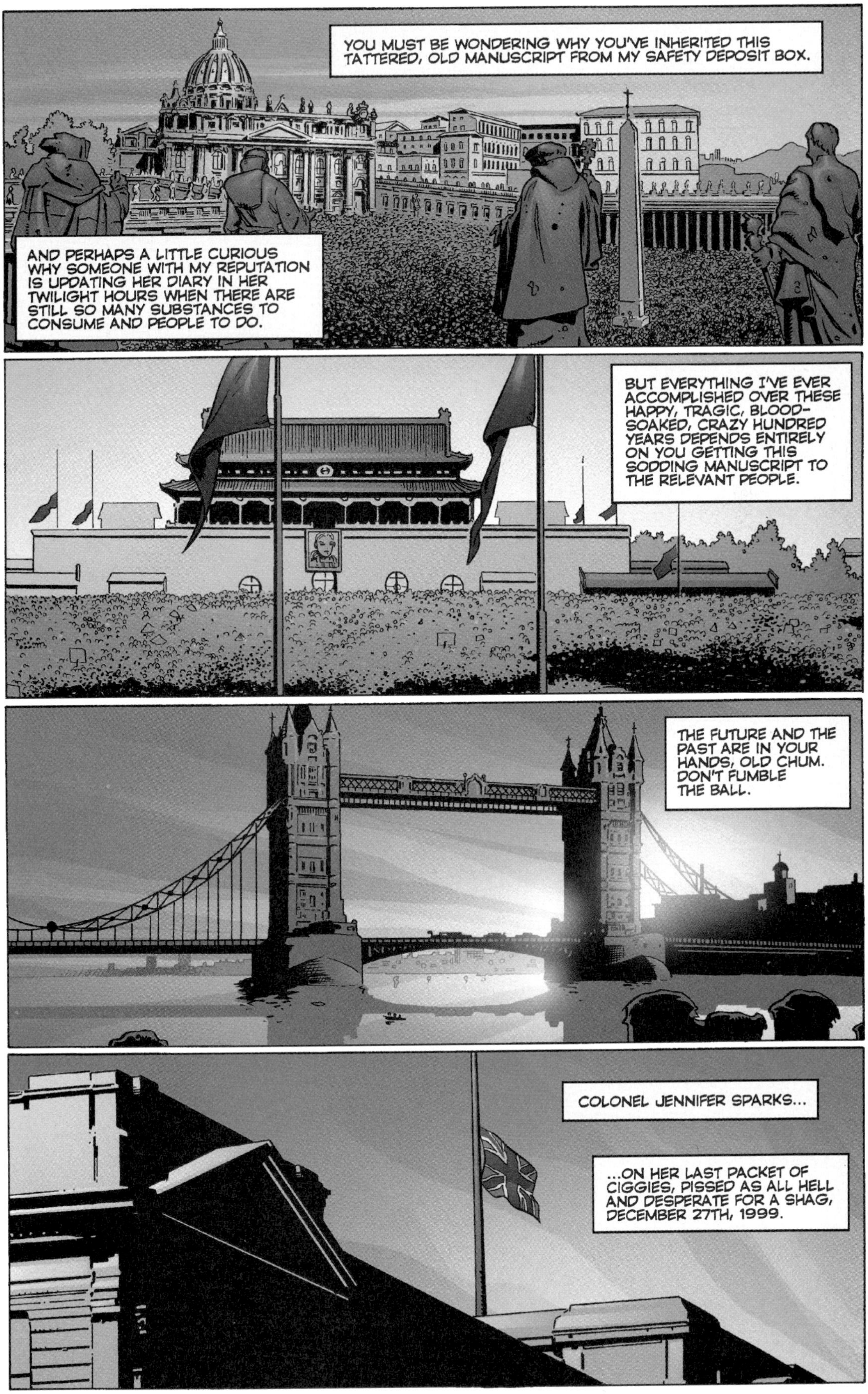
YOU MUST BE WONDERING WHY YOU'VE INHERITED THIS TATTERED, OLD MANUSCRIPT FROM MY SAFETY DEPOSIT BOX.
AND PERHAPS A LITTLE CURIOUS WHY SOMEONE WITH MY REPUTATION IS UPDATING HER DIARY IN HER TWILIGHT HOURS WHEN THERE ARE STILL SO MANY SUBSTANCES TO CONSUME AND PEOPLE TO DO.
BUT EVERYTHING I'VE EVER ACCOMPLISHED OVER THESE HAPPY, TRAGIC, BLOOD-SOAKED, CRAZY HUNDRED YEARS DEPENDS ENTIRELY ON YOU GETTING THIS SODDING MANUSCRIPT TO THE RELEVANT PEOPLE.
THE FUTURE AND THE PAST ARE IN YOUR HANDS, OLD CHUM. DON'T FUMBLE THE BALL.
COLONEL JENNIFER SPARKS...
...ON HER LAST PACKET OF CIGGIES, PISSED AS ALL HELL AND DESPERATE FOR A SHAG, DECEMBER 27TH, 1999.

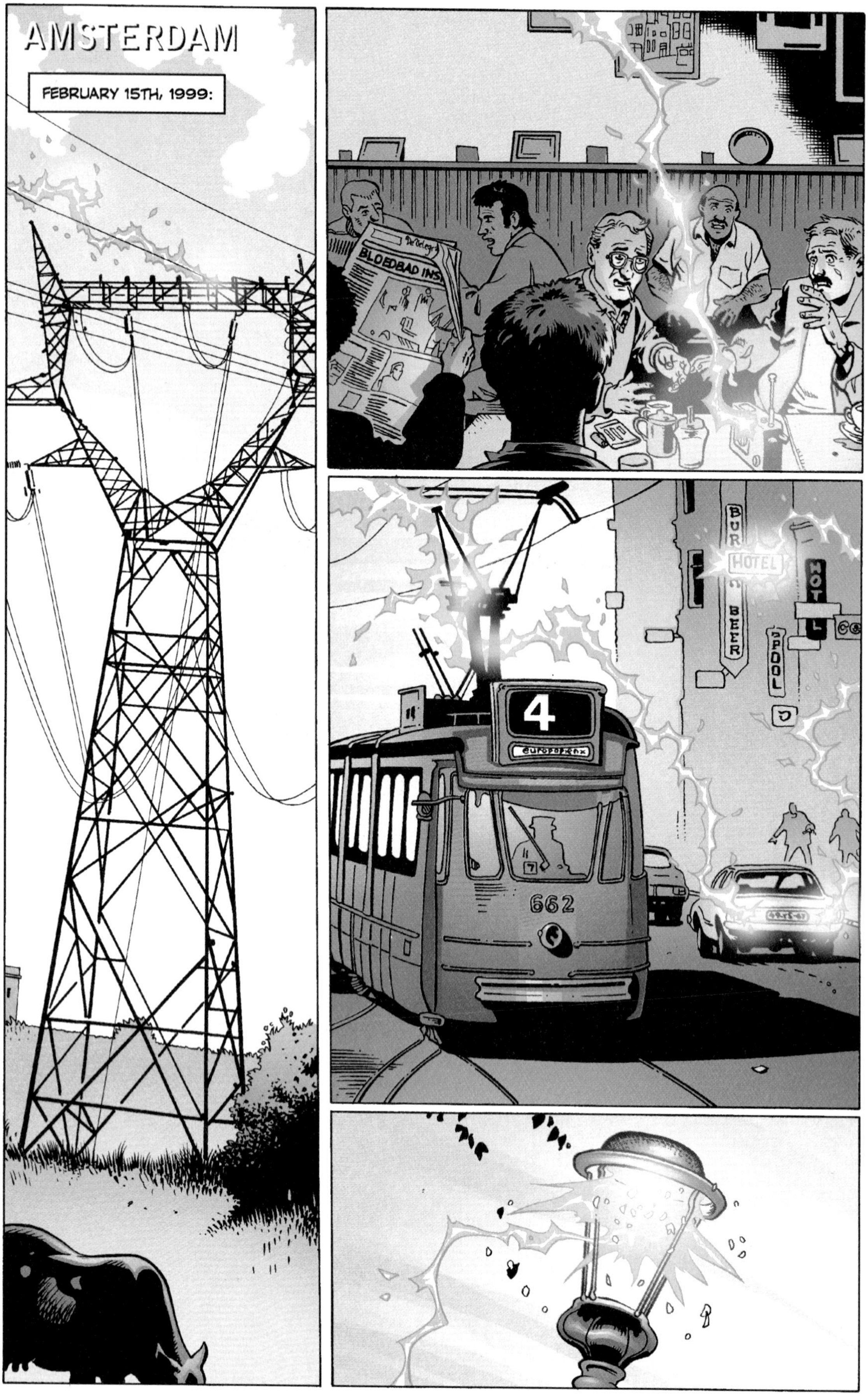

AMSTERDAM
FEBRUARY 15TH, 1999:
BLOEDBAD
4
662
HOTEL
BEER

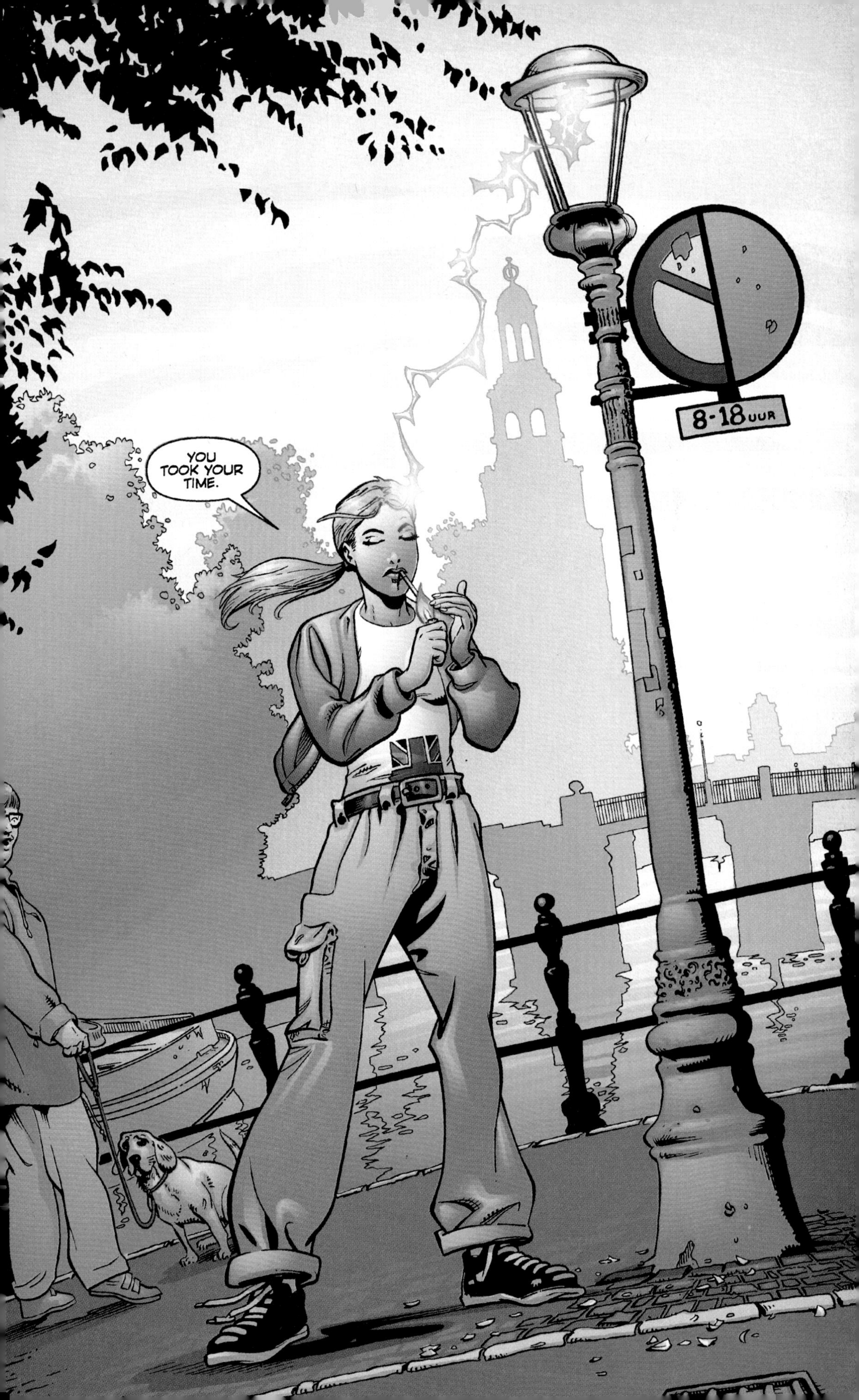
8-18 UUR
YOU TOOK YOUR TIME.

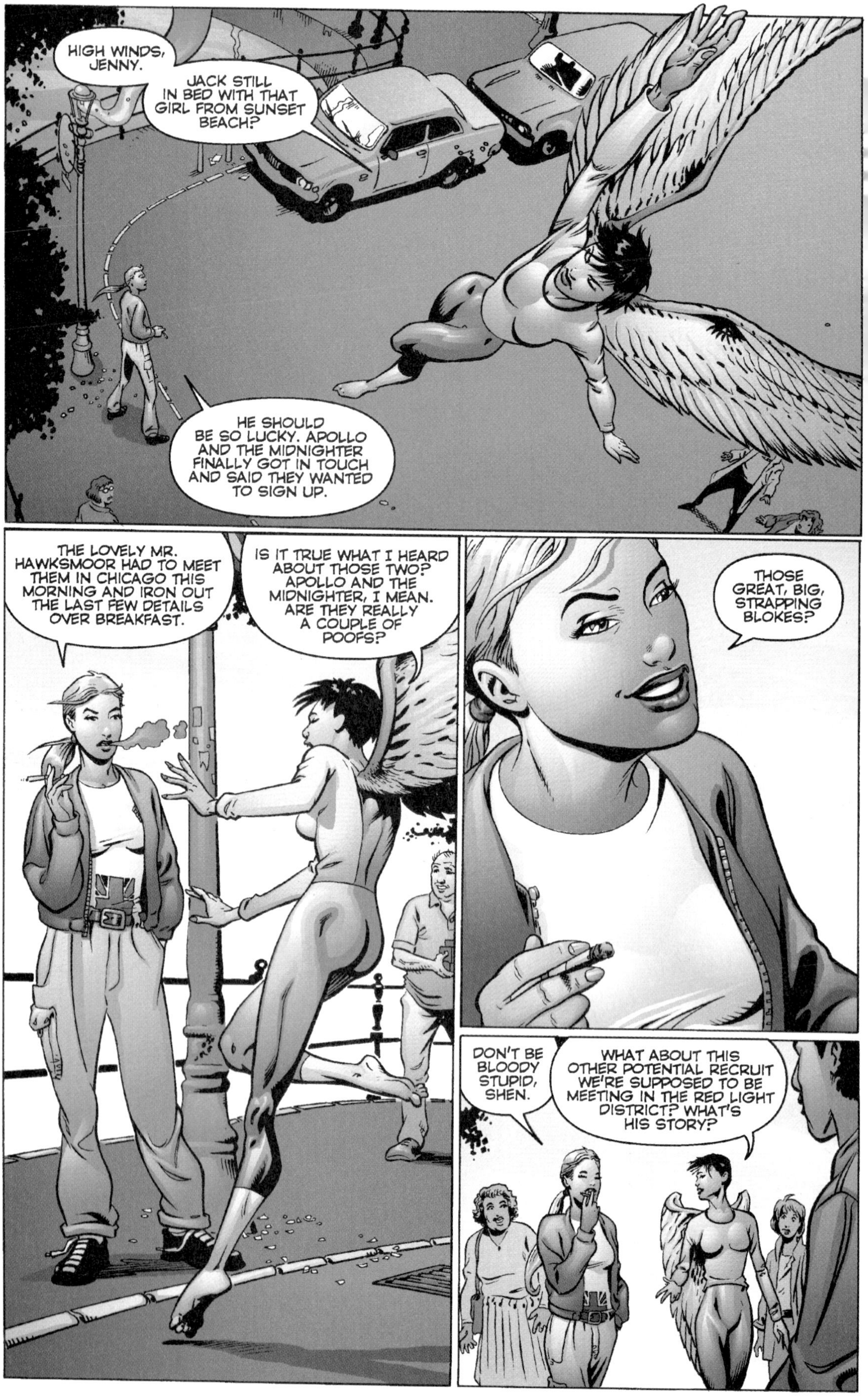
HIGH WINDS, JENNY.
JACK STILL IN BED WITH THAT GIRL FROM SUNSET BEACH?
HE SHOULD BE SO LUCKY. APOLLO AND THE MIDNIGHTER FINALLY GOT IN TOUCH AND SAID THEY WANTED TO SIGN UP.
THE LOVELY MR. HAWKSMOOR HAD TO MEET THEM IN CHICAGO THIS MORNING AND IRON OUT THE LAST FEW DETAILS OVER BREAKFAST.
IS IT TRUE WHAT I HEARD ABOUT THOSE TWO? APOLLO AND THE MIDNIGHTER, I MEAN. ARE THEY REALLY A COUPLE OF POOFS?
THOSE GREAT, BIG, STRAPPING BLOKES?
DON'T BE BLOODY STUPID, SHEN.
WHAT ABOUT THIS OTHER POTENTIAL RECRUIT WE'RE SUPPOSED TO BE MEETING IN THE RED LIGHT DISTRICT? WHAT'S HIS STORY?

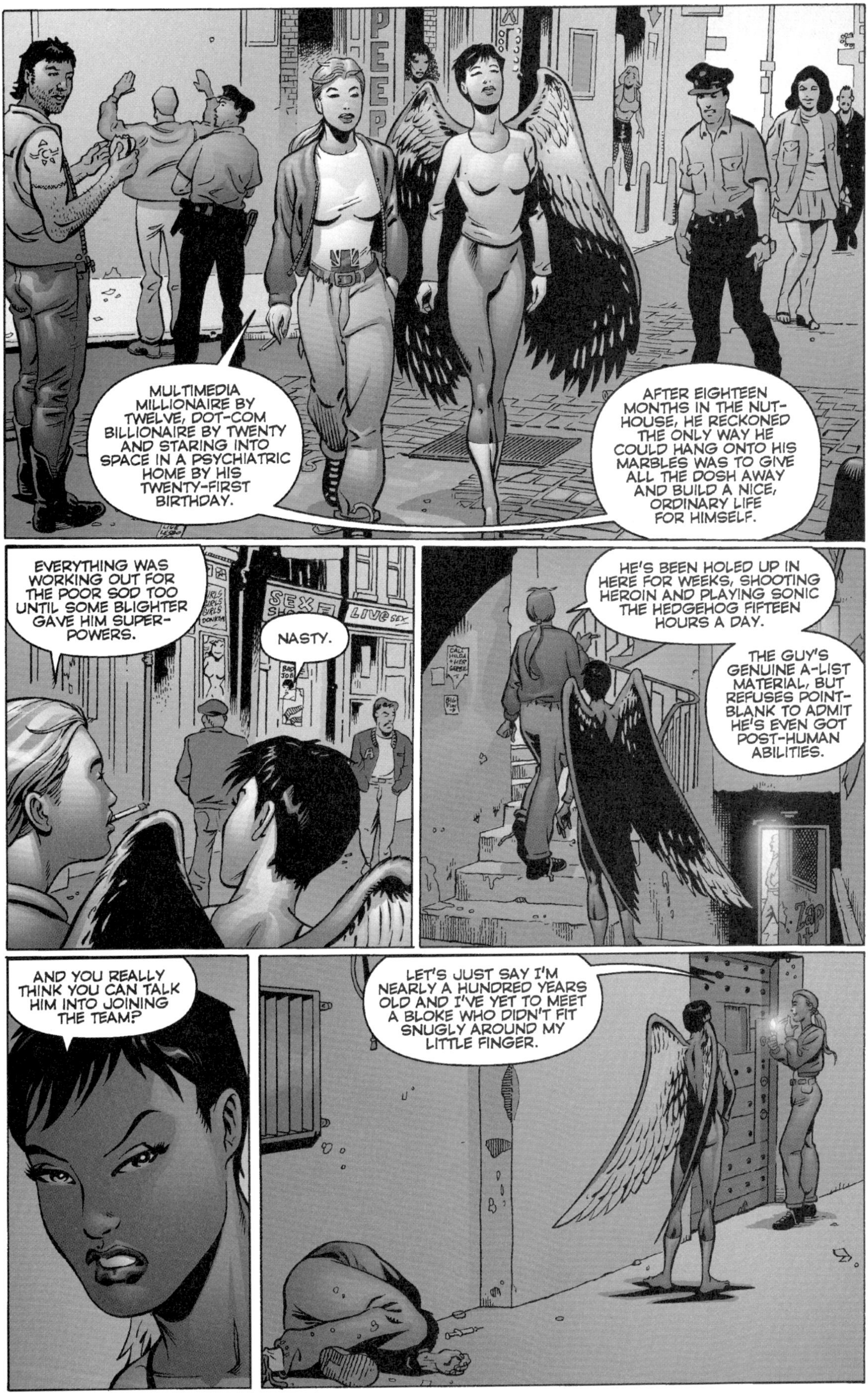
PEEP
MULTIMEDIA MILLIONAIRE BY TWELVE, DOT-COM BILLIONAIRE BY TWENTY AND STARING INTO SPACE IN A PSYCHIATRIC HOME BY HIS TWENTY-FIRST BIRTHDAY.
AFTER EIGHTEEN MONTHS IN THE NUT-HOUSE, HE RECKONED THE ONLY WAY HE COULD HANG ONTO HIS MARBLES WAS TO GIVE ALL THE DOSH AWAY AND BUILD A NICE, ORDINARY LIFE FOR HIMSELF.
EVERYTHING WAS WORKING OUT FOR THE POOR SOD TOO UNTIL SOME BLIGHTER GAVE HIM SUPER-POWERS.
SEX
LIVE SEX
NASTY.
HE'S BEEN HOLED UP IN HERE FOR WEEKS, SHOOTING HEROIN AND PLAYING SONIC THE HEDGEHOG FIFTEEN HOURS A DAY.
THE GUY'S GENUINE A-LIST MATERIAL, BUT REFUSES POINT-BLANK TO ADMIT HE'S EVEN GOT POST-HUMAN ABILITIES.
AND YOU REALLY THINK YOU CAN TALK HIM INTO JOINING THE TEAM?
LET'S JUST SAY I'M NEARLY A HUNDRED YEARS OLD AND I'VE YET TO MEET A BLOKE WHO DIDN'T FIT SNUGLY AROUND MY LITTLE FINGER.

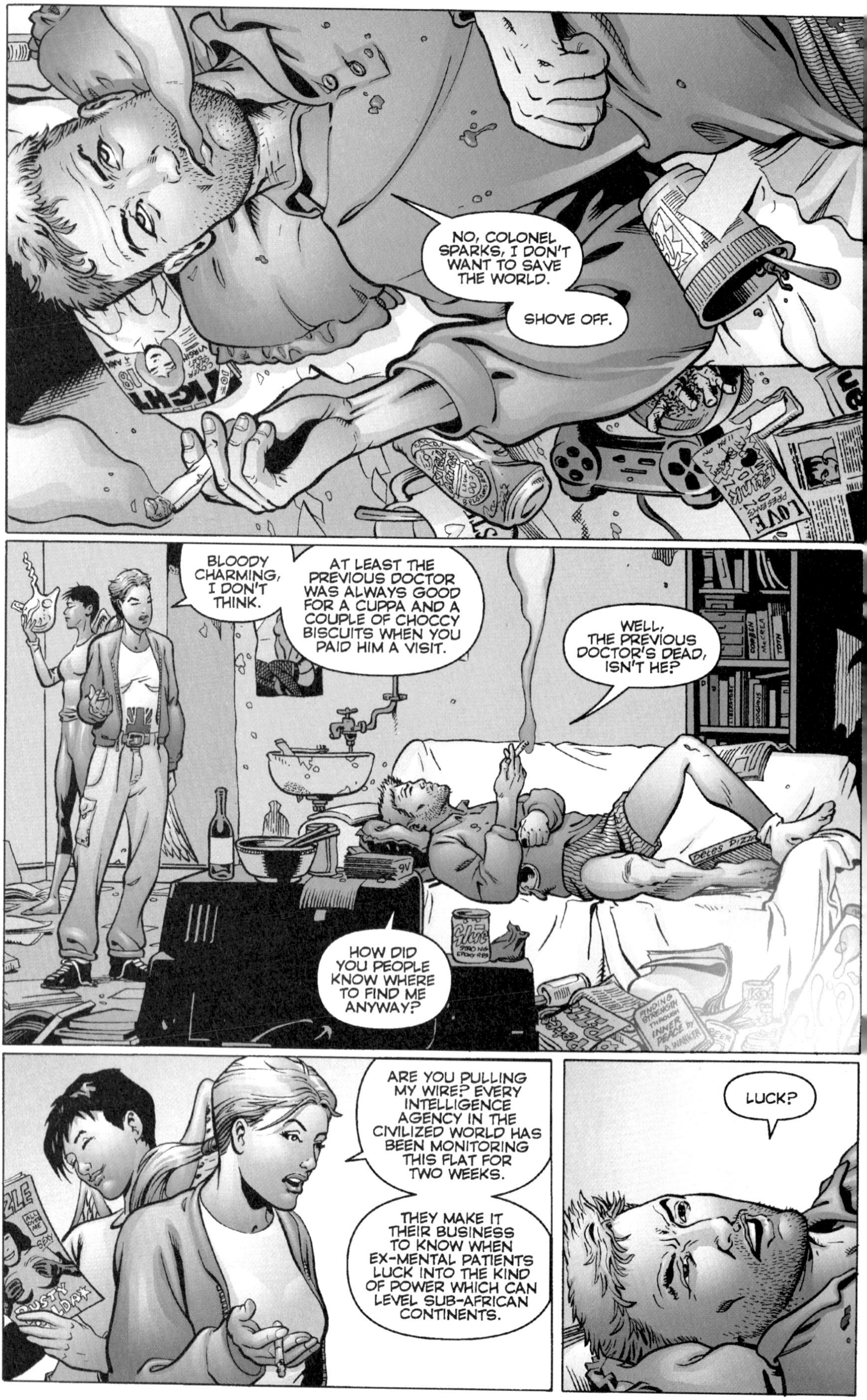

NO, COLONEL SPARKS, I DON'T WANT TO SAVE THE WORLD.
SHOVE OFF.
BLOODY CHARMING, I DON'T THINK.
AT LEAST THE PREVIOUS DOCTOR WAS ALWAYS GOOD FOR A CUPPA AND A COUPLE OF CHOCCY BISCUITS WHEN YOU PAID HIM A VISIT.
WELL, THE PREVIOUS DOCTOR'S DEAD, ISN'T HE?
HOW DID YOU PEOPLE KNOW WHERE TO FIND ME ANYWAY?
ARE YOU PULLING MY WIRE? EVERY INTELLIGENCE AGENCY IN THE CIVILIZED WORLD HAS BEEN MONITORING THIS FLAT FOR TWO WEEKS.
THEY MAKE IT THEIR BUSINESS TO KNOW WHEN EX-MENTAL PATIENTS LUCK INTO THE KIND OF POWER WHICH CAN LEVEL SUB-AFRICAN CONTINENTS.
LUCK?

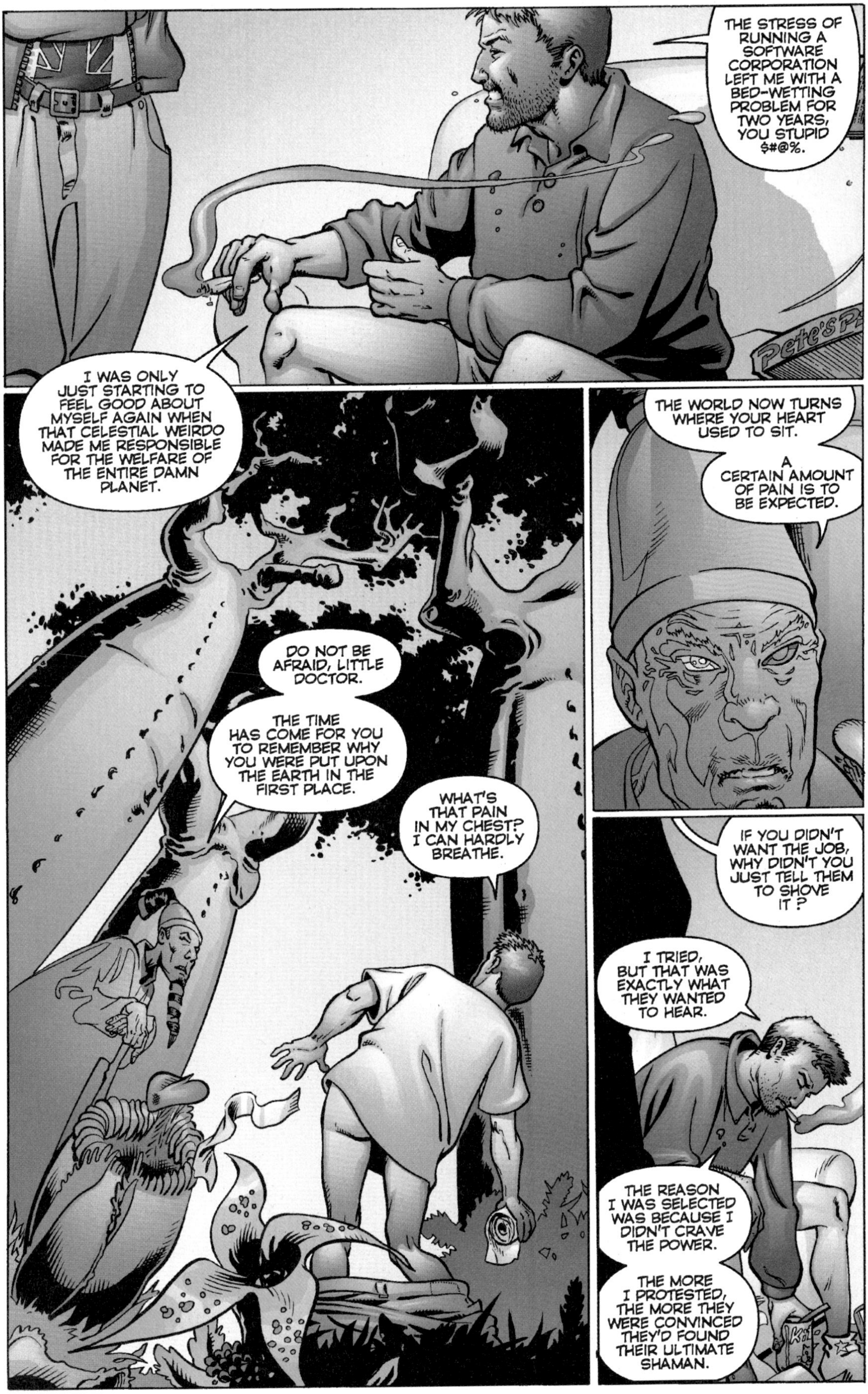

THE STRESS OF RUNNING A SOFTWARE CORPORATION LEFT ME WITH A BED-WETTING PROBLEM FOR TWO YEARS, YOU STUPID $#@%.
Pete's P
I WAS ONLY JUST STARTING TO FEEL GOOD ABOUT MYSELF AGAIN WHEN THAT CELESTIAL WEIRDO MADE ME RESPONSIBLE FOR THE WELFARE OF THE ENTIRE DAMN PLANET.
DO NOT BE AFRAID, LITTLE DOCTOR.
THE TIME HAS COME FOR YOU TO REMEMBER WHY YOU WERE PUT UPON THE EARTH IN THE FIRST PLACE.
WHAT'S THAT PAIN IN MY CHEST? I CAN HARDLY BREATHE.
THE WORLD NOW TURNS WHERE YOUR HEART USED TO SIT.
A CERTAIN AMOUNT OF PAIN IS TO BE EXPECTED.
IF YOU DIDN'T WANT THE JOB, WHY DIDN'T YOU JUST TELL THEM TO SHOVE IT ?
I TRIED, BUT THAT WAS EXACTLY WHAT THEY WANTED TO HEAR.
THE REASON I WAS SELECTED WAS BECAUSE I DIDN'T CRAVE THE POWER.
THE MORE I PROTESTED, THE MORE THEY WERE CONVINCED THEY'D FOUND THEIR ULTIMATE SHAMAN.

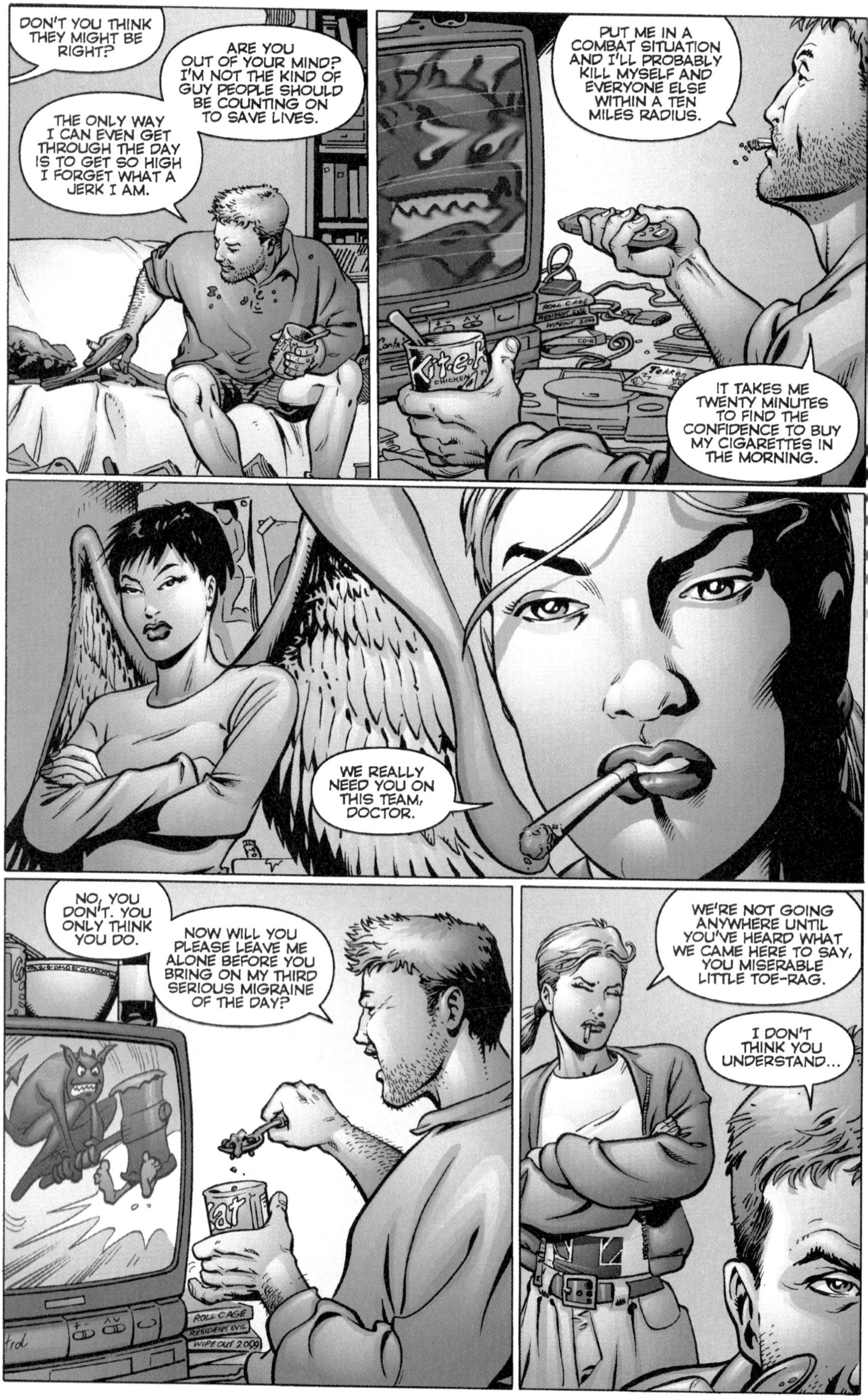
DON'T YOU THINK THEY MIGHT BE RIGHT?
ARE YOU OUT OF YOUR MIND? I'M NOT THE KIND OF GUY PEOPLE SHOULD BE COUNTING ON TO SAVE LIVES.
THE ONLY WAY I CAN EVEN GET THROUGH THE DAY IS TO GET SO HIGH I FORGET WHAT A JERK I AM.
PUT ME IN A COMBAT SITUATION AND I'LL PROBABLY KILL MYSELF AND EVERYONE ELSE WITHIN A TEN MILES RADIUS.
ROLL CAGE
RESIDENT EVIL
WIPEOUT 2097
CD-R
Tekken
Kit-e-h
CHICKEN
IT TAKES ME TWENTY MINUTES TO FIND THE CONFIDENCE TO BUY MY CIGARETTES IN THE MORNING.
WE REALLY NEED YOU ON THIS TEAM, DOCTOR.
NO, YOU DON'T. YOU ONLY THINK YOU DO.
NOW WILL YOU PLEASE LEAVE ME ALONE BEFORE YOU BRING ON MY THIRD SERIOUS MIGRAINE OF THE DAY?
ROLL CAGE
RESIDENT EVIL
WIPEOUT 2099
WE'RE NOT GOING ANYWHERE UNTIL YOU'VE HEARD WHAT WE CAME HERE TO SAY, YOU MISERABLE LITTLE TOE-RAG.
I DON'T THINK YOU UNDERSTAND...

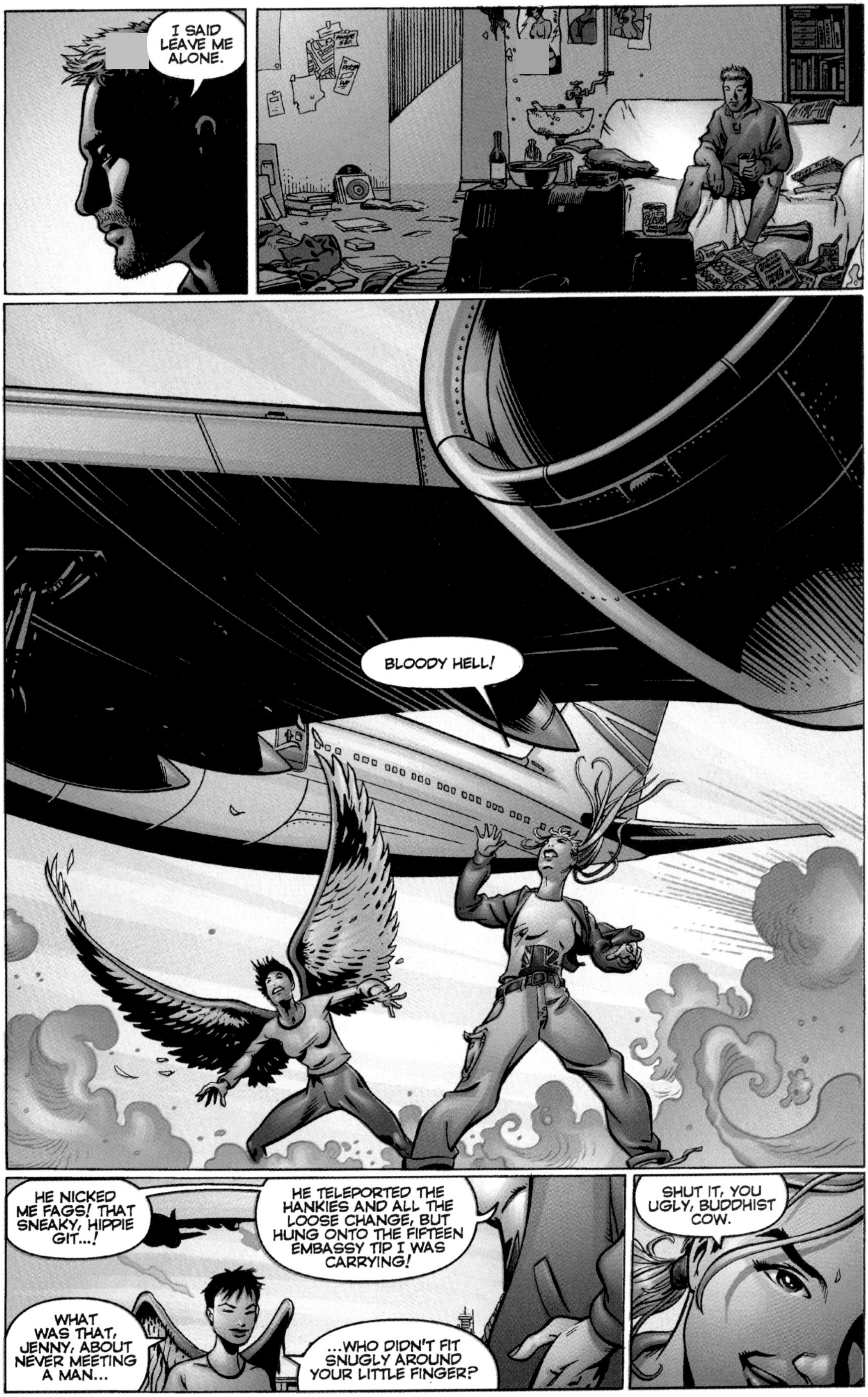

I SAID LEAVE ME ALONE.
BLOODY HELL!
HE NICKED ME FAGS! THAT SNEAKY, HIPPIE GIT...!
HE TELEPORTED THE HANKIES AND ALL THE LOOSE CHANGE, BUT HUNG ONTO THE FIFTEEN EMBASSY TIP I WAS CARRYING!
WHAT WAS THAT, JENNY, ABOUT NEVER MEETING A MAN...
...WHO DIDN'T FIT SNUGLY AROUND YOUR LITTLE FINGER?
SHUT IT, YOU UGLY, BUDDHIST COW.

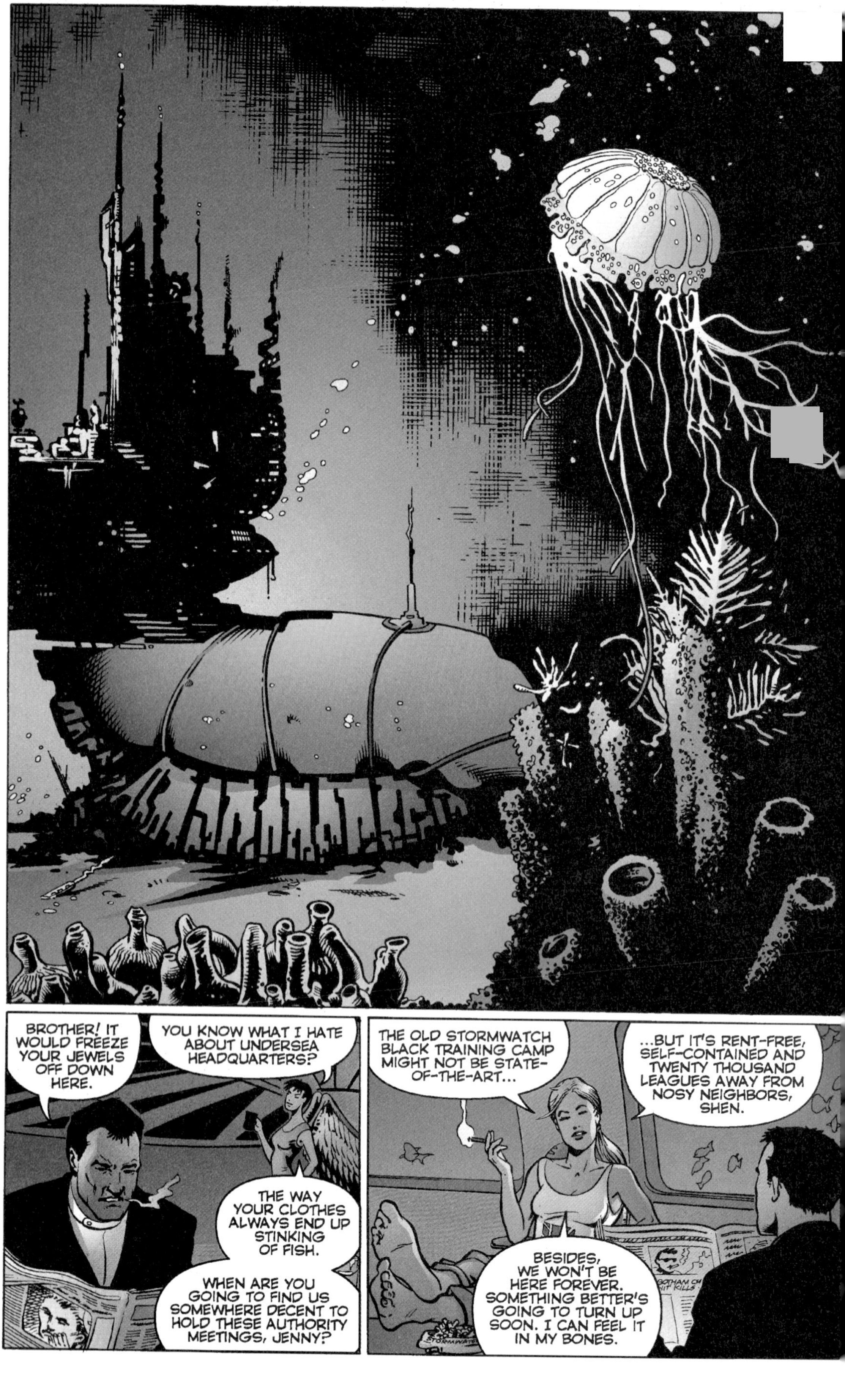
BROTHER! IT WOULD FREEZE YOUR JEWELS OFF DOWN HERE.
YOU KNOW WHAT I HATE ABOUT UNDERSEA HEADQUARTERS?
THE WAY YOUR CLOTHES ALWAYS END UP STINKING OF FISH.
WHEN ARE YOU GOING TO FIND US SOMEWHERE DECENT TO HOLD THESE AUTHORITY MEETINGS, JENNY?
THE OLD STORMWATCH BLACK TRAINING CAMP MIGHT NOT BE STATE-OF-THE-ART...
...BUT IT'S RENT-FREE, SELF-CONTAINED AND TWENTY THOUSAND LEAGUES AWAY FROM NOSY NEIGHBORS, SHEN.
BESIDES, WE WON'T BE HERE FOREVER. SOMETHING BETTER'S GOING TO TURN UP SOON. I CAN FEEL IT IN MY BONES.

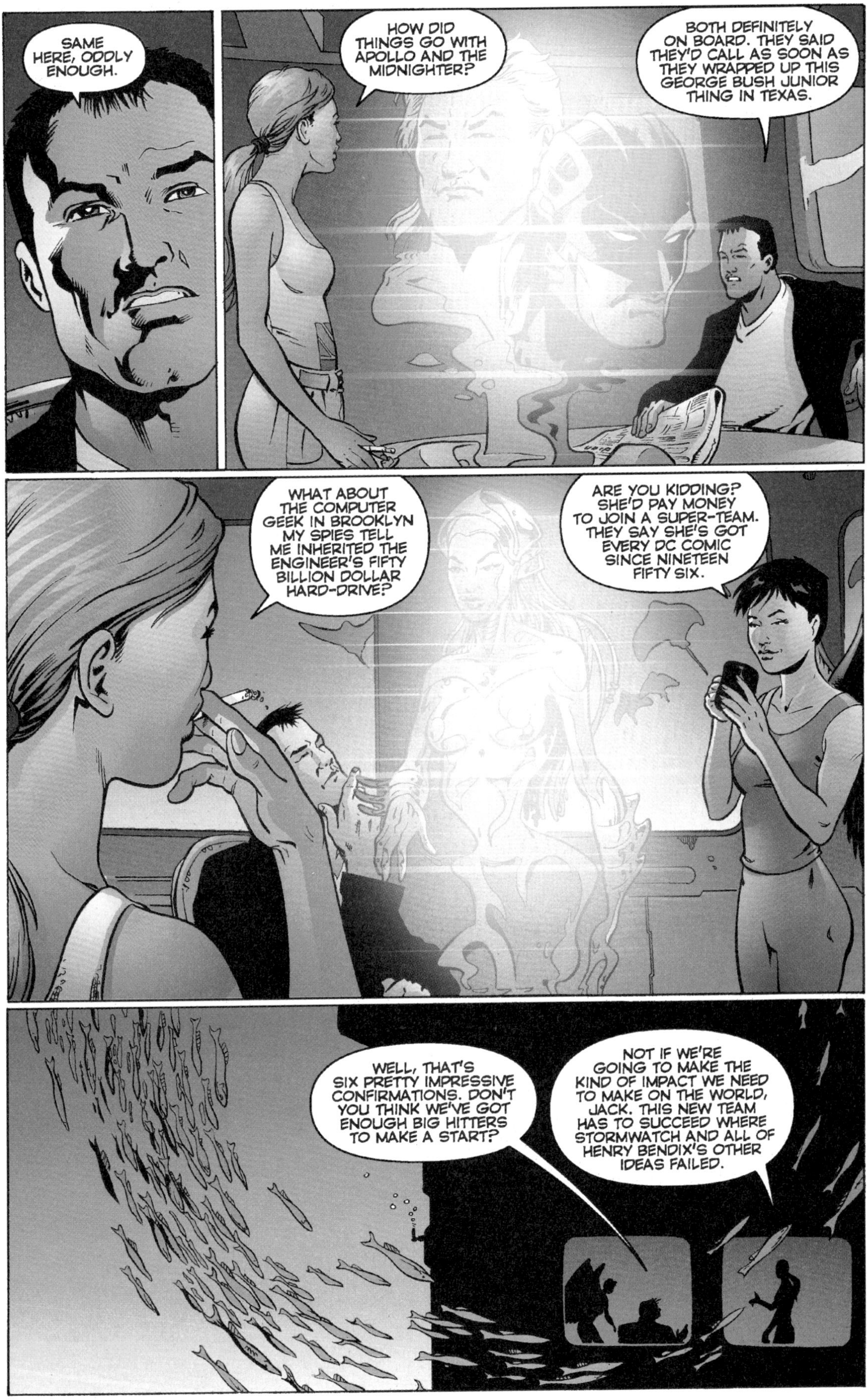
SAME HERE, ODDLY ENOUGH.
HOW DID THINGS GO WITH APOLLO AND THE MIDNIGHTER?
BOTH DEFINITELY ON BOARD. THEY SAID THEY'D CALL AS SOON AS THEY WRAPPED UP THIS GEORGE BUSH JUNIOR THING IN TEXAS.
WHAT ABOUT THE COMPUTER GEEK IN BROOKLYN MY SPIES TELL ME INHERITED THE ENGINEER'S FIFTY BILLION DOLLAR HARD-DRIVE?
ARE YOU KIDDING? SHE'D PAY MONEY TO JOIN A SUPER-TEAM. THEY SAY SHE'S GOT EVERY DC COMIC SINCE NINETEEN FIFTY SIX.
WELL, THAT'S SIX PRETTY IMPRESSIVE CONFIRMATIONS. DON'T YOU THINK WE'VE GOT ENOUGH BIG HITTERS TO MAKE A START?
NOT IF WE'RE GOING TO MAKE THE KIND OF IMPACT WE NEED TO MAKE ON THE WORLD, JACK. THIS NEW TEAM HAS TO SUCCEED WHERE STORMWATCH AND ALL OF HENRY BENDIX'S OTHER IDEAS FAILED.

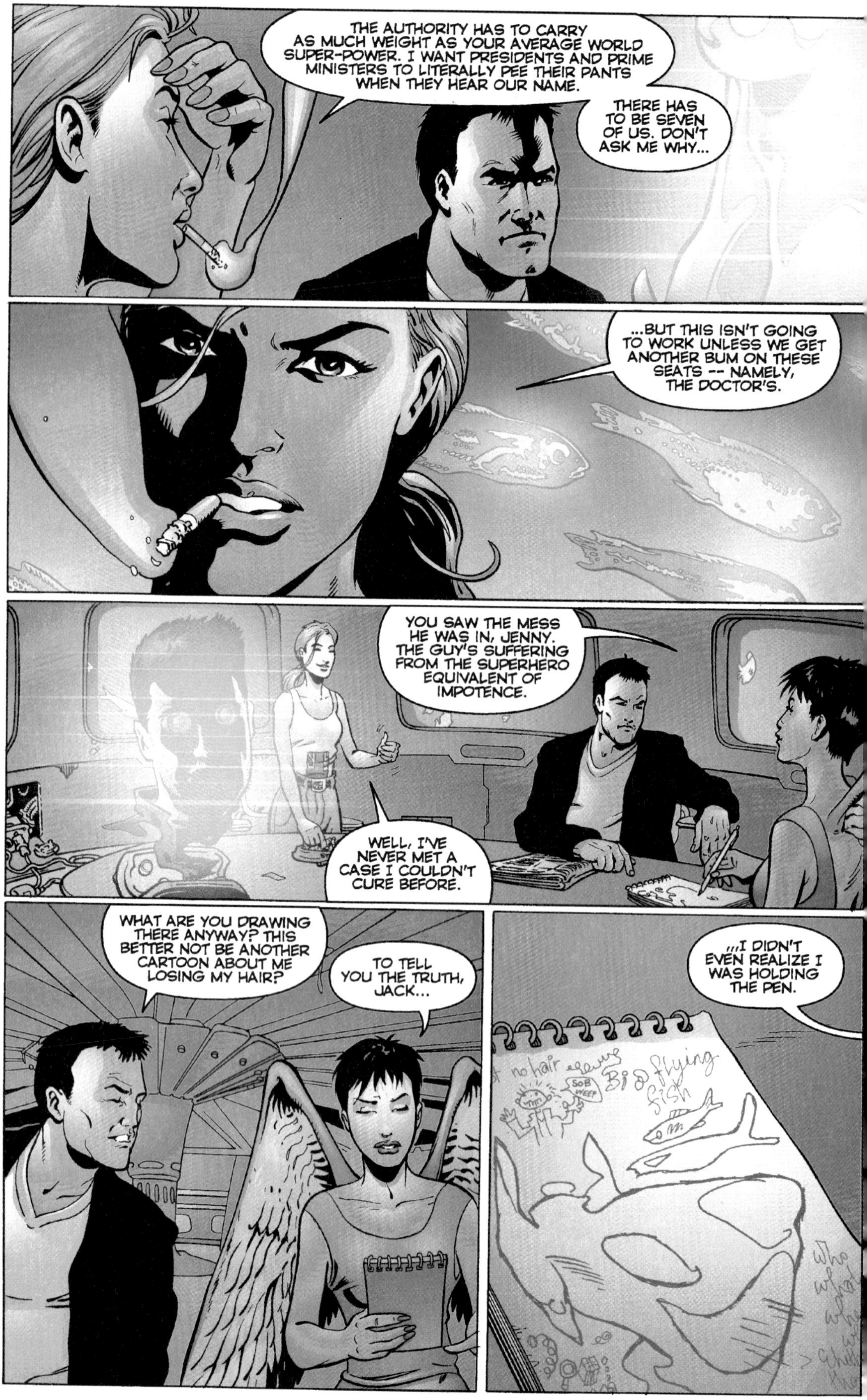
THE AUTHORITY HAS TO CARRY AS MUCH WEIGHT AS YOUR AVERAGE WORLD SUPER-POWER. I WANT PRESIDENTS AND PRIME MINISTERS TO LITERALLY PEE THEIR PANTS WHEN THEY HEAR OUR NAME.
THERE HAS TO BE SEVEN OF US. DON'T ASK ME WHY...
...BUT THIS ISN'T GOING TO WORK UNLESS WE GET ANOTHER BUM ON THESE SEATS -- NAMELY, THE DOCTOR'S.
YOU SAW THE MESS HE WAS IN, JENNY. THE GUY'S SUFFERING FROM THE SUPERHERO EQUIVALENT OF IMPOTENCE.
WELL, I'VE NEVER MET A CASE I COULDN'T CURE BEFORE.
WHAT ARE YOU DRAWING THERE ANYWAY? THIS BETTER NOT BE ANOTHER CARTOON ABOUT ME LOSING MY HAIR?
TO TELL YOU THE TRUTH, JACK...
...I DIDN'T EVEN REALIZE I WAS HOLDING THE PEN.
no hair
SOB WEEP
Big flying fish

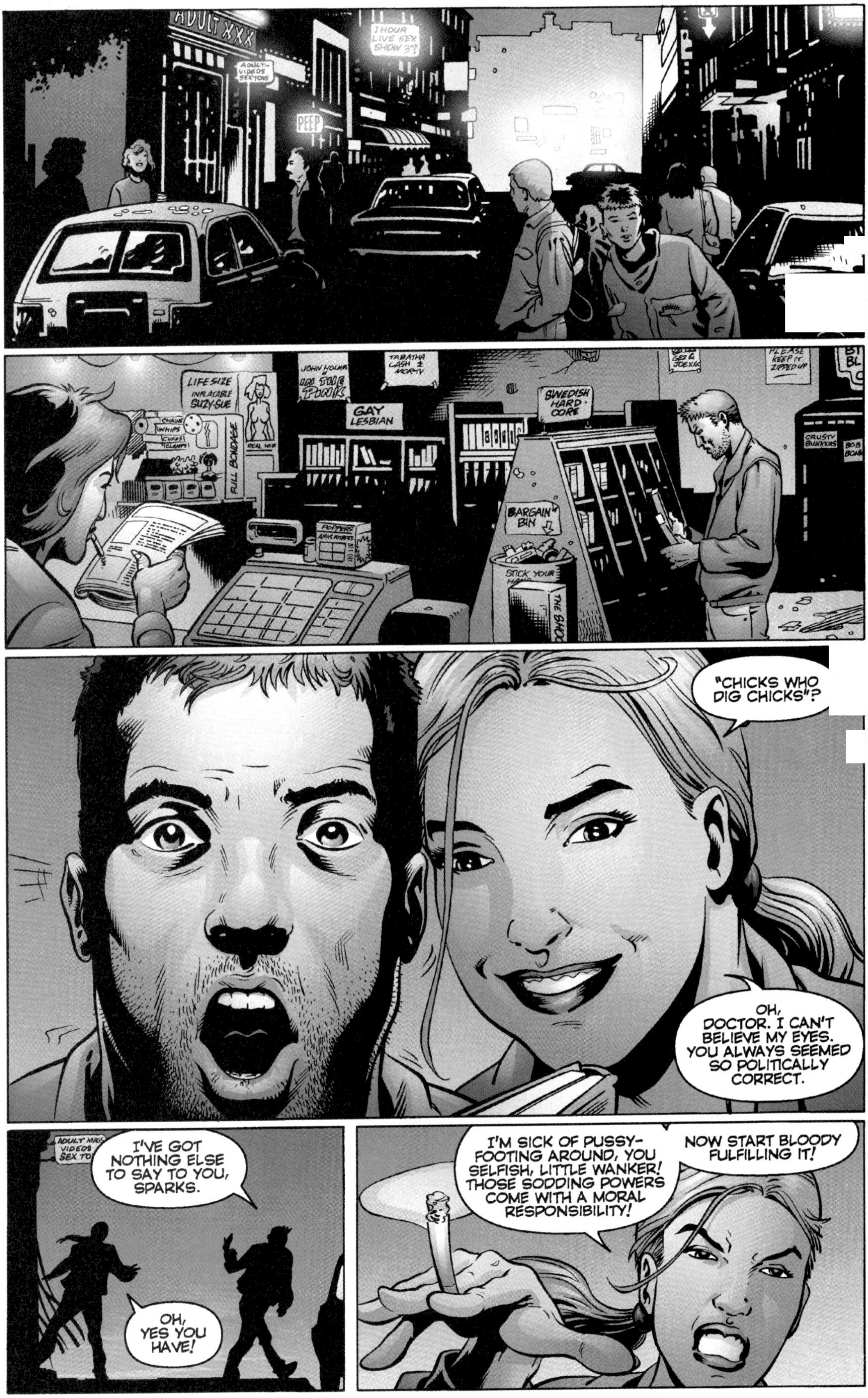
ADULT XXX
PEEP
LIFE SIZE INFLATABLE SUZY-SUE
FULL BONDAGE
GAY LESBIAN
SWEDISH HARD-CORE
BARGAIN BIN
"CHICKS WHO DIG CHICKS"?
OH, DOCTOR. I CAN'T BELIEVE MY EYES. YOU ALWAYS SEEMED SO POLITICALLY CORRECT.
I'VE GOT NOTHING ELSE TO SAY TO YOU, SPARKS.
OH, YES YOU HAVE!
I'M SICK OF PUSSY-FOOTING AROUND, YOU SELFISH, LITTLE WANKER! THOSE SODDING POWERS COME WITH A MORAL RESPONSIBILITY!
NOW START BLOODY FULFILLING IT!

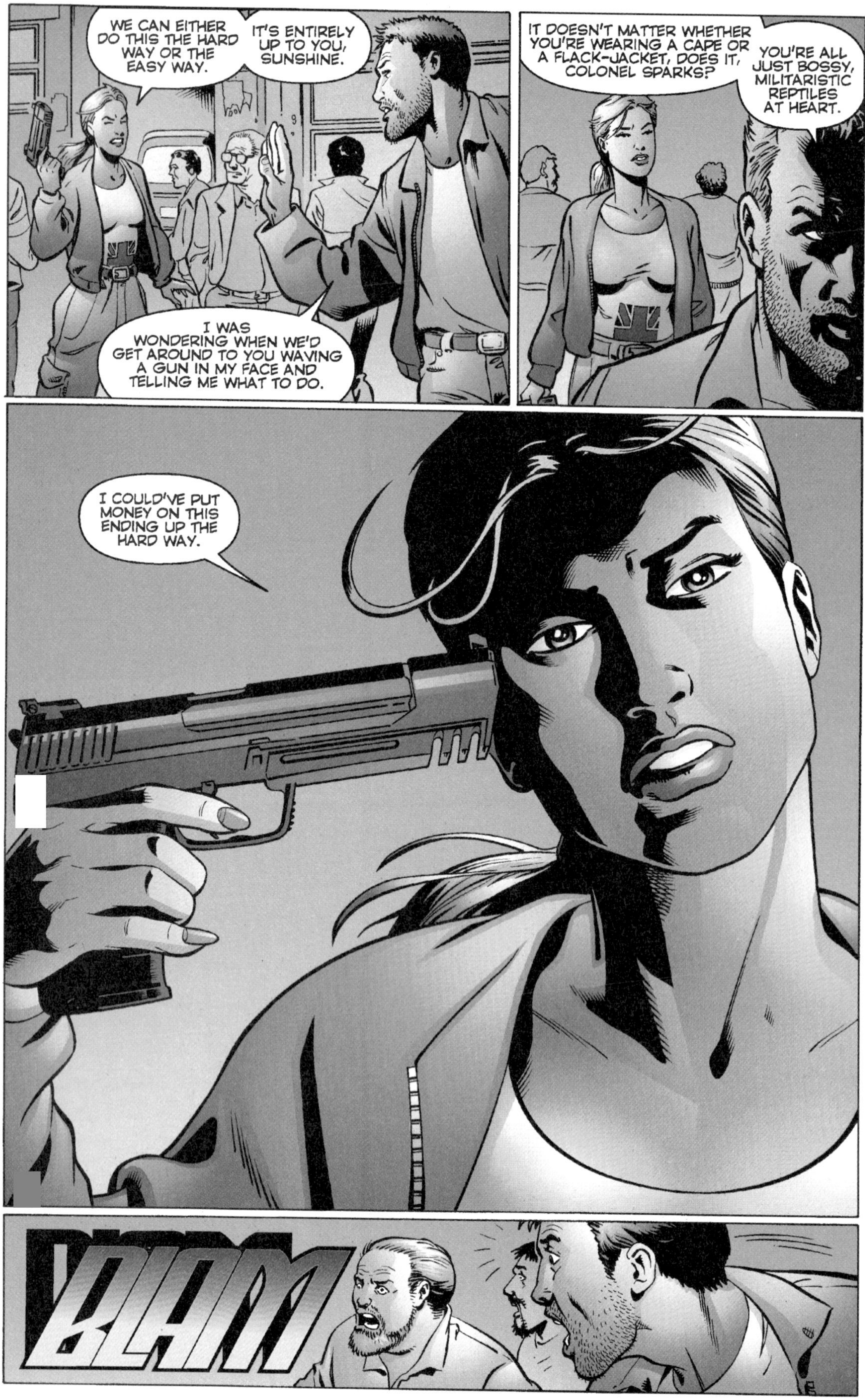
WE CAN EITHER DO THIS THE HARD WAY OR THE EASY WAY.
IT'S ENTIRELY UP TO YOU, SUNSHINE.
I WAS WONDERING WHEN WE'D GET AROUND TO YOU WAVING A GUN IN MY FACE AND TELLING ME WHAT TO DO.
IT DOESN'T MATTER WHETHER YOU'RE WEARING A CAPE OR A FLACK-JACKET, DOES IT, COLONEL SPARKS?
YOU'RE ALL JUST BOSSY, MILITARISTIC REPTILES AT HEART.
I COULD'VE PUT MONEY ON THIS ENDING UP THE HARD WAY.
BLAM

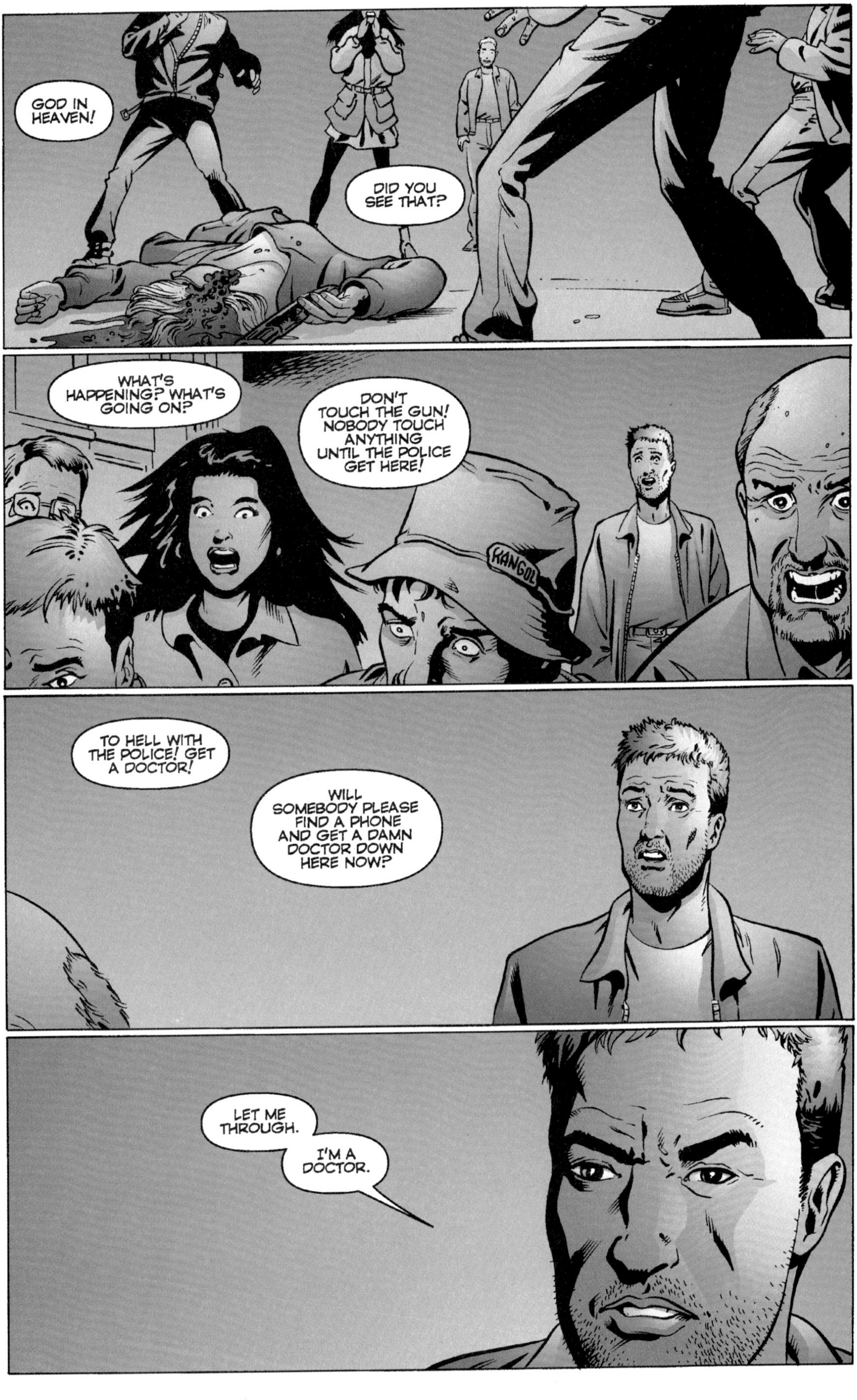
GOD IN HEAVEN!
DID YOU SEE THAT?
WHAT'S HAPPENING? WHAT'S GOING ON?
DON'T TOUCH THE GUN! NOBODY TOUCH ANYTHING UNTIL THE POLICE GET HERE!
KANGOL
TO HELL WITH THE POLICE! GET A DOCTOR!
WILL SOMEBODY PLEASE FIND A PHONE AND GET A DAMN DOCTOR DOWN HERE NOW?
LET ME THROUGH.
I'M A DOCTOR.

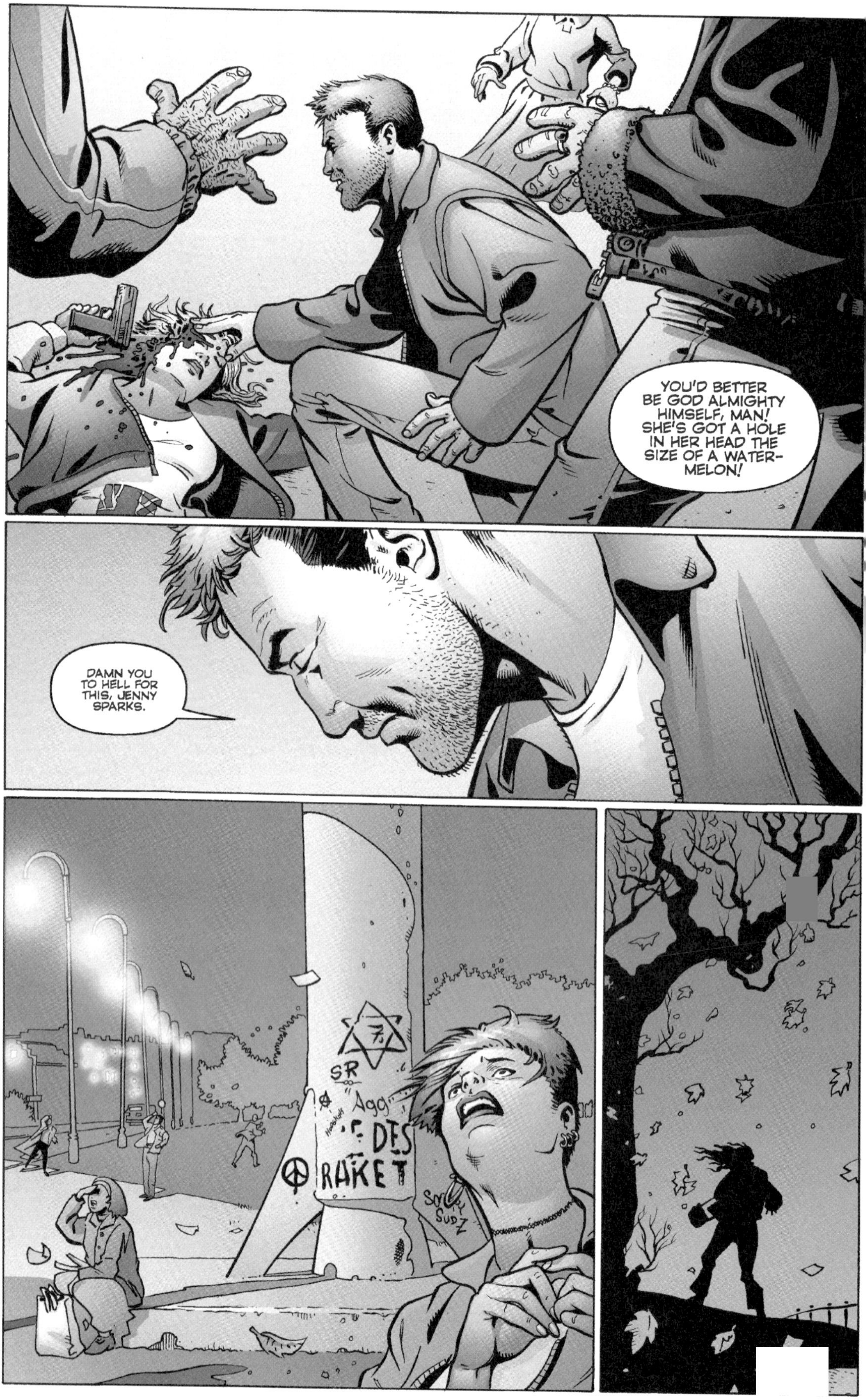
YOU'D BETTER BE GOD ALMIGHTY HIMSELF, MAN! SHE'S GOT A HOLE IN HER HEAD THE SIZE OF A WATER-MELON!
DAMN YOU TO HELL FOR THIS, JENNY SPARKS.
SR
RAKET

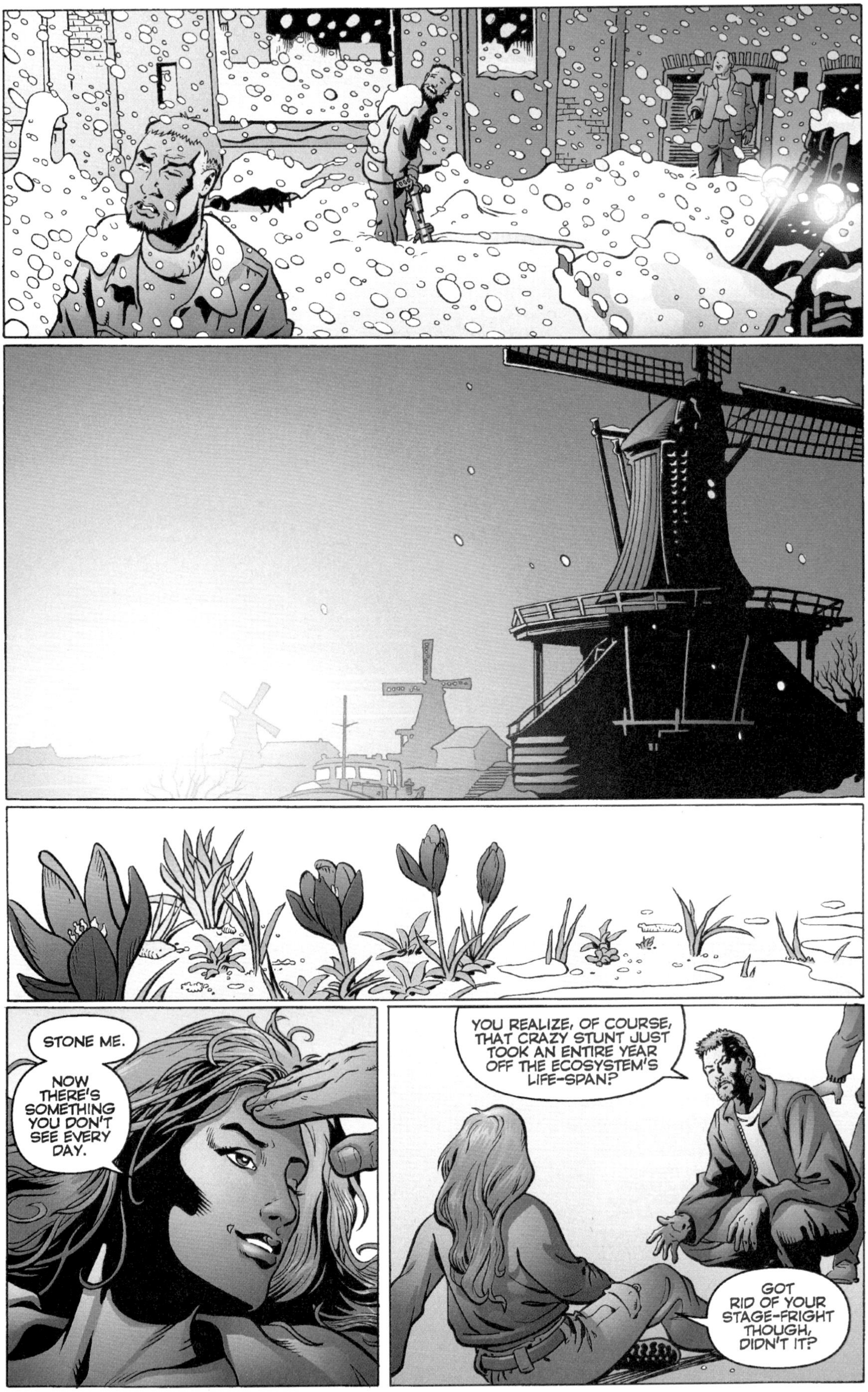
STONE ME.
NOW THERE'S SOMETHING YOU DON'T SEE EVERY DAY.
YOU REALIZE, OF COURSE, THAT CRAZY STUNT JUST TOOK AN ENTIRE YEAR OFF THE ECOSYSTEM'S LIFE-SPAN?
GOT RID OF YOUR STAGE-FRIGHT THOUGH, DIDN'T IT?

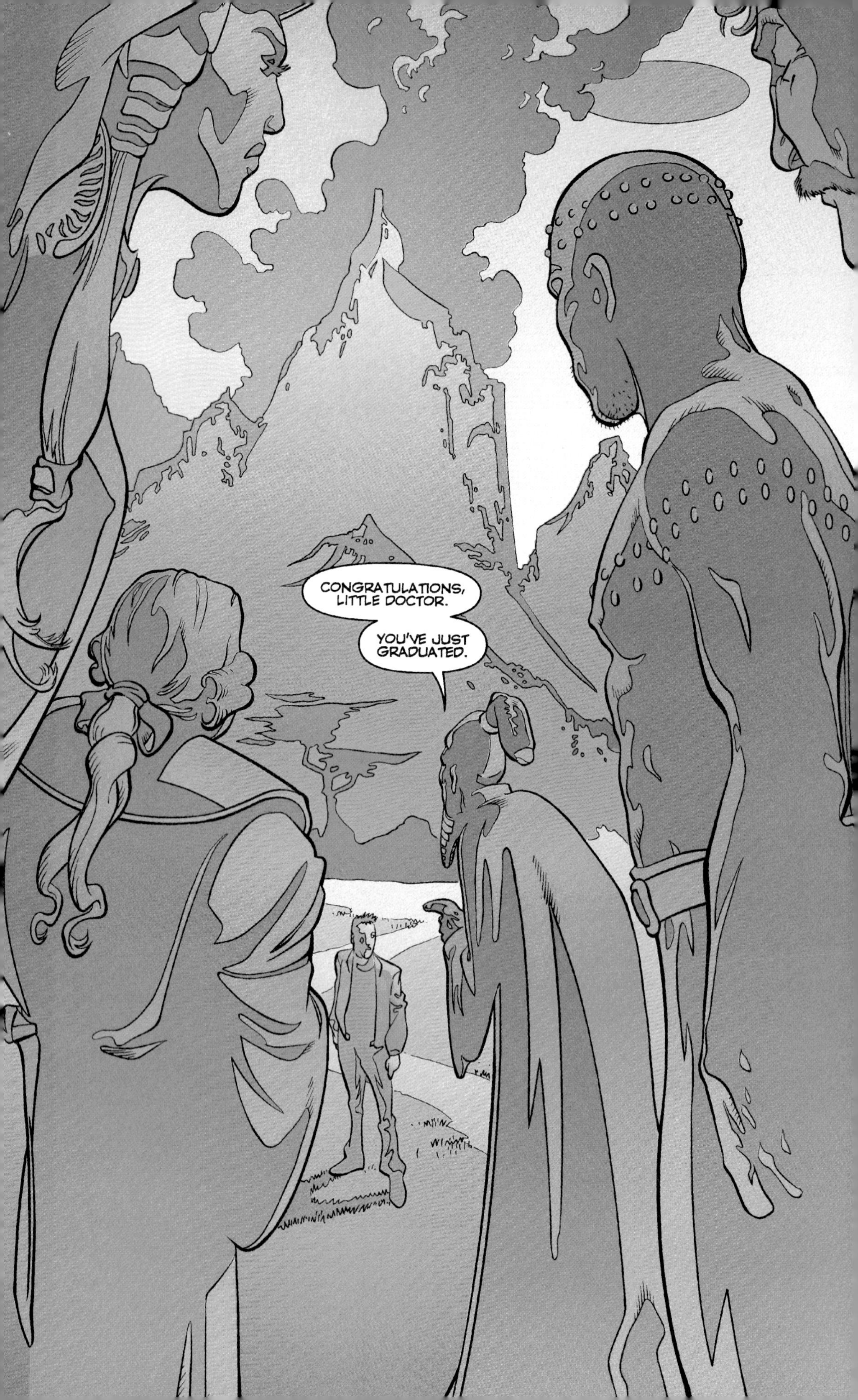
CONGRATULATIONS, LITTLE DOCTOR.
YOU'VE JUST GRADUATED.

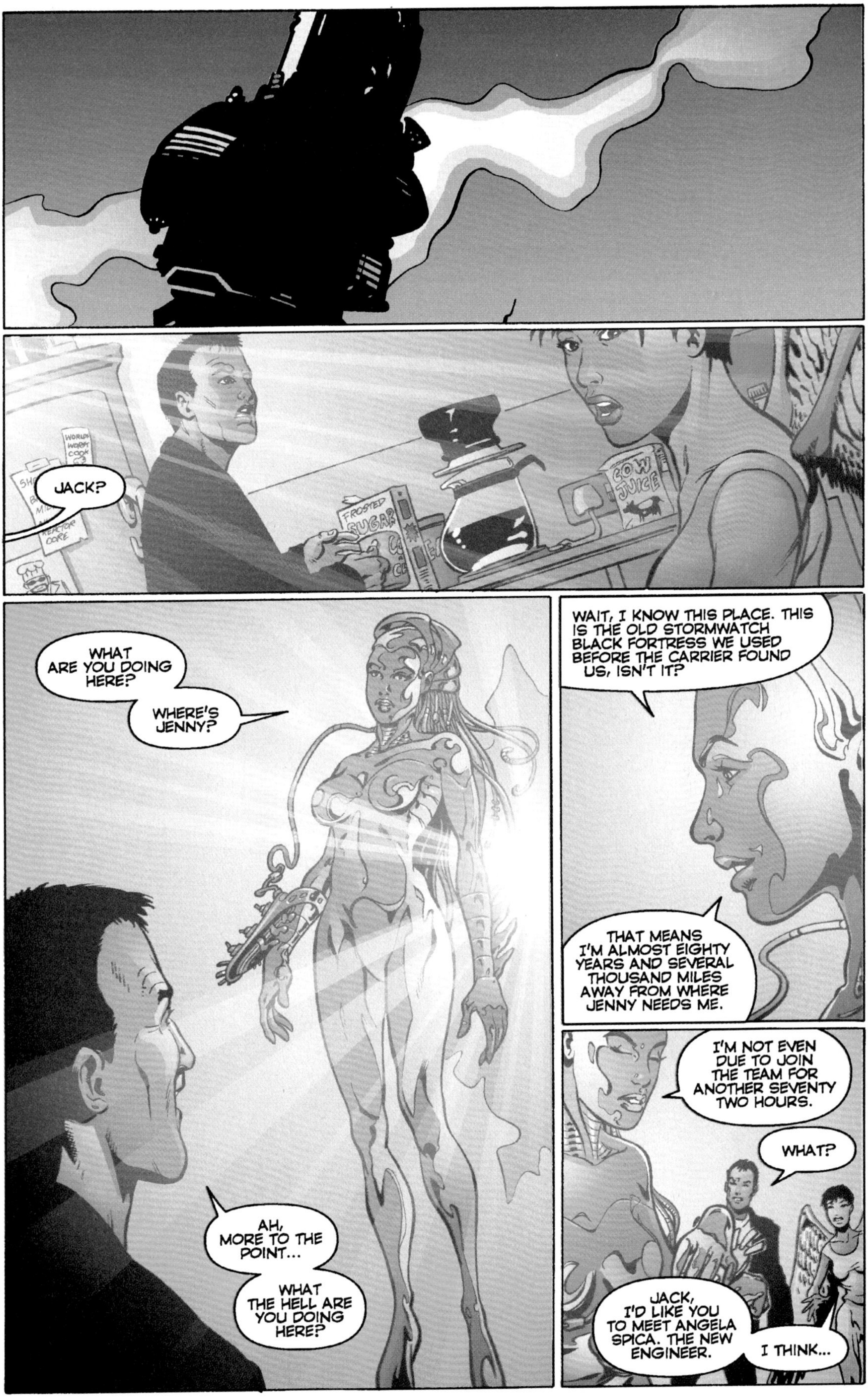
JACK?
WORLD'S WORST COOK
REACTOR CORE
FROSTED SUGAR
COW JUICE
WHAT ARE YOU DOING HERE?
WHERE'S JENNY?
AH, MORE TO THE POINT...
WHAT THE HELL ARE YOU DOING HERE?
WAIT, I KNOW THIS PLACE. THIS IS THE OLD STORMWATCH BLACK FORTRESS WE USED BEFORE THE CARRIER FOUND US, ISN'T IT?
THAT MEANS I'M ALMOST EIGHTY YEARS AND SEVERAL THOUSAND MILES AWAY FROM WHERE JENNY NEEDS ME.
I'M NOT EVEN DUE TO JOIN THE TEAM FOR ANOTHER SEVENTY TWO HOURS.
WHAT?
JACK, I'D LIKE YOU TO MEET ANGELA SPICA. THE NEW ENGINEER.
I THINK...

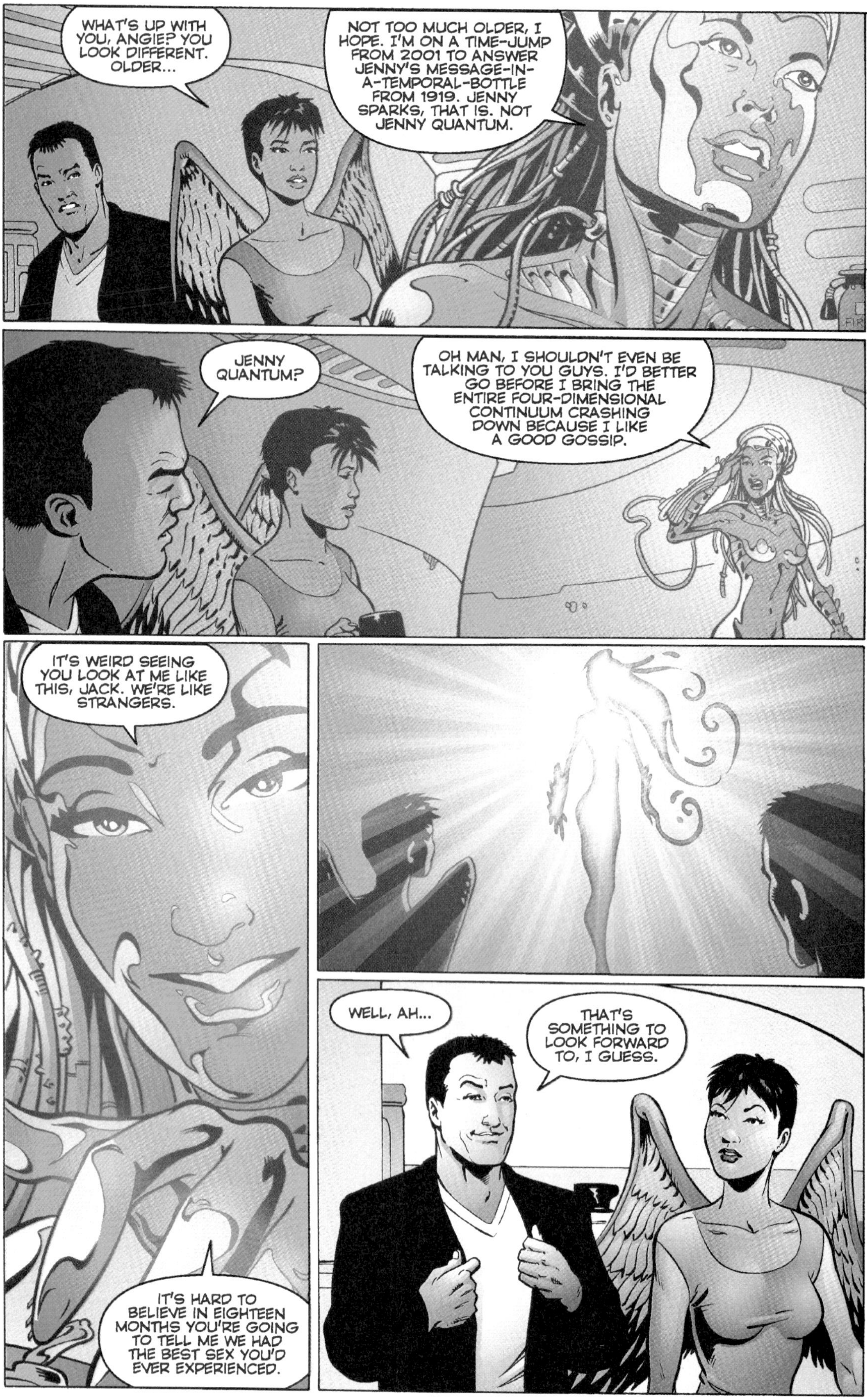
WHAT'S UP WITH YOU, ANGIE? YOU LOOK DIFFERENT. OLDER...
NOT TOO MUCH OLDER, I HOPE. I'M ON A TIME-JUMP FROM 2001 TO ANSWER JENNY'S MESSAGE-IN-A-TEMPORAL-BOTTLE FROM 1919. JENNY SPARKS, THAT IS. NOT JENNY QUANTUM.
JENNY QUANTUM?
OH MAN, I SHOULDN'T EVEN BE TALKING TO YOU GUYS. I'D BETTER GO BEFORE I BRING THE ENTIRE FOUR-DIMENSIONAL CONTINUUM CRASHING DOWN BECAUSE I LIKE A GOOD GOSSIP.
IT'S WEIRD SEEING YOU LOOK AT ME LIKE THIS, JACK. WE'RE LIKE STRANGERS.
IT'S HARD TO BELIEVE IN EIGHTEEN MONTHS YOU'RE GOING TO TELL ME WE HAD THE BEST SEX YOU'D EVER EXPERIENCED.
WELL, AH...
THAT'S SOMETHING TO LOOK FORWARD TO, I GUESS.

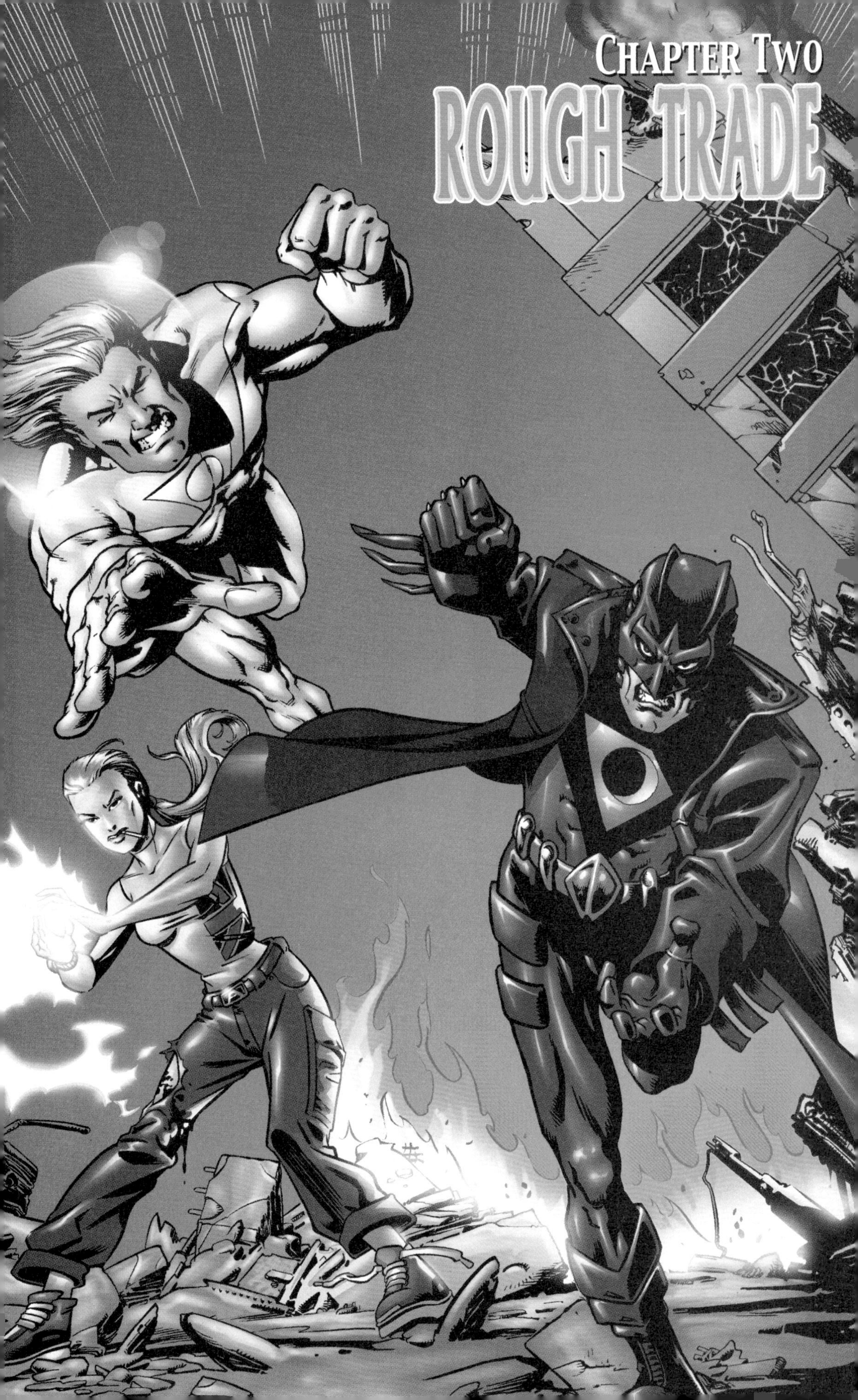
CHAPTER TWO
ROUGH TRADE

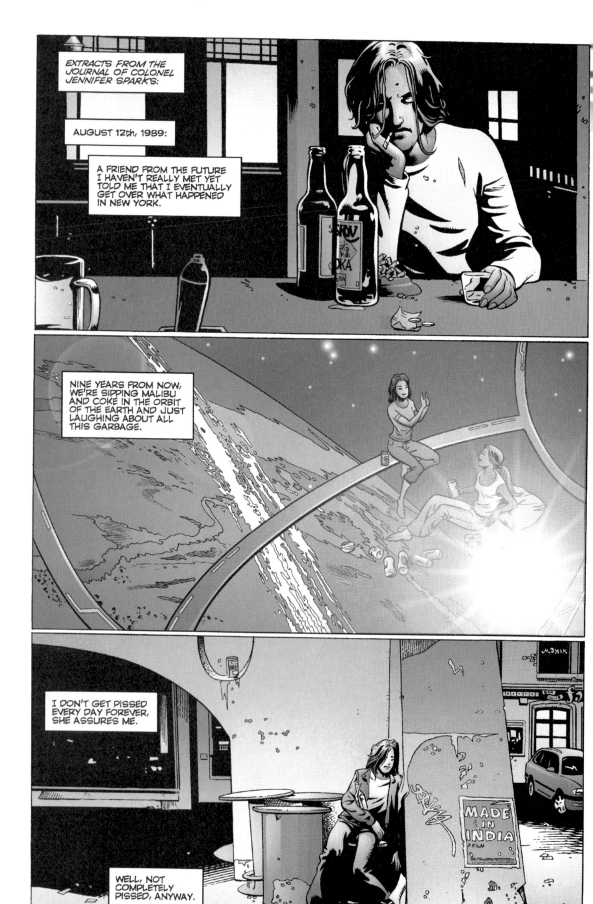

EXTRACTS FROM THE JOURNAL OF COLONEL JENNIFER SPARKS:

AUGUST 12th, 1989:

A FRIEND FROM THE FUTURE I HAVEN'T REALLY MET YET TOLD ME THAT I EVENTUALLY GET OVER WHAT HAPPENED IN NEW YORK.

NINE YEARS FROM NOW, WE'RE SIPPING MALIBU AND COKE IN THE ORBIT OF THE EARTH AND JUST LAUGHING ABOUT ALL THIS GARBAGE.

I DON'T GET PISSED EVERY DAY FOREVER, SHE ASSURES ME.

WELL, NOT COMPLETELY PISSED, ANYWAY.

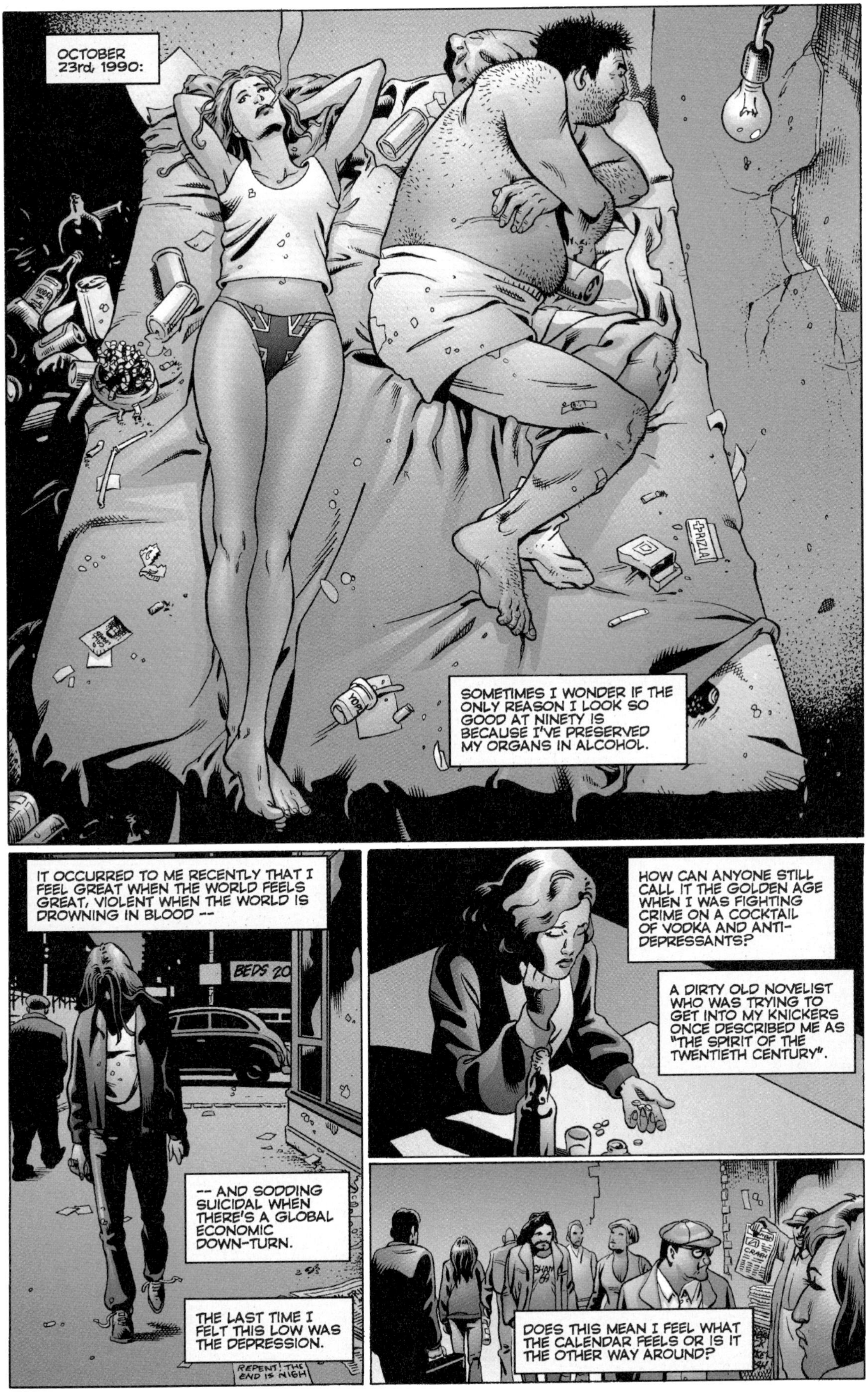
OCTOBER 23rd, 1990:
SOMETIMES I WONDER IF THE ONLY REASON I LOOK SO GOOD AT NINETY IS BECAUSE I'VE PRESERVED MY ORGANS IN ALCOHOL.
IT OCCURRED TO ME RECENTLY THAT I FEEL GREAT WHEN THE WORLD FEELS GREAT, VIOLENT WHEN THE WORLD IS DROWNING IN BLOOD --
BEDS 20
-- AND SODDING SUICIDAL WHEN THERE'S A GLOBAL ECONOMIC DOWN-TURN.
THE LAST TIME I FELT THIS LOW WAS THE DEPRESSION.
REPENT! THE END IS NIGH
HOW CAN ANYONE STILL CALL IT THE GOLDEN AGE WHEN I WAS FIGHTING CRIME ON A COCKTAIL OF VODKA AND ANTI-DEPRESSANTS?
A DIRTY OLD NOVELIST WHO WAS TRYING TO GET INTO MY KNICKERS ONCE DESCRIBED ME AS "THE SPIRIT OF THE TWENTIETH CENTURY".
DOES THIS MEAN I FEEL WHAT THE CALENDAR FEELS OR IS IT THE OTHER WAY AROUND?

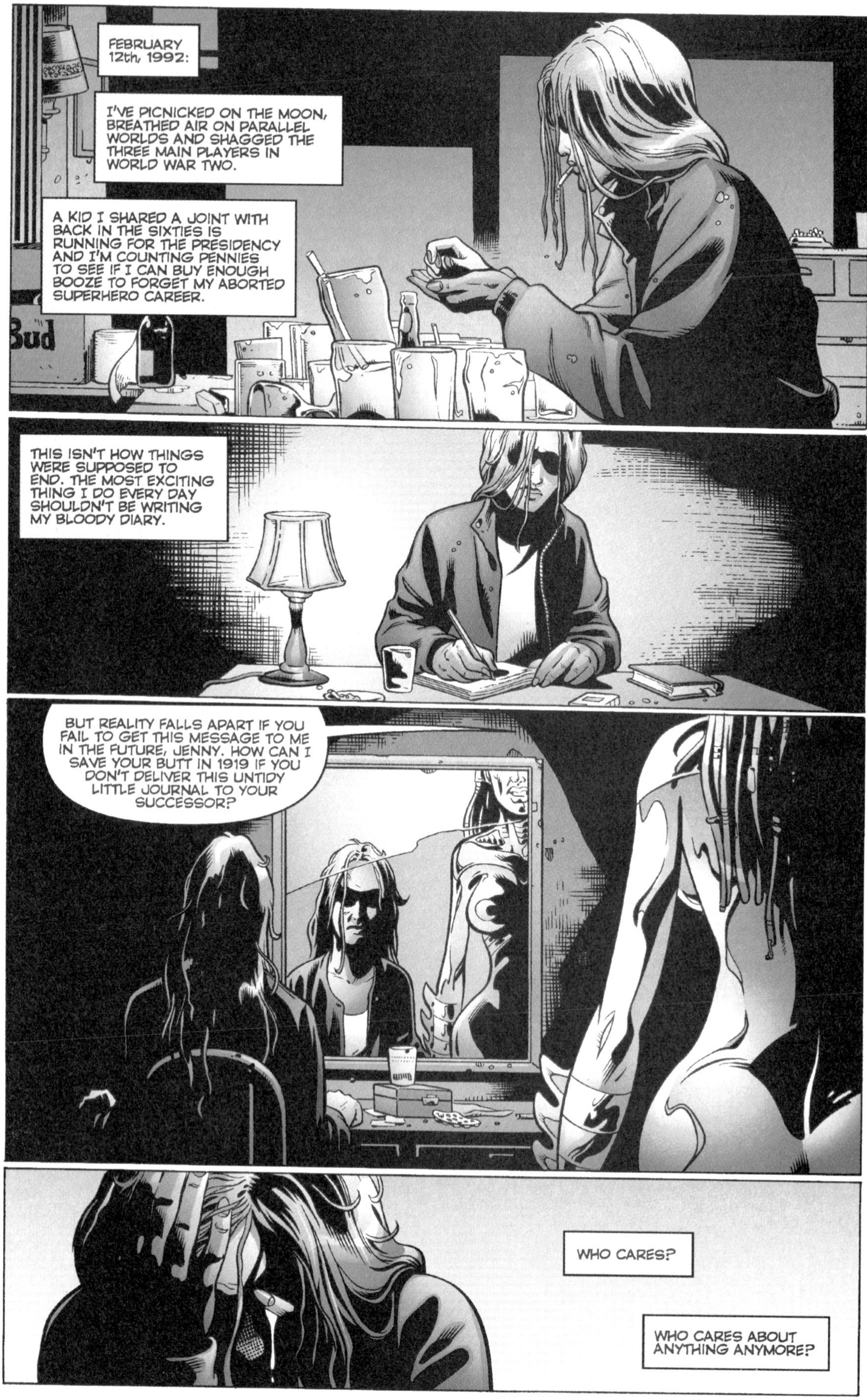
FEBRUARY 12th, 1992:
I'VE PICNICKED ON THE MOON, BREATHED AIR ON PARALLEL WORLDS AND SHAGGED THE THREE MAIN PLAYERS IN WORLD WAR TWO.
A KID I SHARED A JOINT WITH BACK IN THE SIXTIES IS RUNNING FOR THE PRESIDENCY AND I'M COUNTING PENNIES TO SEE IF I CAN BUY ENOUGH BOOZE TO FORGET MY ABORTED SUPERHERO CAREER.
Bud
THIS ISN'T HOW THINGS WERE SUPPOSED TO END. THE MOST EXCITING THING I DO EVERY DAY SHOULDN'T BE WRITING MY BLOODY DIARY.
BUT REALITY FALLS APART IF YOU FAIL TO GET THIS MESSAGE TO ME IN THE FUTURE, JENNY. HOW CAN I SAVE YOUR BUTT IN 1919 IF YOU DON'T DELIVER THIS UNTIDY LITTLE JOURNAL TO YOUR SUCCESSOR?
WHO CARES?
WHO CARES ABOUT ANYTHING ANYMORE?

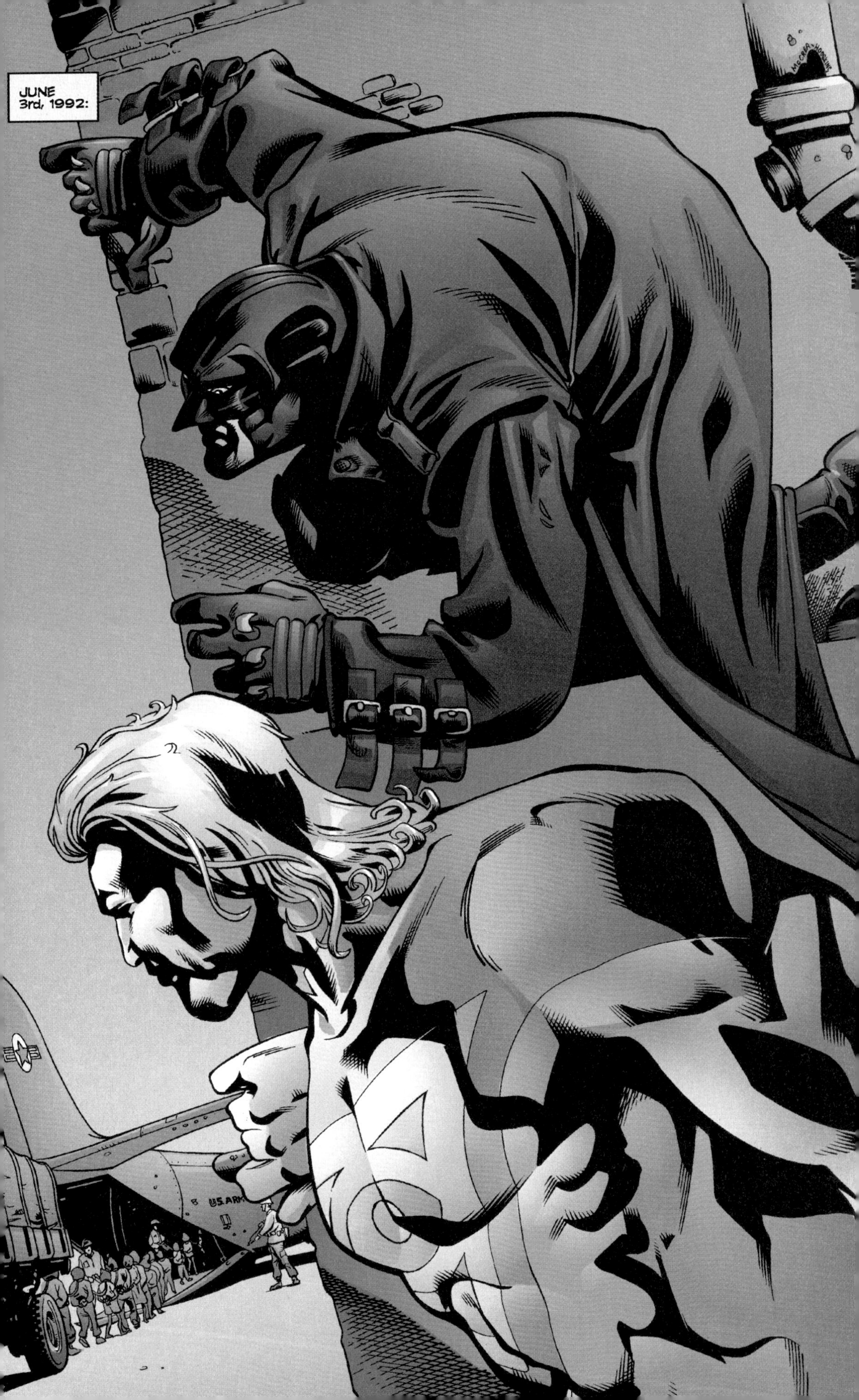
JUNE 3rd, 1992:

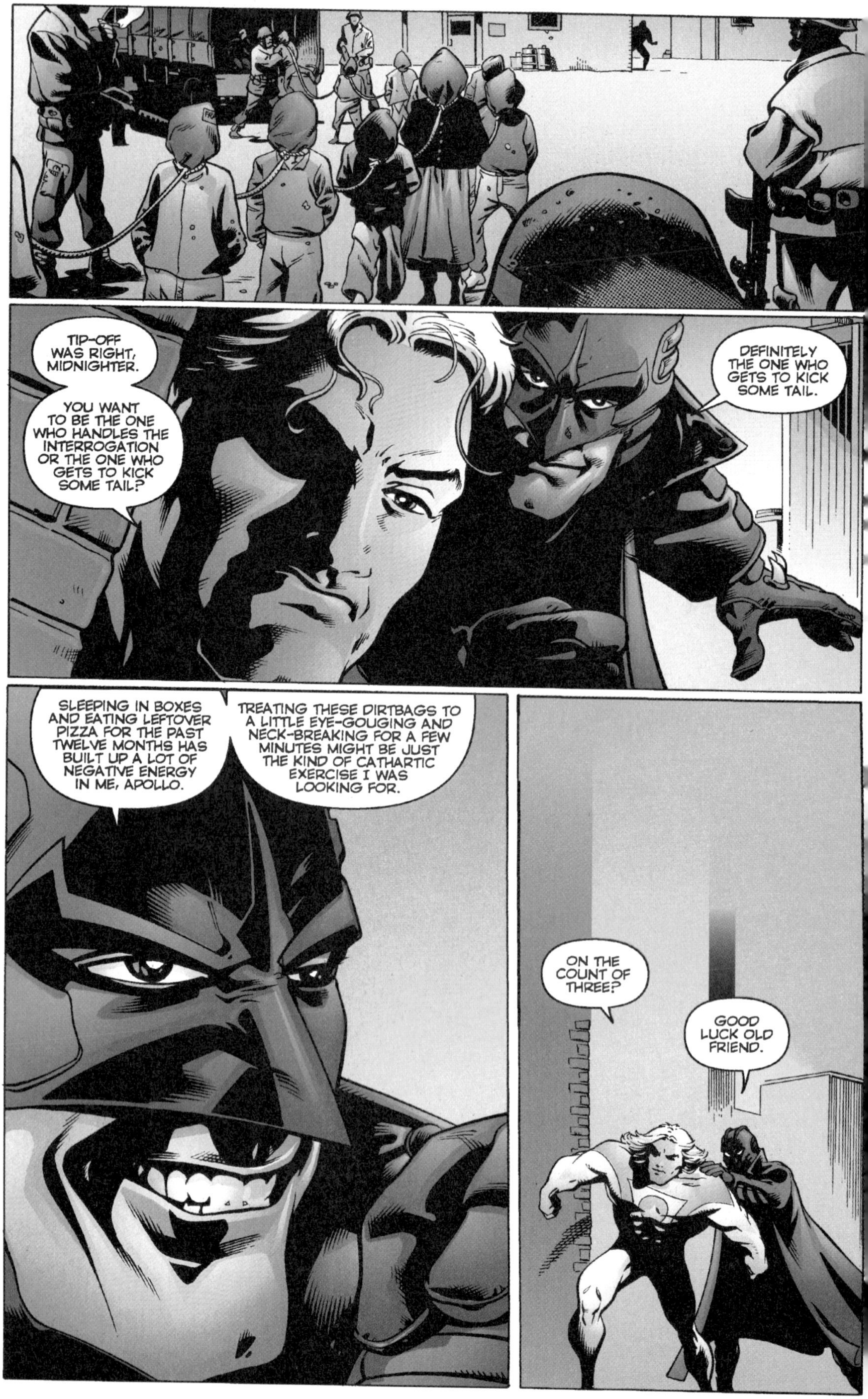

TIP-OFF WAS RIGHT, MIDNIGHTER.
YOU WANT TO BE THE ONE WHO HANDLES THE INTERROGATION OR THE ONE WHO GETS TO KICK SOME TAIL?
DEFINITELY THE ONE WHO GETS TO KICK SOME TAIL.
SLEEPING IN BOXES AND EATING LEFTOVER PIZZA FOR THE PAST TWELVE MONTHS HAS BUILT UP A LOT OF NEGATIVE ENERGY IN ME, APOLLO.
TREATING THESE DIRTBAGS TO A LITTLE EYE-GOUGING AND NECK-BREAKING FOR A FEW MINUTES MIGHT BE JUST THE KIND OF CATHARTIC EXERCISE I WAS LOOKING FOR.
ON THE COUNT OF THREE?
GOOD LUCK OLD FRIEND.

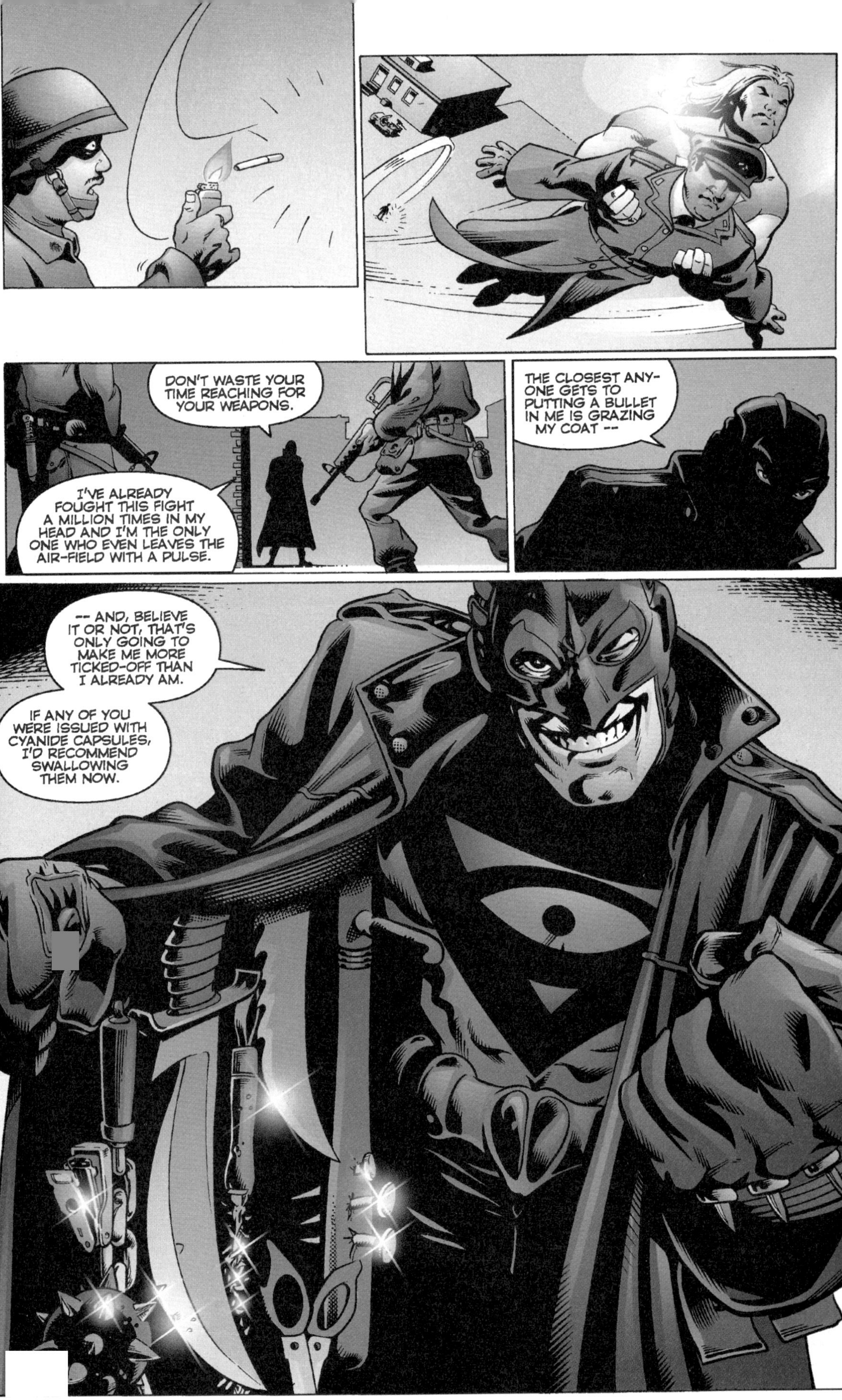
DON'T WASTE YOUR TIME REACHING FOR YOUR WEAPONS.
I'VE ALREADY FOUGHT THIS FIGHT A MILLION TIMES IN MY HEAD AND I'M THE ONLY ONE WHO EVEN LEAVES THE AIR-FIELD WITH A PULSE.
THE CLOSEST ANY-ONE GETS TO PUTTING A BULLET IN ME IS GRAZING MY COAT --
-- AND, BELIEVE IT OR NOT, THAT'S ONLY GOING TO MAKE ME MORE TICKED-OFF THAN I ALREADY AM.
IF ANY OF YOU WERE ISSUED WITH CYANIDE CAPSULES, I'D RECOMMEND SWALLOWING THEM NOW.

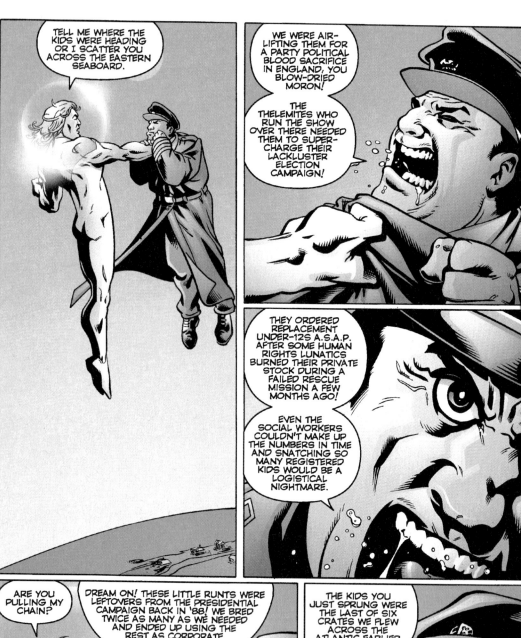

TELL ME WHERE THE KIDS WERE HEADING OR I SCATTER YOU ACROSS THE EASTERN SEABOARD.

WE WERE AIR-LIFTING THEM FOR A PARTY POLITICAL BLOOD SACRIFICE IN ENGLAND, YOU BLOW-DRIED MORON!

THE THELEMITES WHO RUN THE SHOW OVER THERE NEEDED THEM TO SUPER-CHARGE THEIR LACKLUSTER ELECTION CAMPAIGN!

THEY ORDERED REPLACEMENT UNDER-12S A.S.A.P. AFTER SOME HUMAN RIGHTS LUNATICS BURNED THEIR PRIVATE STOCK DURING A FAILED RESCUE MISSION A FEW MONTHS AGO!

EVEN THE SOCIAL WORKERS COULDN'T MAKE UP THE NUMBERS IN TIME AND SNATCHING SO MANY REGISTERED KIDS WOULD BE A LOGISTICAL NIGHTMARE.

ARE YOU PULLING MY CHAIN?

DREAM ON! THESE LITTLE RUNTS WERE LEFTOVERS FROM THE PRESIDENTIAL CAMPAIGN BACK IN '88! WE BRED TWICE AS MANY AS WE NEEDED AND ENDED UP USING THE REST AS CORPORATE WHORES, MOSTLY!

THE KIDS YOU JUST SPRUNG WERE THE LAST OF SIX CRATES WE FLEW ACROSS THE ATLANTIC EARLIER IN THE WEEK!

THEIR LITTLE BROTHERS AND SISTERS ARE PROBABLY ROASTING ON KEBAB-STICKS AS WE SPEAK!

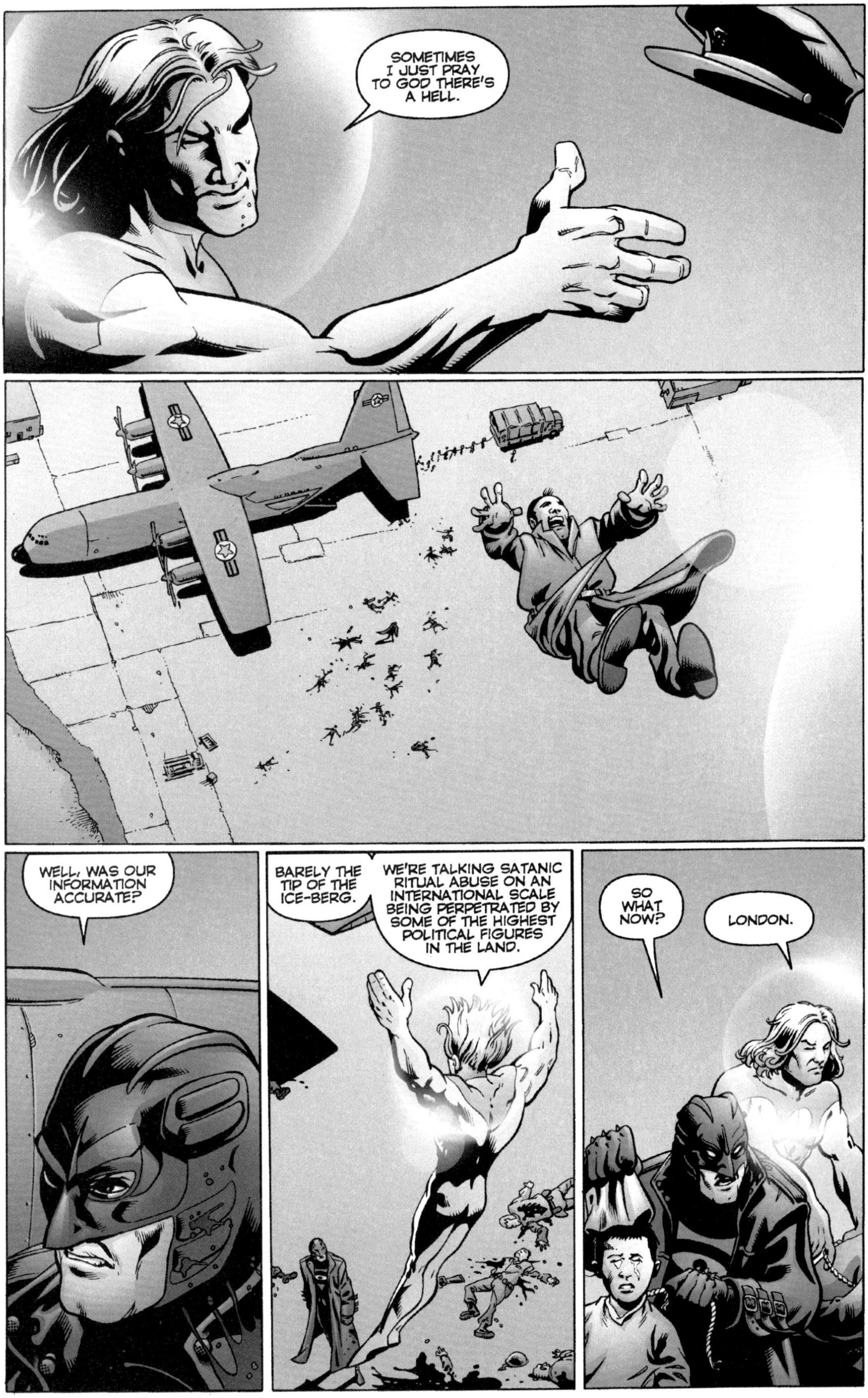
SOMETIMES I JUST PRAY TO GOD THERE'S A HELL.
WELL, WAS OUR INFORMATION ACCURATE?
BARELY THE TIP OF THE ICE-BERG.
WE'RE TALKING SATANIC RITUAL ABUSE ON AN INTERNATIONAL SCALE BEING PERPETRATED BY SOME OF THE HIGHEST POLITICAL FIGURES IN THE LAND.
SO WHAT NOW?
LONDON.

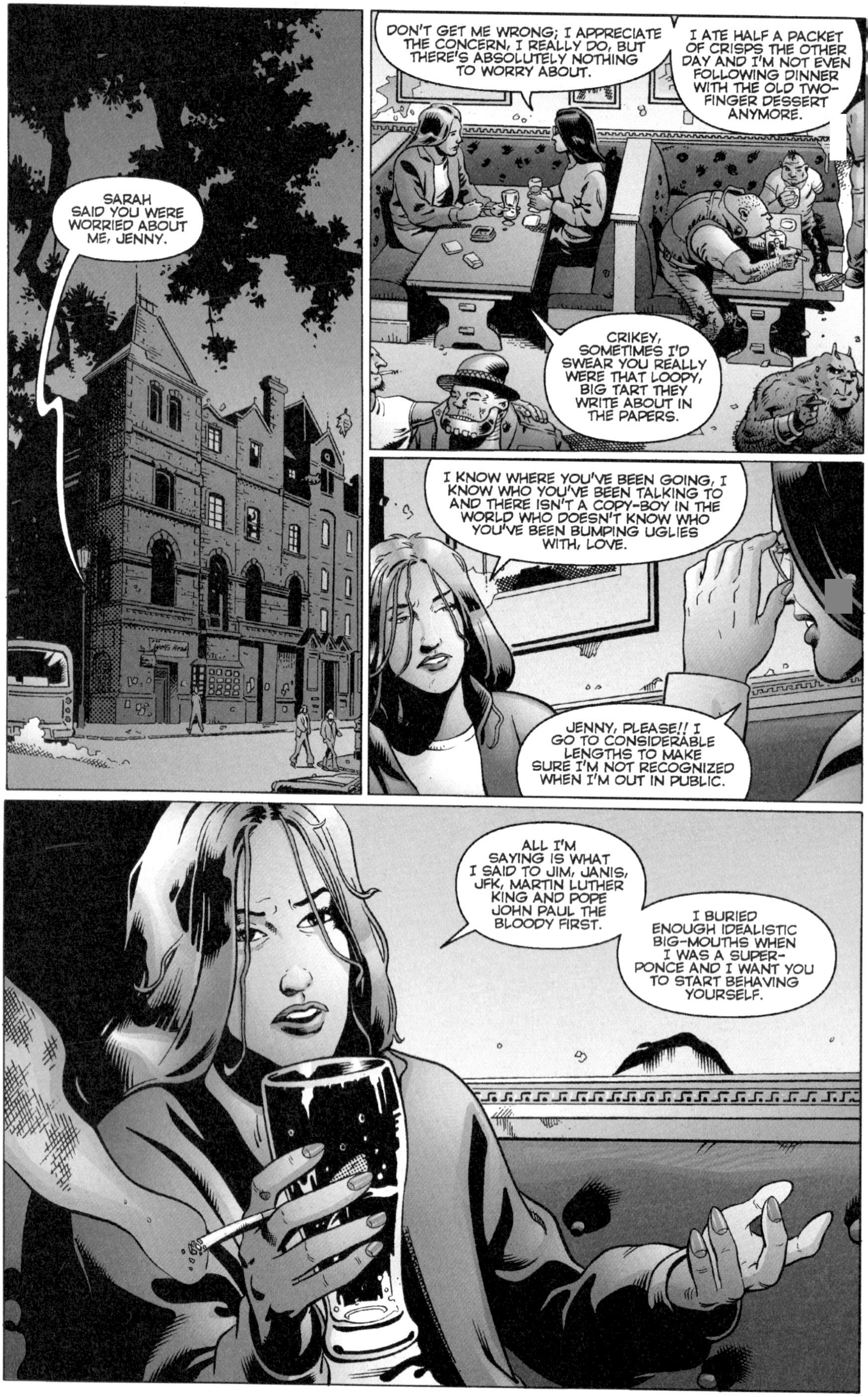
SARAH SAID YOU WERE WORRIED ABOUT ME, JENNY.
DON'T GET ME WRONG; I APPRECIATE THE CONCERN, I REALLY DO, BUT THERE'S ABSOLUTELY NOTHING TO WORRY ABOUT.
I ATE HALF A PACKET OF CRISPS THE OTHER DAY AND I'M NOT EVEN FOLLOWING DINNER WITH THE OLD TWO-FINGER DESSERT ANYMORE.
CRIKEY, SOMETIMES I'D SWEAR YOU REALLY WERE THAT LOOPY, BIG TART THEY WRITE ABOUT IN THE PAPERS.
I KNOW WHERE YOU'VE BEEN GOING, I KNOW WHO YOU'VE BEEN TALKING TO AND THERE ISN'T A COPY-BOY IN THE WORLD WHO DOESN'T KNOW WHO YOU'VE BEEN BUMPING UGLIES WITH, LOVE.
JENNY, PLEASE!! I GO TO CONSIDERABLE LENGTHS TO MAKE SURE I'M NOT RECOGNIZED WHEN I'M OUT IN PUBLIC.
ALL I'M SAYING IS WHAT I SAID TO JIM, JANIS, JFK, MARTIN LUTHER KING AND POPE JOHN PAUL THE BLOODY FIRST.
I BURIED ENOUGH IDEALISTIC BIG-MOUTHS WHEN I WAS A SUPER-PONCE AND I WANT YOU TO START BEHAVING YOURSELF.

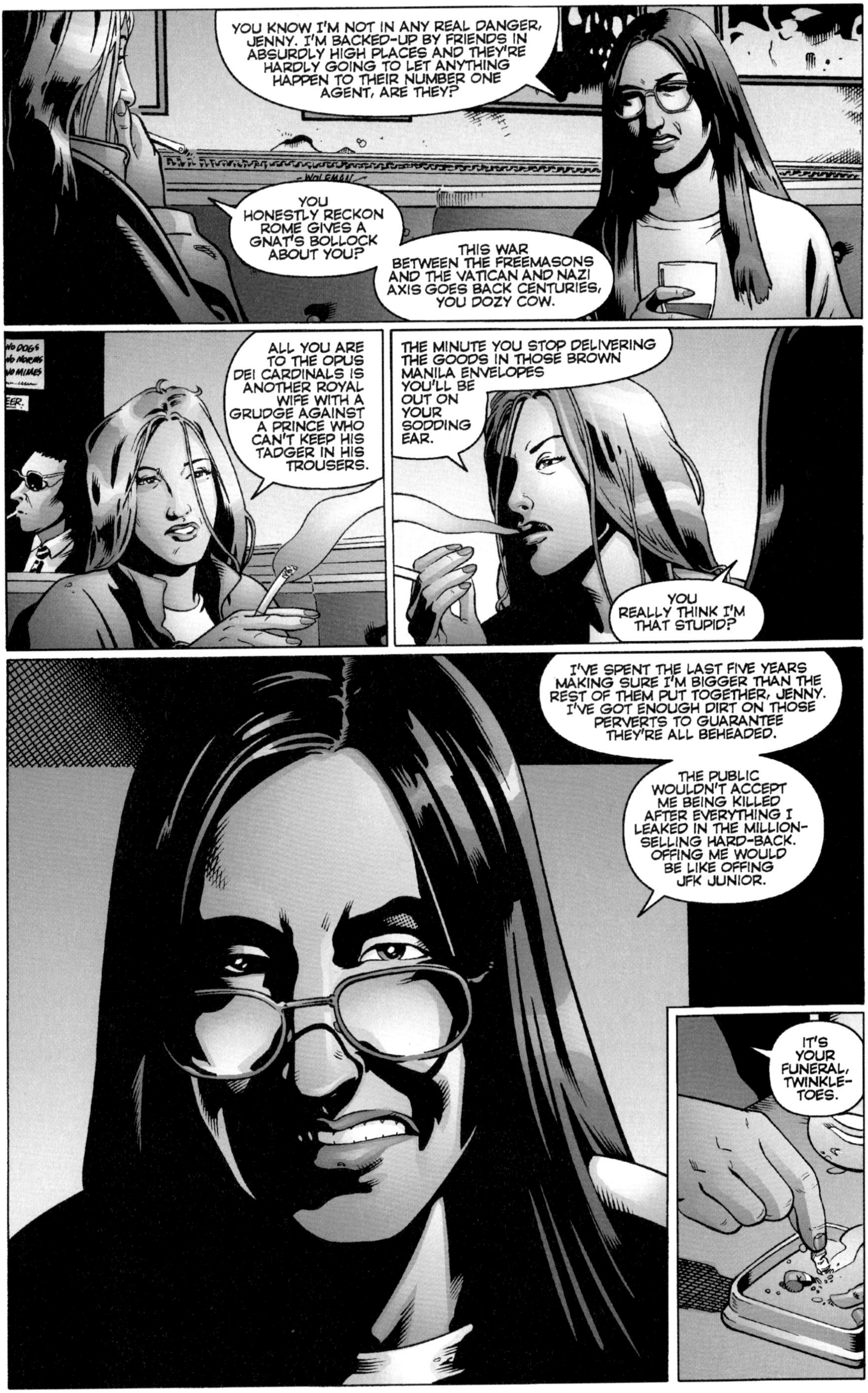
YOU KNOW I'M NOT IN ANY REAL DANGER, JENNY. I'M BACKED-UP BY FRIENDS IN ABSURDLY HIGH PLACES AND THEY'RE HARDLY GOING TO LET ANYTHING HAPPEN TO THEIR NUMBER ONE AGENT, ARE THEY?
YOU HONESTLY RECKON ROME GIVES A GNAT'S BOLLOCK ABOUT YOU?
THIS WAR BETWEEN THE FREEMASONS AND THE VATICAN AND NAZI AXIS GOES BACK CENTURIES, YOU DOZY COW.
NO DOGS NO NORMS NO MIMES
ALL YOU ARE TO THE OPUS DEI CARDINALS IS ANOTHER ROYAL WIFE WITH A GRUDGE AGAINST A PRINCE WHO CAN'T KEEP HIS TADGER IN HIS TROUSERS.
THE MINUTE YOU STOP DELIVERING THE GOODS IN THOSE BROWN MANILA ENVELOPES YOU'LL BE OUT ON YOUR SODDING EAR.
YOU REALLY THINK I'M THAT STUPID?
I'VE SPENT THE LAST FIVE YEARS MAKING SURE I'M BIGGER THAN THE REST OF THEM PUT TOGETHER, JENNY. I'VE GOT ENOUGH DIRT ON THOSE PERVERTS TO GUARANTEE THEY'RE ALL BEHEADED.
THE PUBLIC WOULDN'T ACCEPT ME BEING KILLED AFTER EVERYTHING I LEAKED IN THE MILLION-SELLING HARD-BACK. OFFING ME WOULD BE LIKE OFFING JFK JUNIOR.
IT'S YOUR FUNERAL, TWINKLE-TOES.

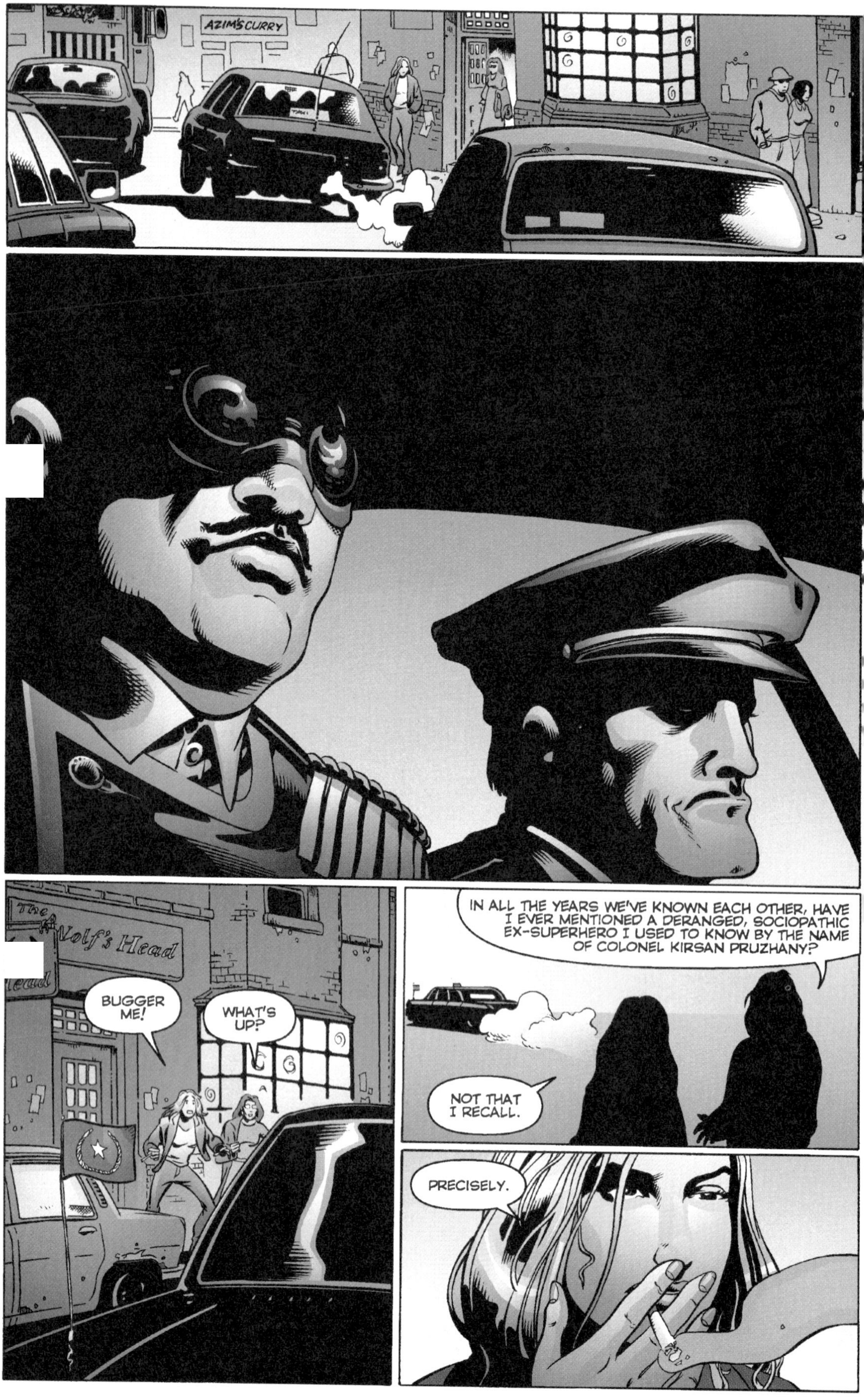
AZIM'S CURRY
BUGGER ME!
WHAT'S UP?
IN ALL THE YEARS WE'VE KNOWN EACH OTHER, HAVE I EVER MENTIONED A DERANGED, SOCIOPATHIC EX-SUPERHERO I USED TO KNOW BY THE NAME OF COLONEL KIRSAN PRUZHANY?
NOT THAT I RECALL.
PRECISELY.

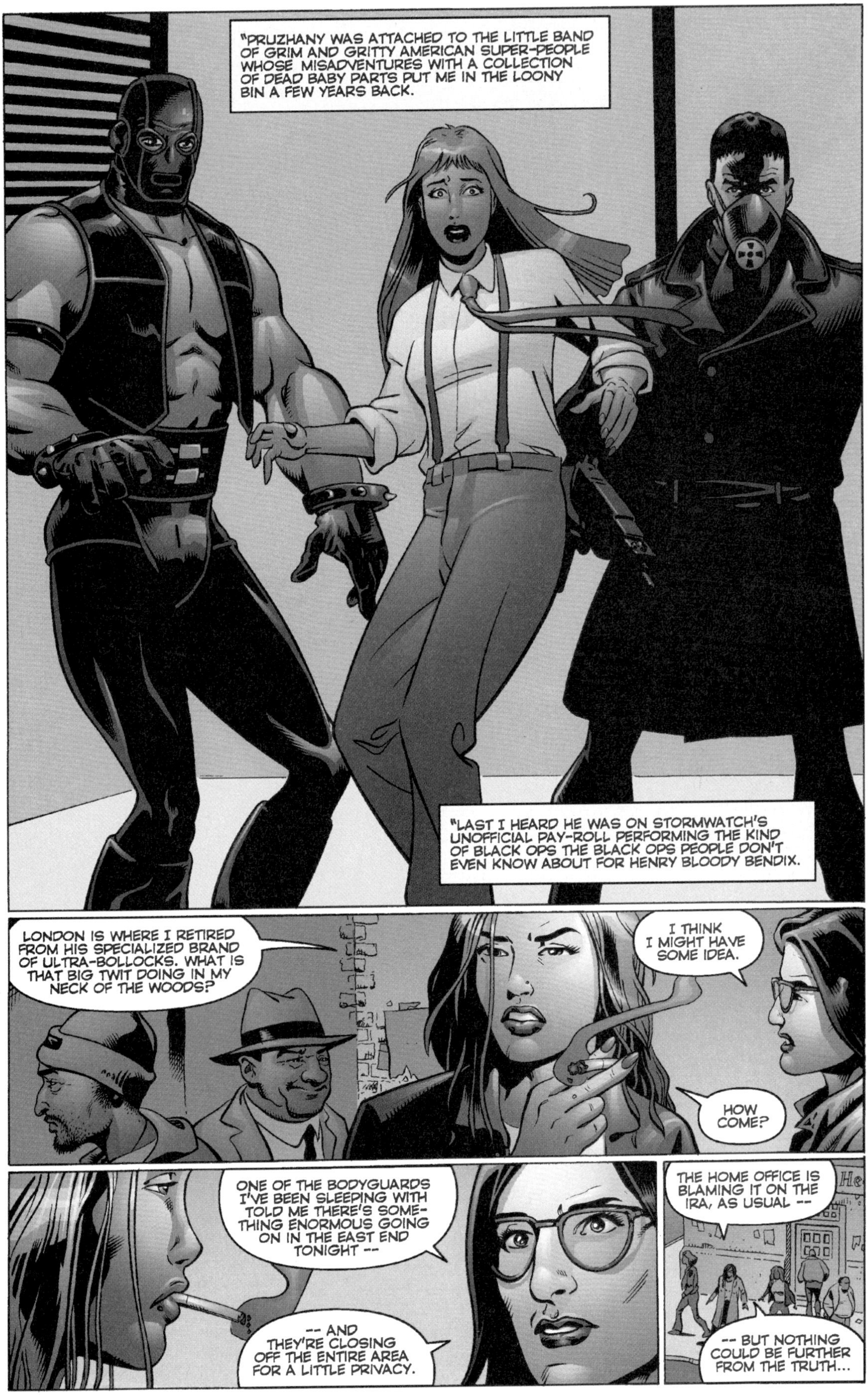
"PRUZHANY WAS ATTACHED TO THE LITTLE BAND OF GRIM AND GRITTY AMERICAN SUPER-PEOPLE WHOSE MISADVENTURES WITH A COLLECTION OF DEAD BABY PARTS PUT ME IN THE LOONY BIN A FEW YEARS BACK.
"LAST I HEARD HE WAS ON STORMWATCH'S UNOFFICIAL PAY-ROLL PERFORMING THE KIND OF BLACK OPS THE BLACK OPS PEOPLE DON'T EVEN KNOW ABOUT FOR HENRY BLOODY BENDIX.
LONDON IS WHERE I RETIRED FROM HIS SPECIALIZED BRAND OF ULTRA-BOLLOCKS. WHAT IS THAT BIG TWIT DOING IN MY NECK OF THE WOODS?
I THINK I MIGHT HAVE SOME IDEA.
HOW COME?
ONE OF THE BODYGUARDS I'VE BEEN SLEEPING WITH TOLD ME THERE'S SOMETHING ENORMOUS GOING ON IN THE EAST END TONIGHT --
-- AND THEY'RE CLOSING OFF THE ENTIRE AREA FOR A LITTLE PRIVACY.
THE HOME OFFICE IS BLAMING IT ON THE IRA, AS USUAL --
-- BUT NOTHING COULD BE FURTHER FROM THE TRUTH...

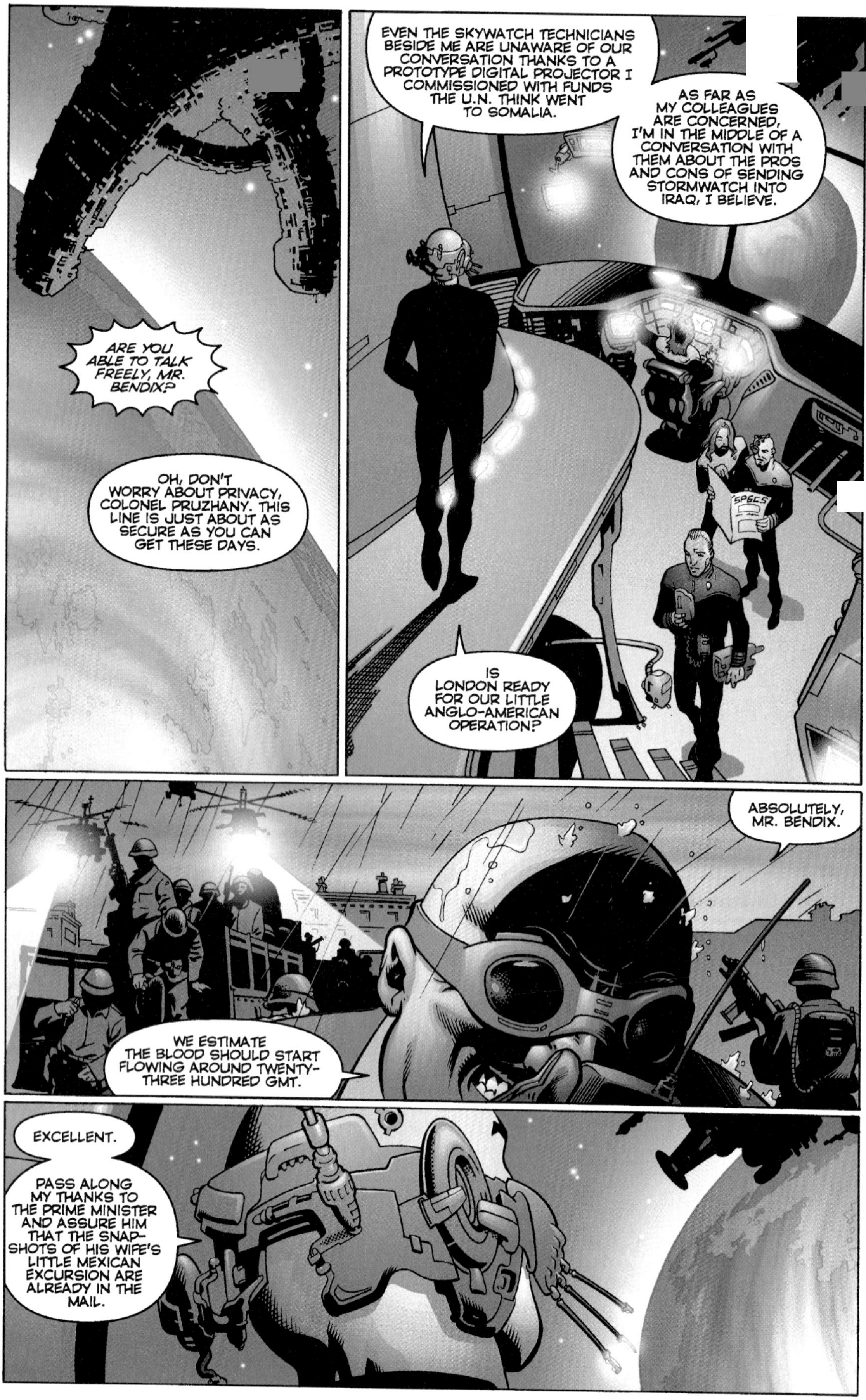
ARE YOU ABLE TO TALK FREELY, MR. BENDIX?
OH, DON'T WORRY ABOUT PRIVACY, COLONEL PRUZHANY. THIS LINE IS JUST ABOUT AS SECURE AS YOU CAN GET THESE DAYS.
EVEN THE SKYWATCH TECHNICIANS BESIDE ME ARE UNAWARE OF OUR CONVERSATION THANKS TO A PROTOTYPE DIGITAL PROJECTOR I COMMISSIONED WITH FUNDS THE U.N. THINK WENT TO SOMALIA.
AS FAR AS MY COLLEAGUES ARE CONCERNED, I'M IN THE MIDDLE OF A CONVERSATION WITH THEM ABOUT THE PROS AND CONS OF SENDING STORMWATCH INTO IRAQ, I BELIEVE.
SPECS
IS LONDON READY FOR OUR LITTLE ANGLO-AMERICAN OPERATION?
ABSOLUTELY, MR. BENDIX.
WE ESTIMATE THE BLOOD SHOULD START FLOWING AROUND TWENTY-THREE HUNDRED GMT.
EXCELLENT.
PASS ALONG MY THANKS TO THE PRIME MINISTER AND ASSURE HIM THAT THE SNAPSHOTS OF HIS WIFE'S LITTLE MEXICAN EXCURSION ARE ALREADY IN THE MAIL.

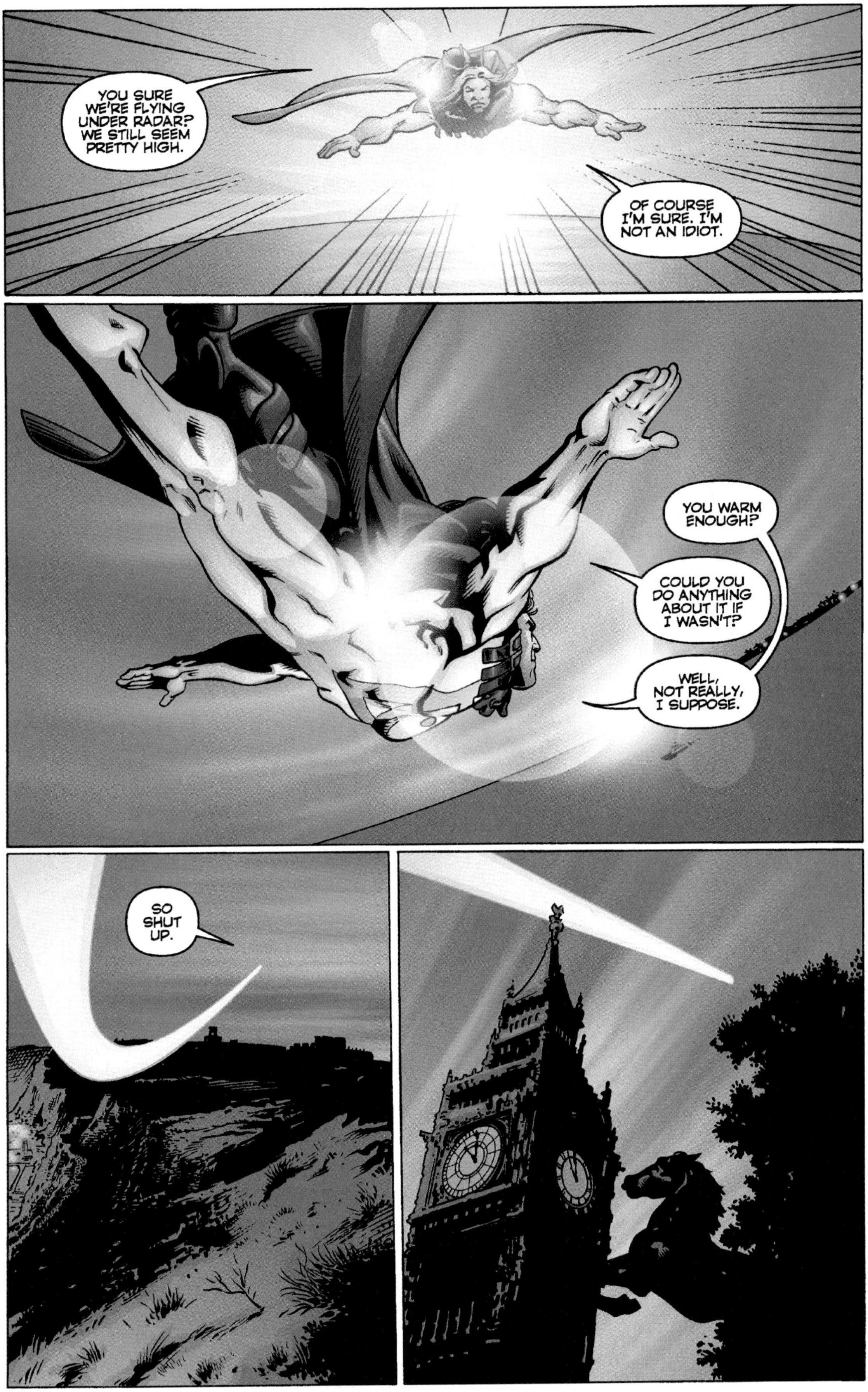
YOU SURE WE'RE FLYING UNDER RADAR? WE STILL SEEM PRETTY HIGH.
OF COURSE I'M SURE. I'M NOT AN IDIOT.
YOU WARM ENOUGH?
COULD YOU DO ANYTHING ABOUT IT IF I WASN'T?
WELL, NOT REALLY, I SUPPOSE.
SO SHUT UP.

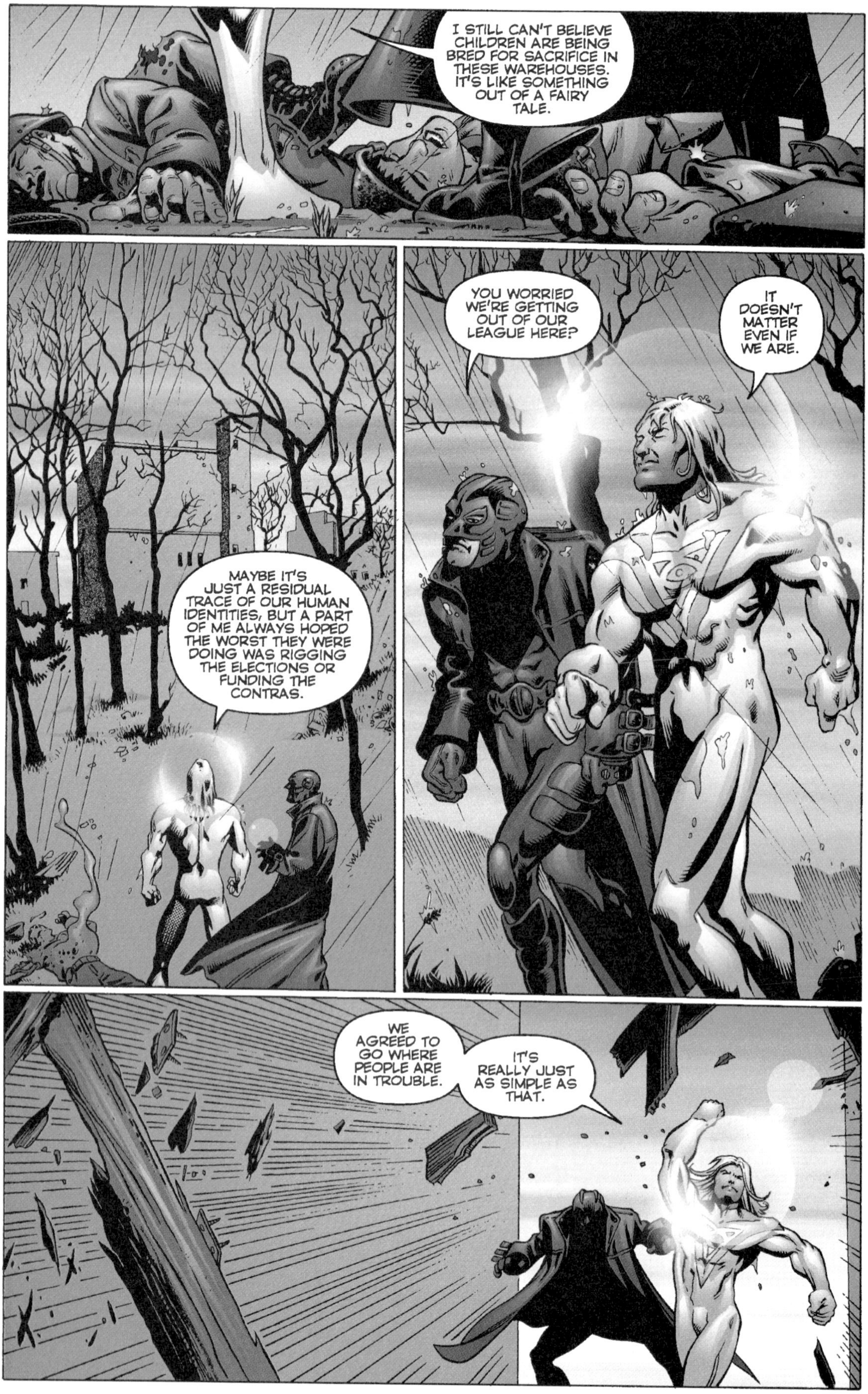
I STILL CAN'T BELIEVE CHILDREN ARE BEING BRED FOR SACRIFICE IN THESE WAREHOUSES. IT'S LIKE SOMETHING OUT OF A FAIRY TALE.
MAYBE IT'S JUST A RESIDUAL TRACE OF OUR HUMAN IDENTITIES, BUT A PART OF ME ALWAYS HOPED THE WORST THEY WERE DOING WAS RIGGING THE ELECTIONS OR FUNDING THE CONTRAS.
YOU WORRIED WE'RE GETTING OUT OF OUR LEAGUE HERE?
IT DOESN'T MATTER EVEN IF WE ARE.
WE AGREED TO GO WHERE PEOPLE ARE IN TROUBLE.
IT'S REALLY JUST AS SIMPLE AS THAT.

WHAT HAPPENED TO THE KIDS?

APOLLO, GET US OUT OF HERE AS QUICKLY AS YOU CAN...

WE'RE STANDING IN THE MIDDLE OF A THREE-DIMENSIONAL CONSTRUCT.

THE WHOLE THING WAS A TRAP.

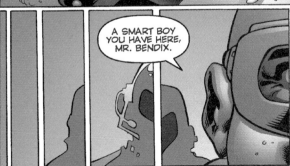

A SMART BOY YOU HAVE HERE, MR. BENDIX.

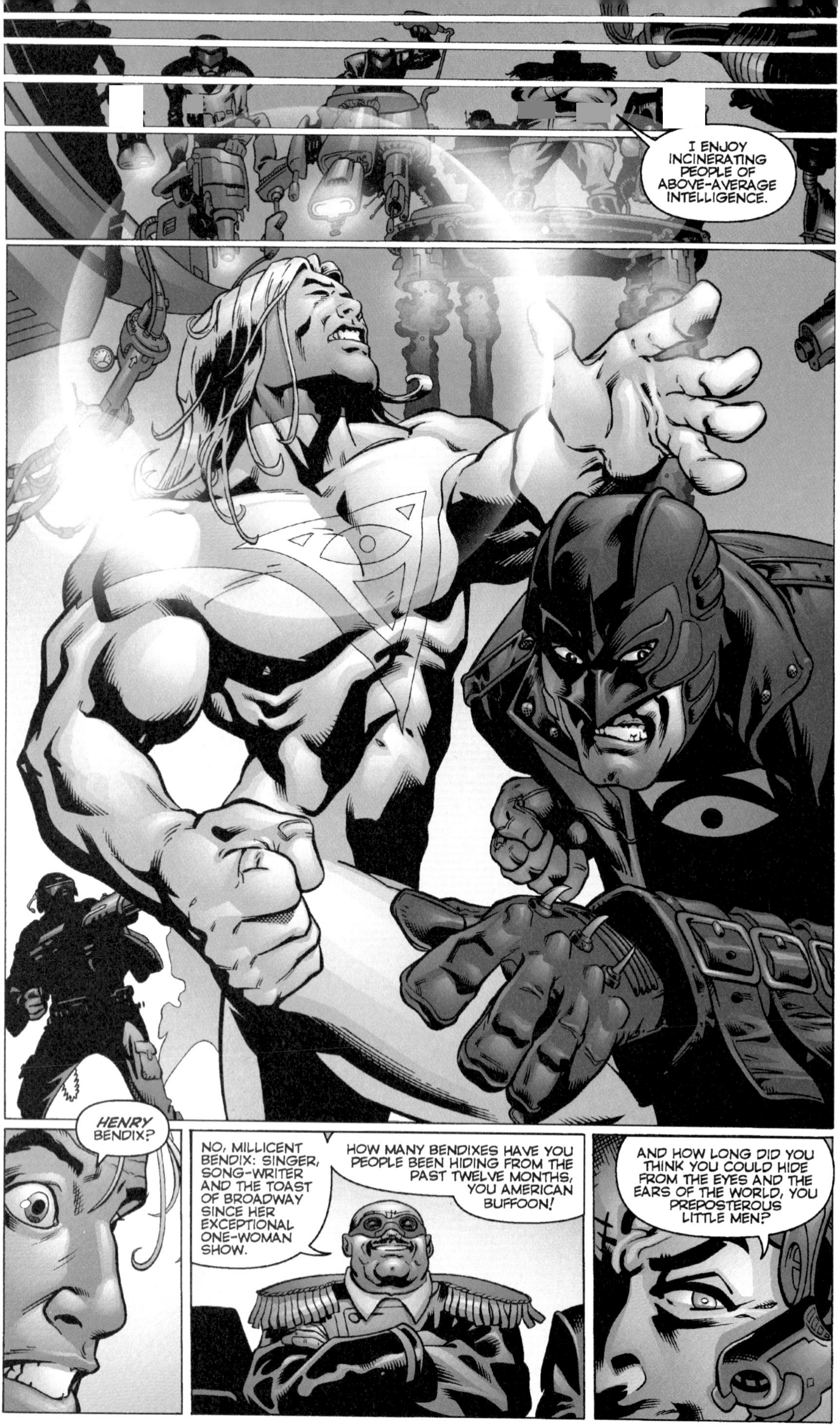
I ENJOY INCINERATING PEOPLE OF ABOVE-AVERAGE INTELLIGENCE.
HENRY BENDIX?
NO, MILLICENT BENDIX: SINGER, SONG-WRITER AND THE TOAST OF BROADWAY SINCE HER EXCEPTIONAL ONE-WOMAN SHOW.
HOW MANY BENDIXES HAVE YOU PEOPLE BEEN HIDING FROM THE PAST TWELVE MONTHS, YOU AMERICAN BUFFOON!
AND HOW LONG DID YOU THINK YOU COULD HIDE FROM THE EYES AND THE EARS OF THE WORLD, YOU PREPOSTEROUS LITTLE MEN?

BENDIX, LISTEN TO US! THERE ARE CHILDREN AT RISK HERE...!

THERE ARE NO CHILDREN AT RISK, APOLLO. THERE WERE NEVER ANY CHILDREN. THIS ENTIRE OPERATION WAS JUST AN ELABORATE RUSE TO DRAW YOU TWO INTO THE OPEN.

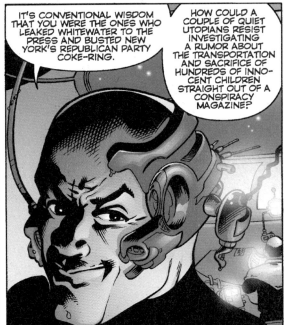

IT'S CONVENTIONAL WISDOM THAT YOU WERE THE ONES WHO LEAKED WHITEWATER TO THE PRESS AND BUSTED NEW YORK'S REPUBLICAN PARTY COKE-RING.

HOW COULD A COUPLE OF QUIET UTOPIANS RESIST INVESTIGATING A RUMOR ABOUT THE TRANSPORTATION AND SACRIFICE OF HUNDREDS OF INNOCENT CHILDREN STRAIGHT OUT OF A CONSPIRACY MAGAZINE?

YOU'RE FIVE THOUSAND MILES FROM HOME IN A COUNTRY WITH NO POST-HUMAN PRESENCE WORTH MENTIONING, GENTLEMEN.

THE LITTLE ROGUE OPERATIONS YOU'VE BEEN INVESTIGATING OUTSIDE MY JURISDICTION THESE PAST TWELVE MONTHS ARE NOW OFFICIALLY OVER.

HENRY, FOR GOD'S SAKE! WE WERE ONLY DOING WHAT YOU DESIGNED US TO DO! WE JUST WANTED TO MAKE THINGS BETTER!

THE WORLD WILL BE BETTER, MIDNIGHTER, BUT ON MY TERMS—

--NOT TWO INSIGNIFICANT PIECES OF GENETIC TRASH WHO ESCAPED FROM ONE OF MY LESS-EXPENSIVE PETRI-DISHES.

YOU CAN KILL THEM NOW, INCIDENTALLY.

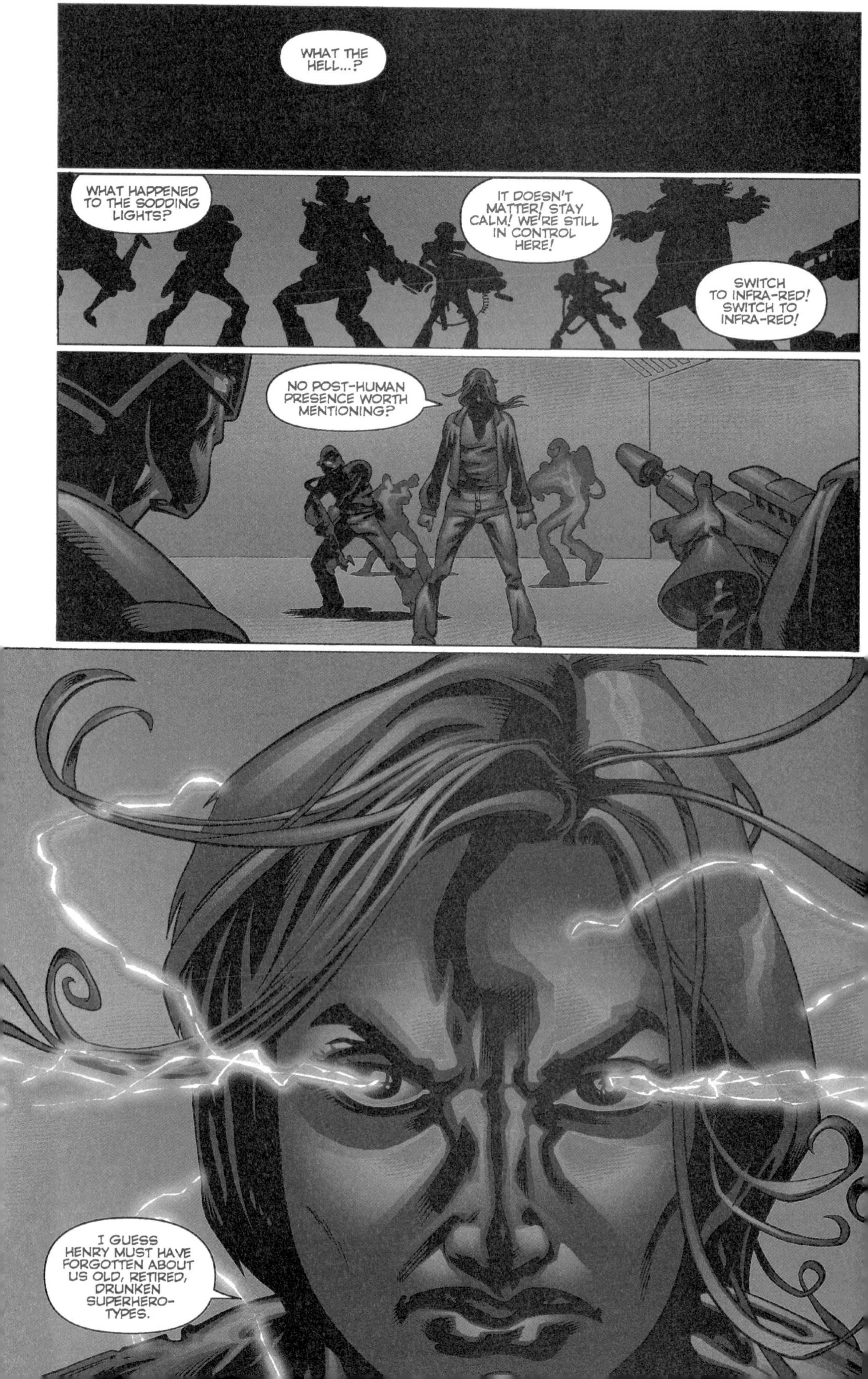
WHAT THE HELL...?
WHAT HAPPENED TO THE SODDING LIGHTS?
IT DOESN'T MATTER! STAY CALM! WE'RE STILL IN CONTROL HERE!
SWITCH TO INFRA-RED! SWITCH TO INFRA-RED!
NO POST-HUMAN PRESENCE WORTH MENTIONING?
I GUESS HENRY MUST HAVE FORGOTTEN ABOUT US OLD, RETIRED, DRUNKEN SUPERHERO-TYPES.

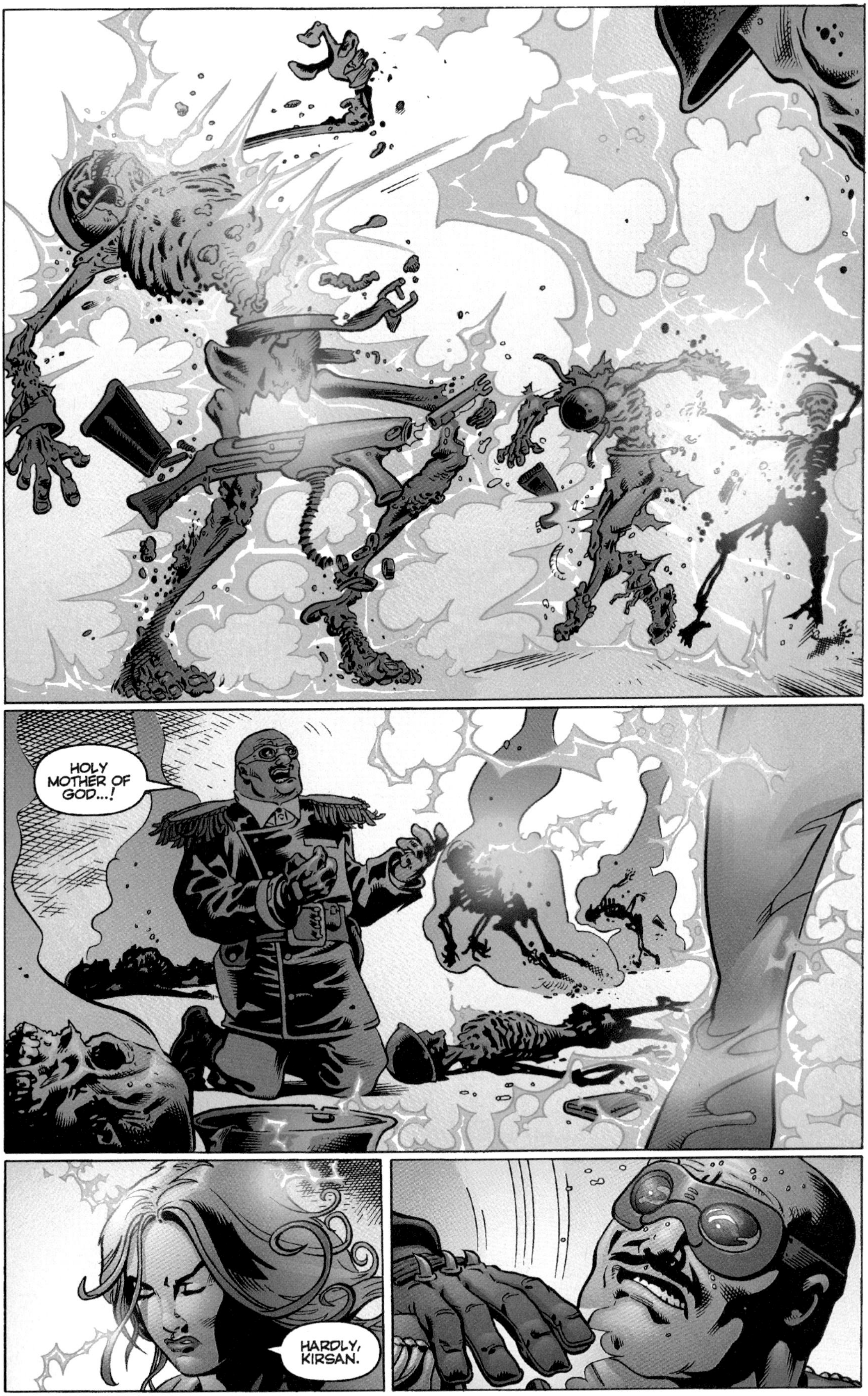
HOLY MOTHER OF GOD...!
HARDLY, KIRSAN.

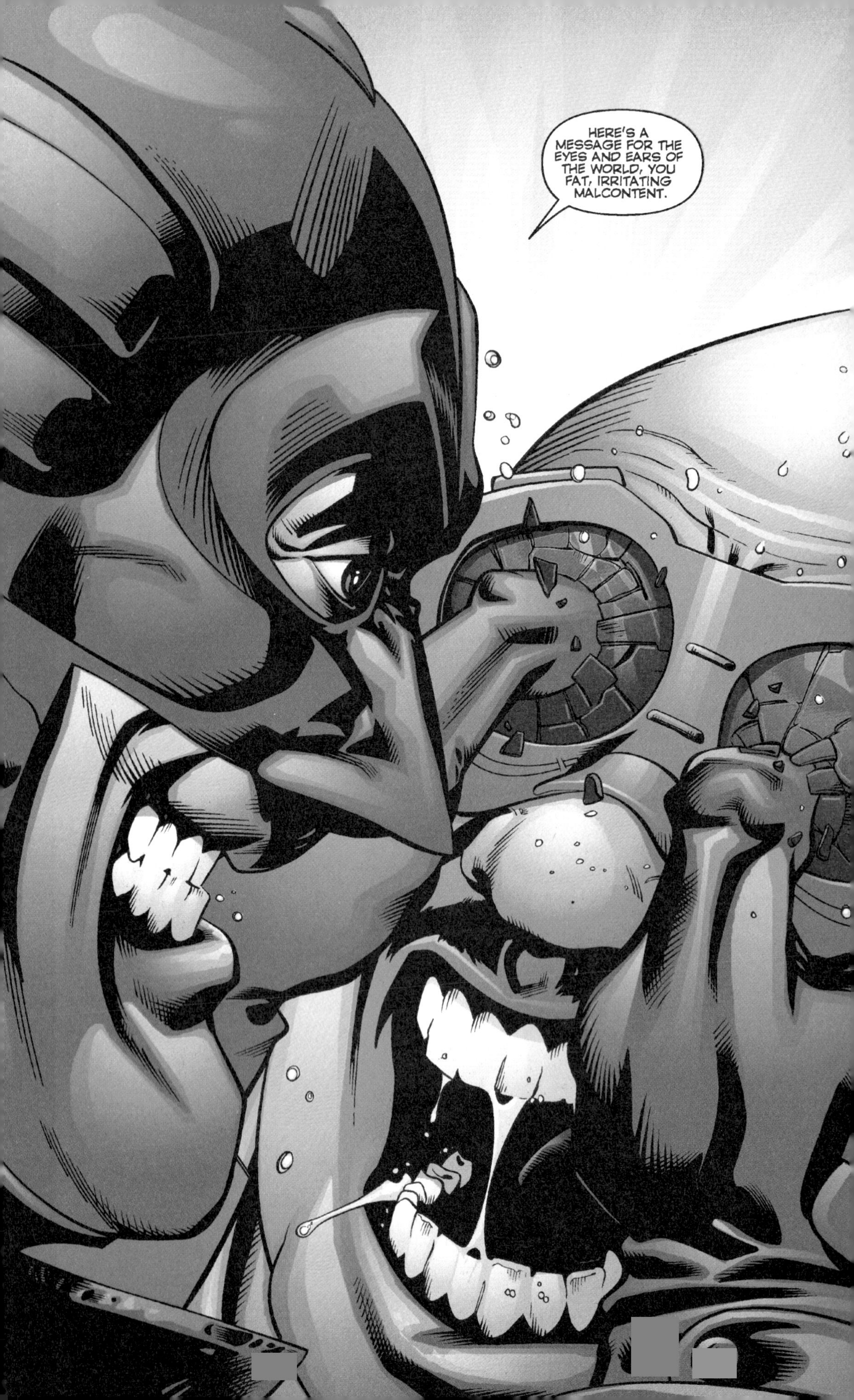
HERE'S A MESSAGE FOR THE EYES AND EARS OF THE WORLD, YOU FAT, IRRITATING MALCONTENT.

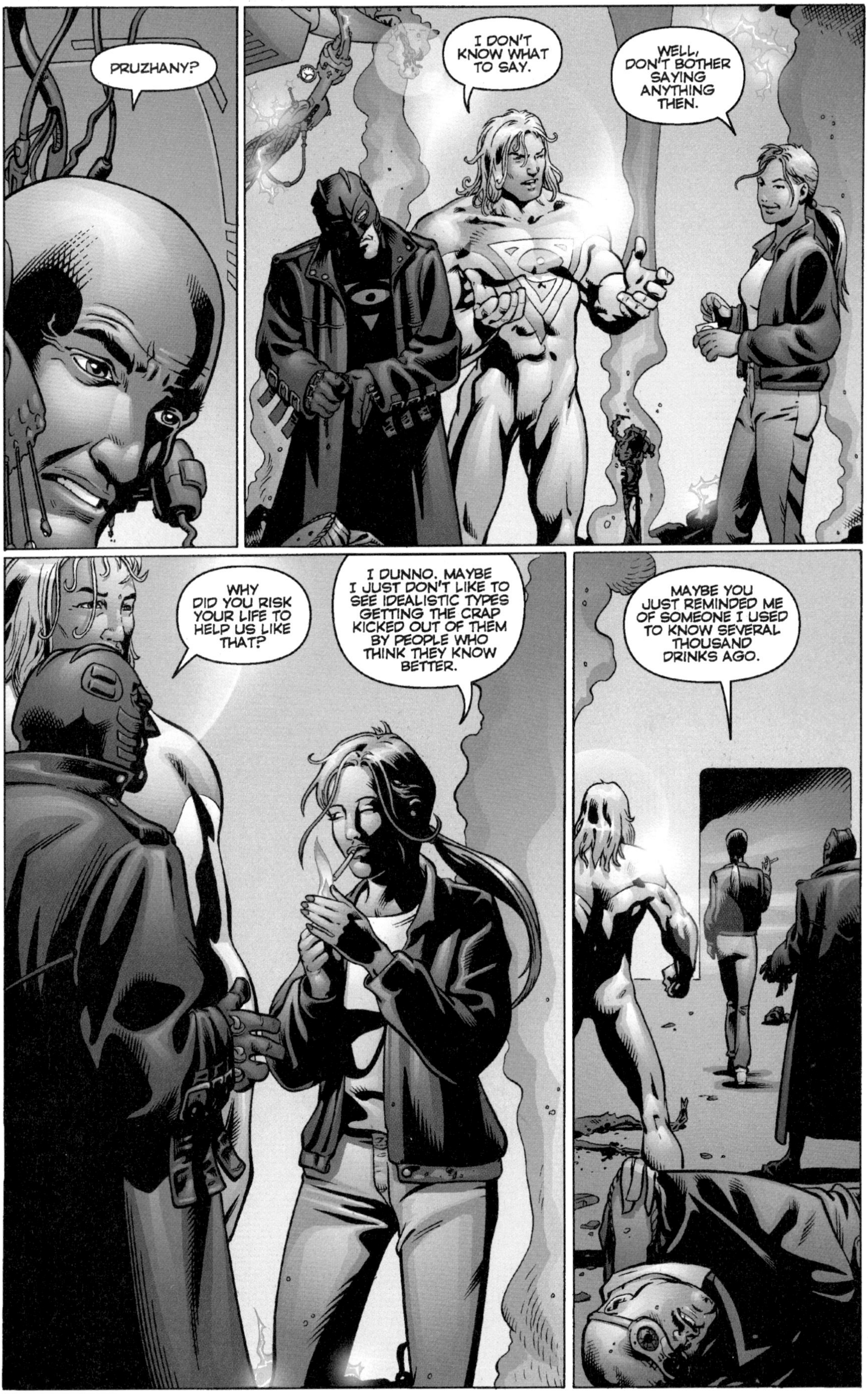
PRUZHANY?
I DON'T KNOW WHAT TO SAY.
WELL, DON'T BOTHER SAYING ANYTHING THEN.
WHY DID YOU RISK YOUR LIFE TO HELP US LIKE THAT?
I DUNNO. MAYBE I JUST DON'T LIKE TO SEE IDEALISTIC TYPES GETTING THE CRAP KICKED OUT OF THEM BY PEOPLE WHO THINK THEY KNOW BETTER.
MAYBE YOU JUST REMINDED ME OF SOMEONE I USED TO KNOW SEVERAL THOUSAND DRINKS AGO.

Chapter Three
A Tale of Two Cities

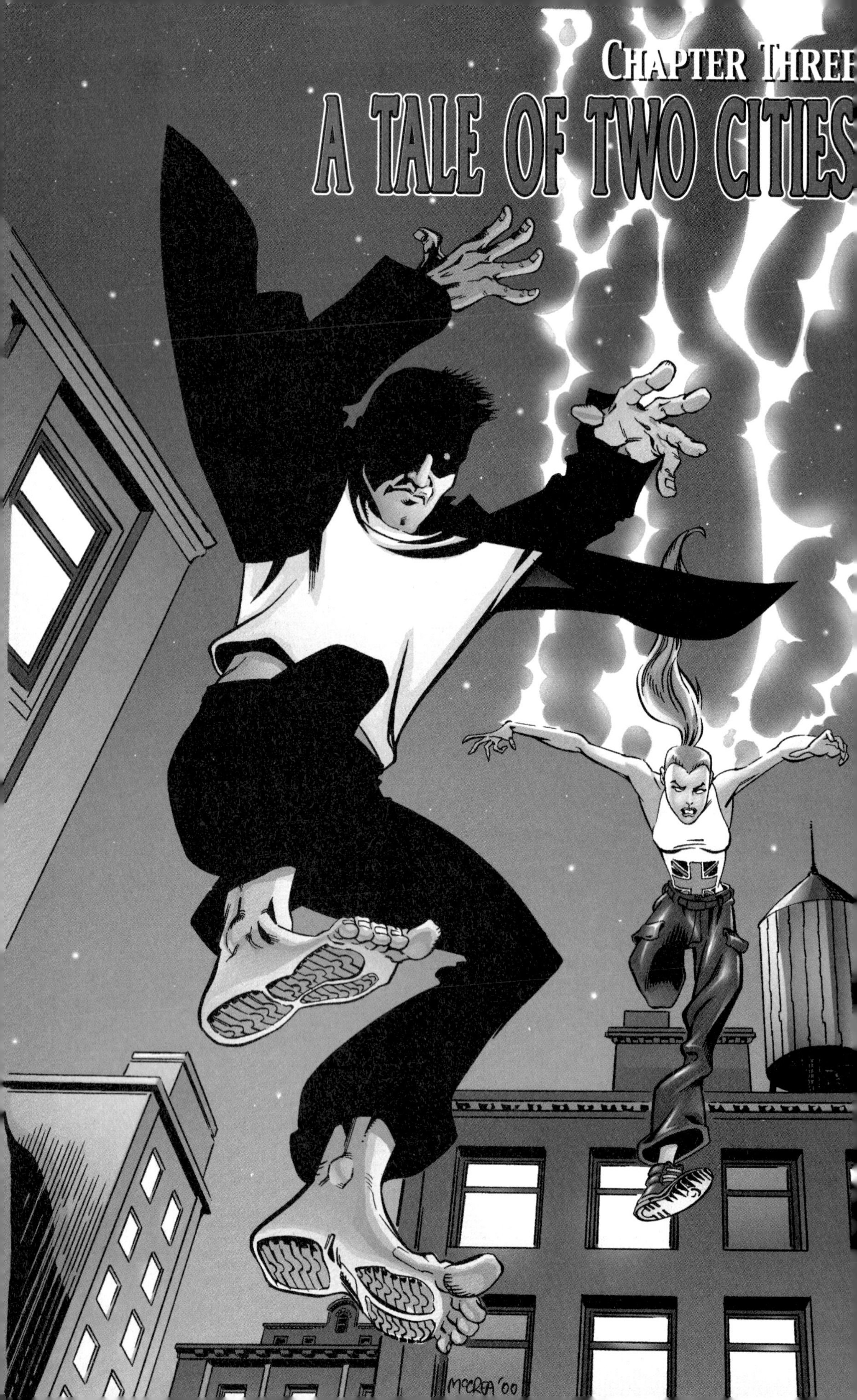
McCREA '00

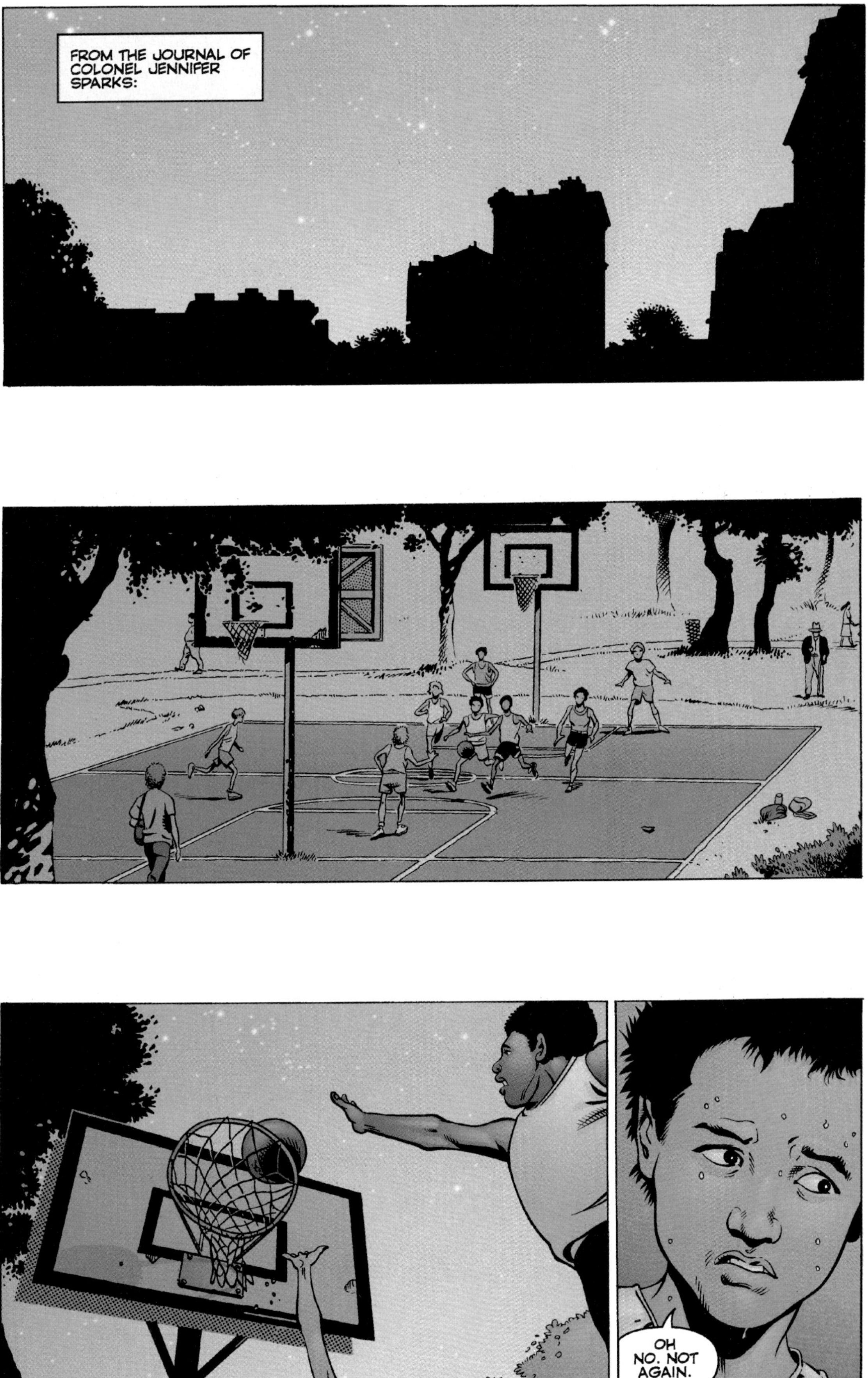
FROM THE JOURNAL OF COLONEL JENNIFER SPARKS:
OH NO. NOT AGAIN.

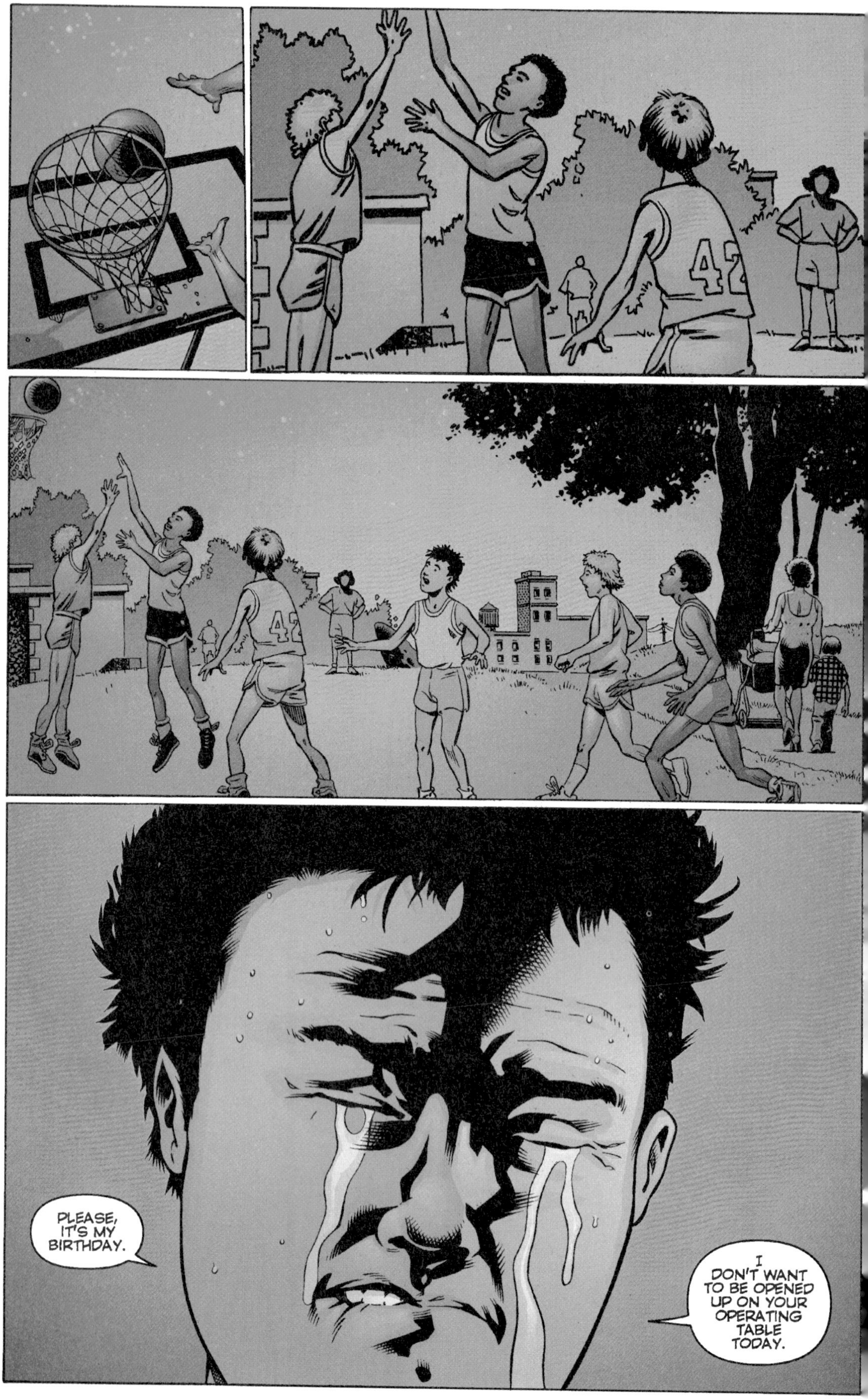

PLEASE, IT'S MY BIRTHDAY.
I DON'T WANT TO BE OPENED UP ON YOUR OPERATING TABLE TODAY.

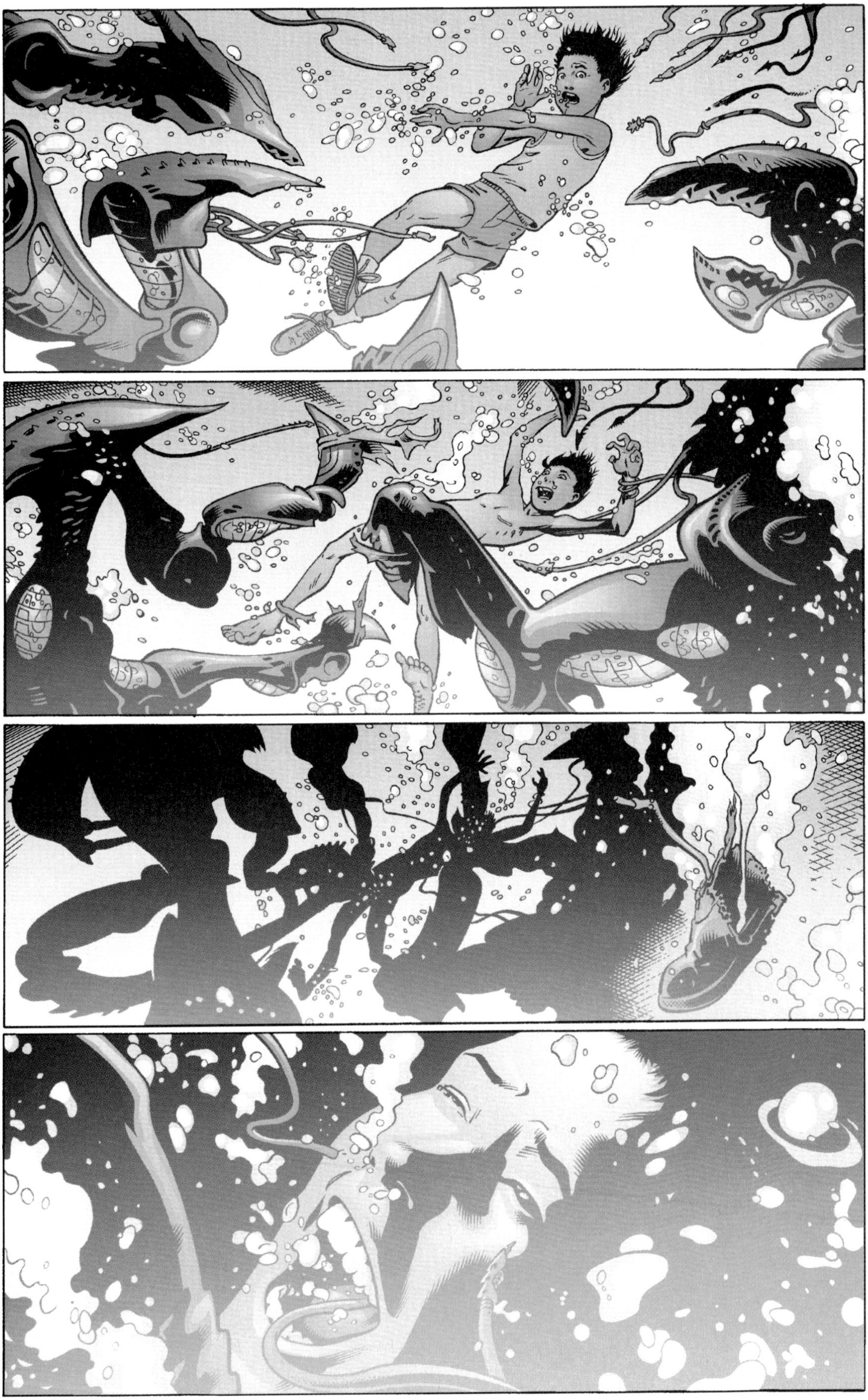

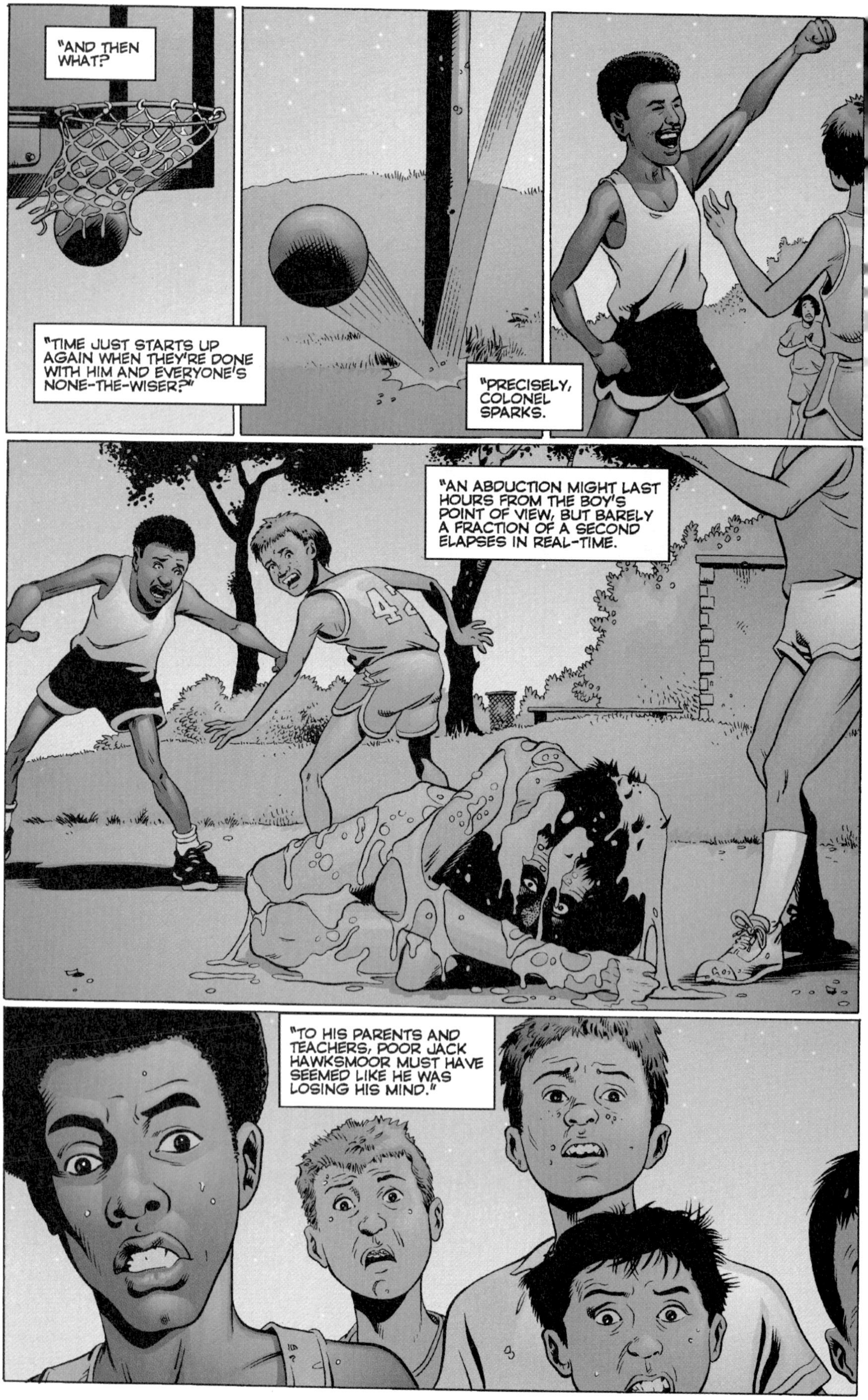
"AND THEN WHAT?
"TIME JUST STARTS UP AGAIN WHEN THEY'RE DONE WITH HIM AND EVERYONE'S NONE-THE-WISER?"
"PRECISELY, COLONEL SPARKS.
"AN ABDUCTION MIGHT LAST HOURS FROM THE BOY'S POINT OF VIEW, BUT BARELY A FRACTION OF A SECOND ELAPSES IN REAL-TIME.
"TO HIS PARENTS AND TEACHERS, POOR JACK HAWKSMOOR MUST HAVE SEEMED LIKE HE WAS LOSING HIS MIND."

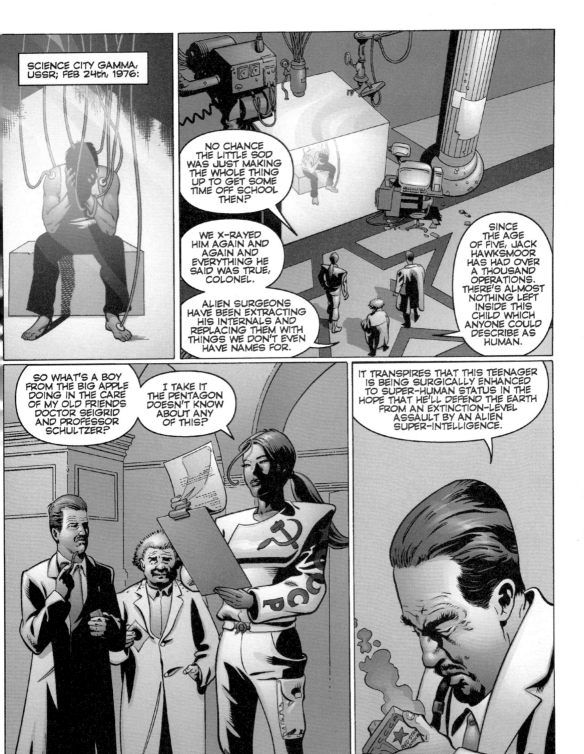

SCIENCE CITY GAMMA, USSR; FEB 24th, 1976:

NO CHANCE THE LITTLE SOD WAS JUST MAKING THE WHOLE THING UP TO GET SOME TIME OFF SCHOOL THEN?

WE X-RAYED HIM AGAIN AND AGAIN AND EVERYTHING HE SAID WAS TRUE, COLONEL.

ALIEN SURGEONS HAVE BEEN EXTRACTING HIS INTERNALS AND REPLACING THEM WITH THINGS WE DON'T EVEN HAVE NAMES FOR.

SINCE THE AGE OF FIVE, JACK HAWKSMOOR HAS HAD OVER A THOUSAND OPERATIONS. THERE'S ALMOST NOTHING LEFT INSIDE THIS CHILD WHICH ANYONE COULD DESCRIBE AS HUMAN.

SO WHAT'S A BOY FROM THE BIG APPLE DOING IN THE CARE OF MY OLD FRIENDS DOCTOR SEIGRID AND PROFESSOR SCHULTZER?

I TAKE IT THE PENTAGON DOESN'T KNOW ABOUT ANY OF THIS?

IT TRANSPIRES THAT THIS TEENAGER IS BEING SURGICALLY ENHANCED TO SUPER-HUMAN STATUS IN THE HOPE THAT HE'LL DEFEND THE EARTH FROM AN EXTINCTION-LEVEL ASSAULT BY AN ALIEN SUPER-INTELLIGENCE.

ACTUALLY, COLONEL, YOUNG HAWKSMOOR IS OUR GUEST AT THE PENTAGON'S REQUEST.

WHAT ELSE COULD THE AMERICANS DO EXCEPT MAKE A SECRET APPEAL FOR INTERNATIONAL COOPERATION IN THE MATTER?

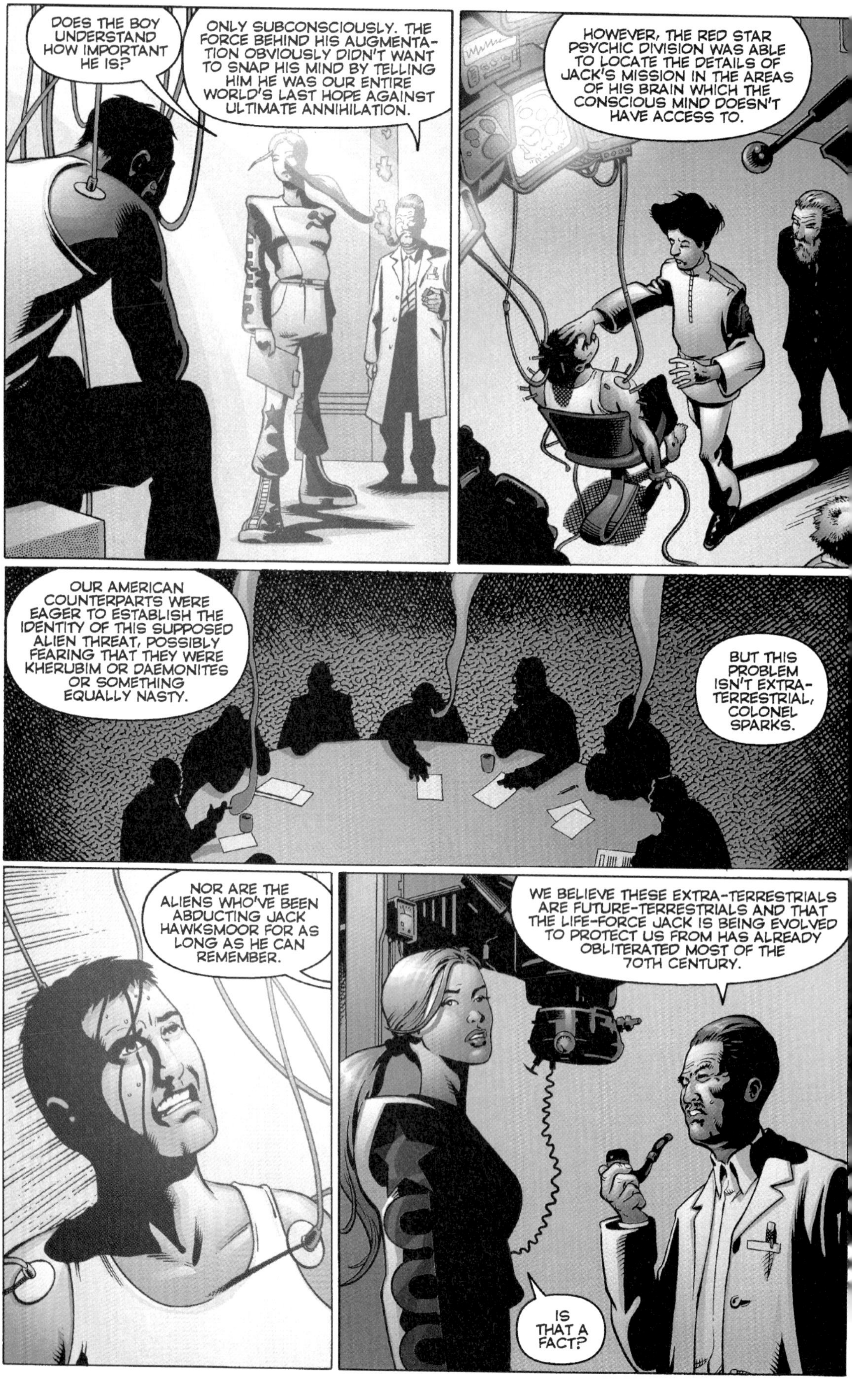
DOES THE BOY UNDERSTAND HOW IMPORTANT HE IS?
ONLY SUBCONSCIOUSLY. THE FORCE BEHIND HIS AUGMENTATION OBVIOUSLY DIDN'T WANT TO SNAP HIS MIND BY TELLING HIM HE WAS OUR ENTIRE WORLD'S LAST HOPE AGAINST ULTIMATE ANNIHILATION.
HOWEVER, THE RED STAR PSYCHIC DIVISION WAS ABLE TO LOCATE THE DETAILS OF JACK'S MISSION IN THE AREAS OF HIS BRAIN WHICH THE CONSCIOUS MIND DOESN'T HAVE ACCESS TO.
OUR AMERICAN COUNTERPARTS WERE EAGER TO ESTABLISH THE IDENTITY OF THIS SUPPOSED ALIEN THREAT, POSSIBLY FEARING THAT THEY WERE KHERUBIM OR DAEMONITES OR SOMETHING EQUALLY NASTY.
BUT THIS PROBLEM ISN'T EXTRA-TERRESTRIAL, COLONEL SPARKS.
NOR ARE THE ALIENS WHO'VE BEEN ABDUCTING JACK HAWKSMOOR FOR AS LONG AS HE CAN REMEMBER.
WE BELIEVE THESE EXTRA-TERRESTRIALS ARE FUTURE-TERRESTRIALS AND THAT THE LIFE-FORCE JACK IS BEING EVOLVED TO PROTECT US FROM HAS ALREADY OBLITERATED MOST OF THE 70TH CENTURY.
IS THAT A FACT?

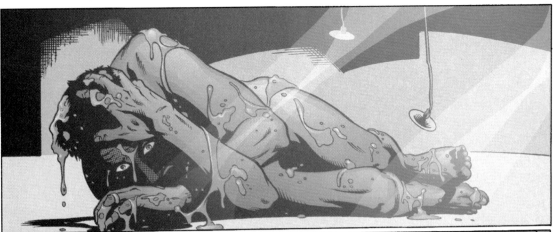

AND HOW OFTEN ARE THESE ABDUCTIONS HAPPENING EXACTLY?

EVERY COUPLE OF HOURS AS WE APPROACH THE INVASION DATE.

OUR ALLIES IN THE FUTURE ARE HOPING TO COMPLETE HIS TRANSFORMATION INTO A POST-HUMAN SOLDIER BY THIS POINT, BUT WE'RE RATHER PESSIMISTIC ABOUT HIS CHANCES.

AS FAR AS WE UNDERSTAND, JACK CAN DRAW INCREDIBLE POWERS FROM THIS AND ANY OTHER CITY. HE EATS POLLUTION, TALKS TO BUILDINGS AND IS VIRTUALLY INDESTRUCTIBLE.

UP AGAINST CONVENTIONAL FORCES, HE'S PROBABLY FORMIDABLE ENOUGH TO TURN A SMALL COUNTRY INTO A GRAVEYARD.

UP AGAINST A FOUR-DIMENSIONAL KILLER WHICH HAS MURDERED ALMOST EVERY LIVING CREATURE IN EARTH'S DISTANT FUTURE?

WELL, I'M SURE YOU CAN APPRECIATE WHY WE FELT IT WAS ESSENTIAL TO MAKE PROVISIONS OF OUR OWN, COLONEL SPARKS.

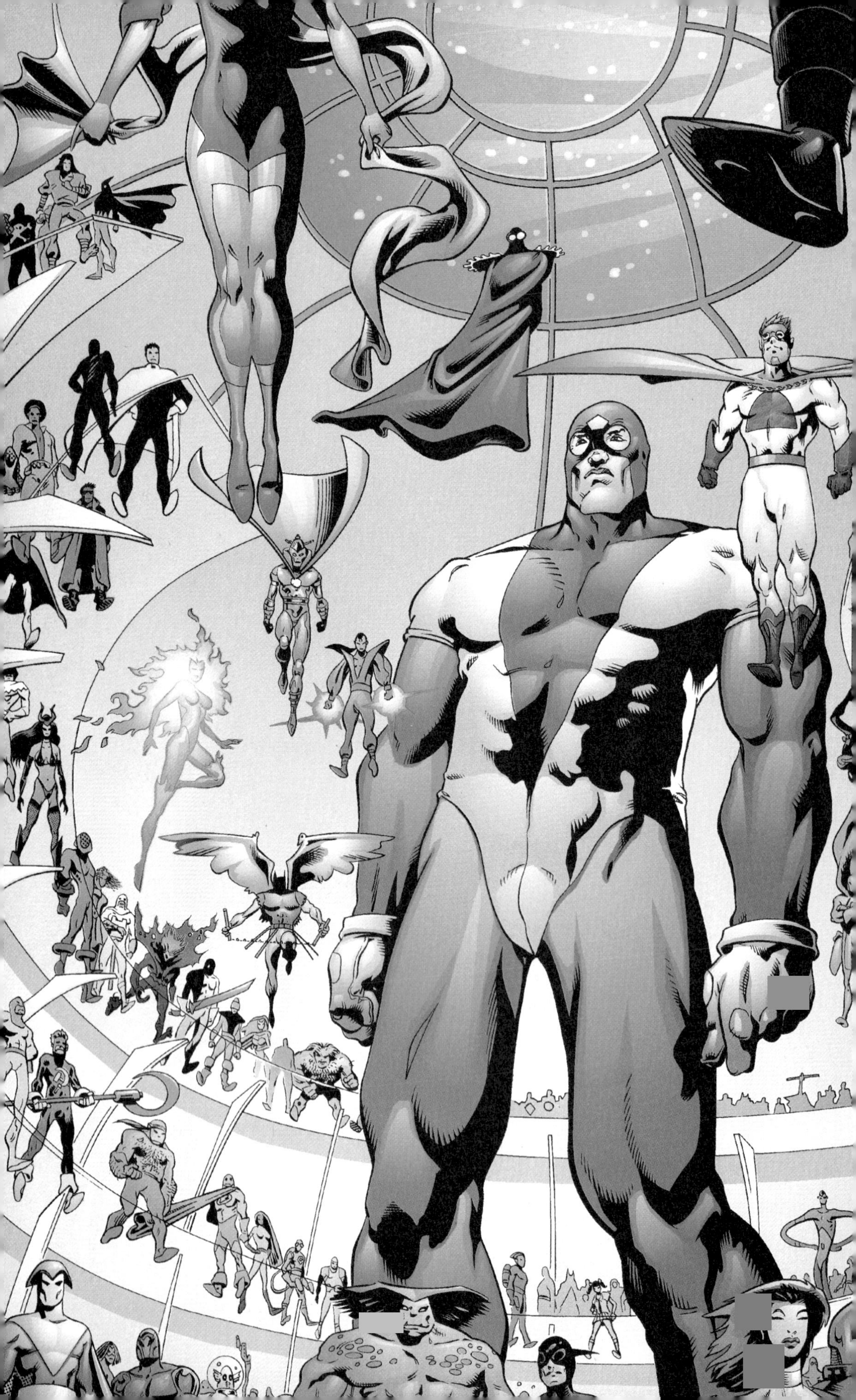

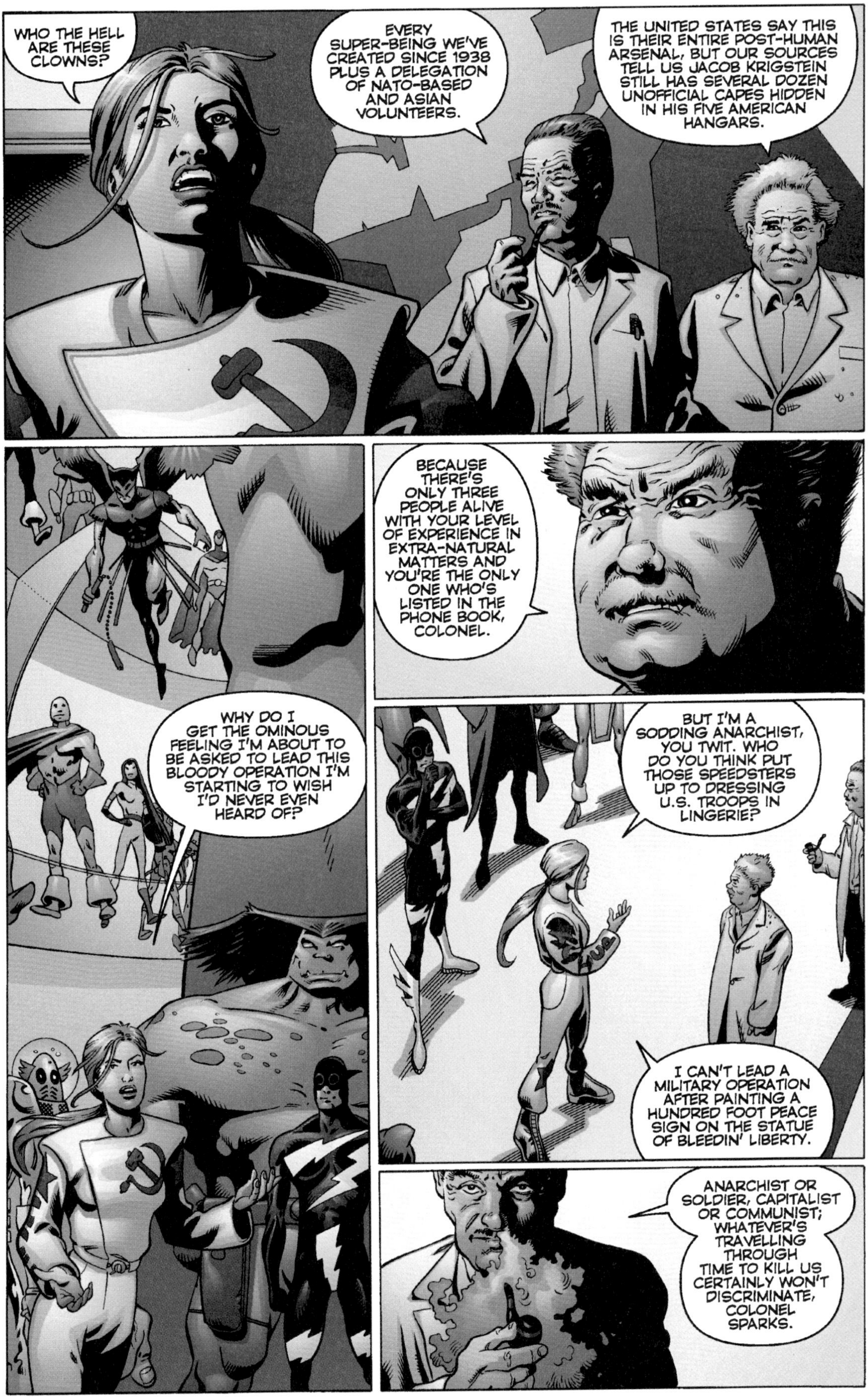
WHO THE HELL ARE THESE CLOWNS?
EVERY SUPER-BEING WE'VE CREATED SINCE 1938 PLUS A DELEGATION OF NATO-BASED AND ASIAN VOLUNTEERS.
THE UNITED STATES SAY THIS IS THEIR ENTIRE POST-HUMAN ARSENAL, BUT OUR SOURCES TELL US JACOB KRIGSTEIN STILL HAS SEVERAL DOZEN UNOFFICIAL CAPES HIDDEN IN HIS FIVE AMERICAN HANGARS.
WHY DO I GET THE OMINOUS FEELING I'M ABOUT TO BE ASKED TO LEAD THIS BLOODY OPERATION I'M STARTING TO WISH I'D NEVER EVEN HEARD OF?
BECAUSE THERE'S ONLY THREE PEOPLE ALIVE WITH YOUR LEVEL OF EXPERIENCE IN EXTRA-NATURAL MATTERS AND YOU'RE THE ONLY ONE WHO'S LISTED IN THE PHONE BOOK, COLONEL.
BUT I'M A SODDING ANARCHIST, YOU TWIT. WHO DO YOU THINK PUT THOSE SPEEDSTERS UP TO DRESSING U.S. TROOPS IN LINGERIE?
I CAN'T LEAD A MILITARY OPERATION AFTER PAINTING A HUNDRED FOOT PEACE SIGN ON THE STATUE OF BLEEDIN' LIBERTY.
ANARCHIST OR SOLDIER, CAPITALIST OR COMMUNIST; WHATEVER'S TRAVELLING THROUGH TIME TO KILL US CERTAINLY WON'T DISCRIMINATE, COLONEL SPARKS.

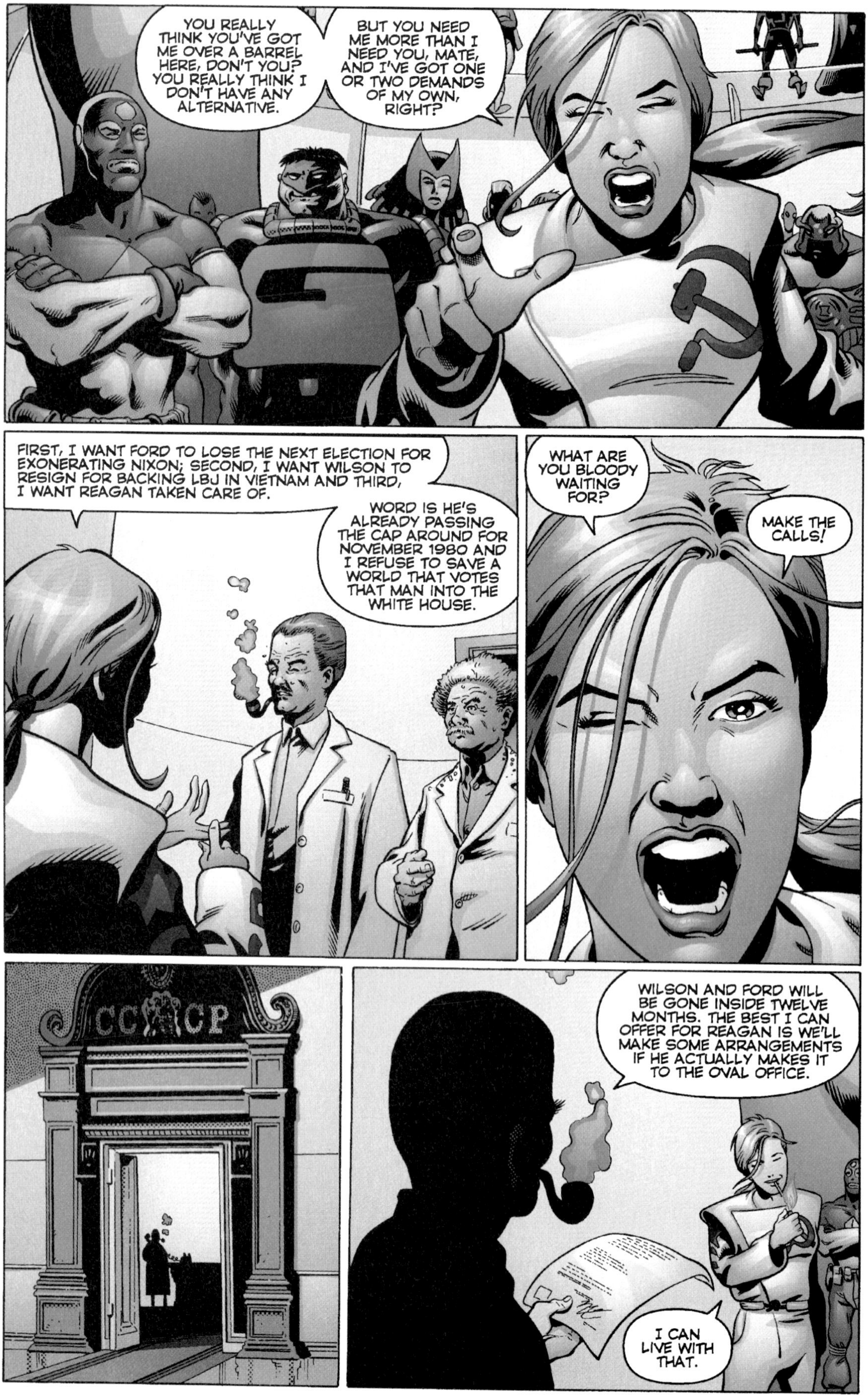
YOU REALLY THINK YOU'VE GOT ME OVER A BARREL HERE, DON'T YOU? YOU REALLY THINK I DON'T HAVE ANY ALTERNATIVE.
BUT YOU NEED ME MORE THAN I NEED YOU, MATE, AND I'VE GOT ONE OR TWO DEMANDS OF MY OWN, RIGHT?
FIRST, I WANT FORD TO LOSE THE NEXT ELECTION FOR EXONERATING NIXON; SECOND, I WANT WILSON TO RESIGN FOR BACKING LBJ IN VIETNAM AND THIRD, I WANT REAGAN TAKEN CARE OF.
WORD IS HE'S ALREADY PASSING THE CAP AROUND FOR NOVEMBER 1980 AND I REFUSE TO SAVE A WORLD THAT VOTES THAT MAN INTO THE WHITE HOUSE.
WHAT ARE YOU BLOODY WAITING FOR?
MAKE THE CALLS!
CCCP
WILSON AND FORD WILL BE GONE INSIDE TWELVE MONTHS. THE BEST I CAN OFFER FOR REAGAN IS WE'LL MAKE SOME ARRANGEMENTS IF HE ACTUALLY MAKES IT TO THE OVAL OFFICE.
I CAN LIVE WITH THAT.

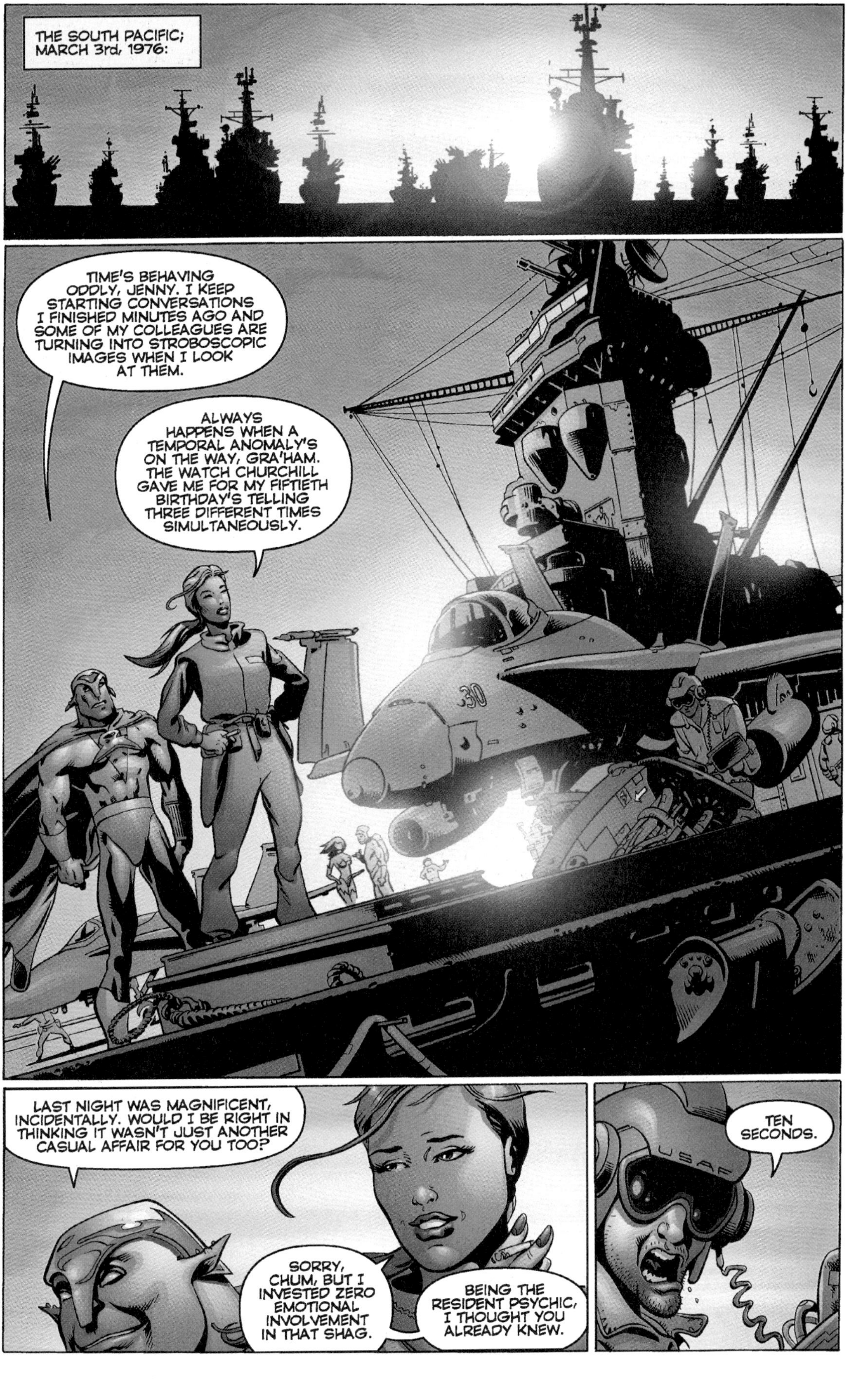
THE SOUTH PACIFIC; MARCH 3rd, 1976:
TIME'S BEHAVING ODDLY, JENNY. I KEEP STARTING CONVERSATIONS I FINISHED MINUTES AGO AND SOME OF MY COLLEAGUES ARE TURNING INTO STROBOSCOPIC IMAGES WHEN I LOOK AT THEM.
ALWAYS HAPPENS WHEN A TEMPORAL ANOMALY'S ON THE WAY, GRA'HAM. THE WATCH CHURCHILL GAVE ME FOR MY FIFTIETH BIRTHDAY'S TELLING THREE DIFFERENT TIMES SIMULTANEOUSLY.
30
LAST NIGHT WAS MAGNIFICENT, INCIDENTALLY. WOULD I BE RIGHT IN THINKING IT WASN'T JUST ANOTHER CASUAL AFFAIR FOR YOU TOO?
SORRY, CHUM, BUT I INVESTED ZERO EMOTIONAL INVOLVEMENT IN THAT SHAG.
BEING THE RESIDENT PSYCHIC, I THOUGHT YOU ALREADY KNEW.
USAF
TEN SECONDS.

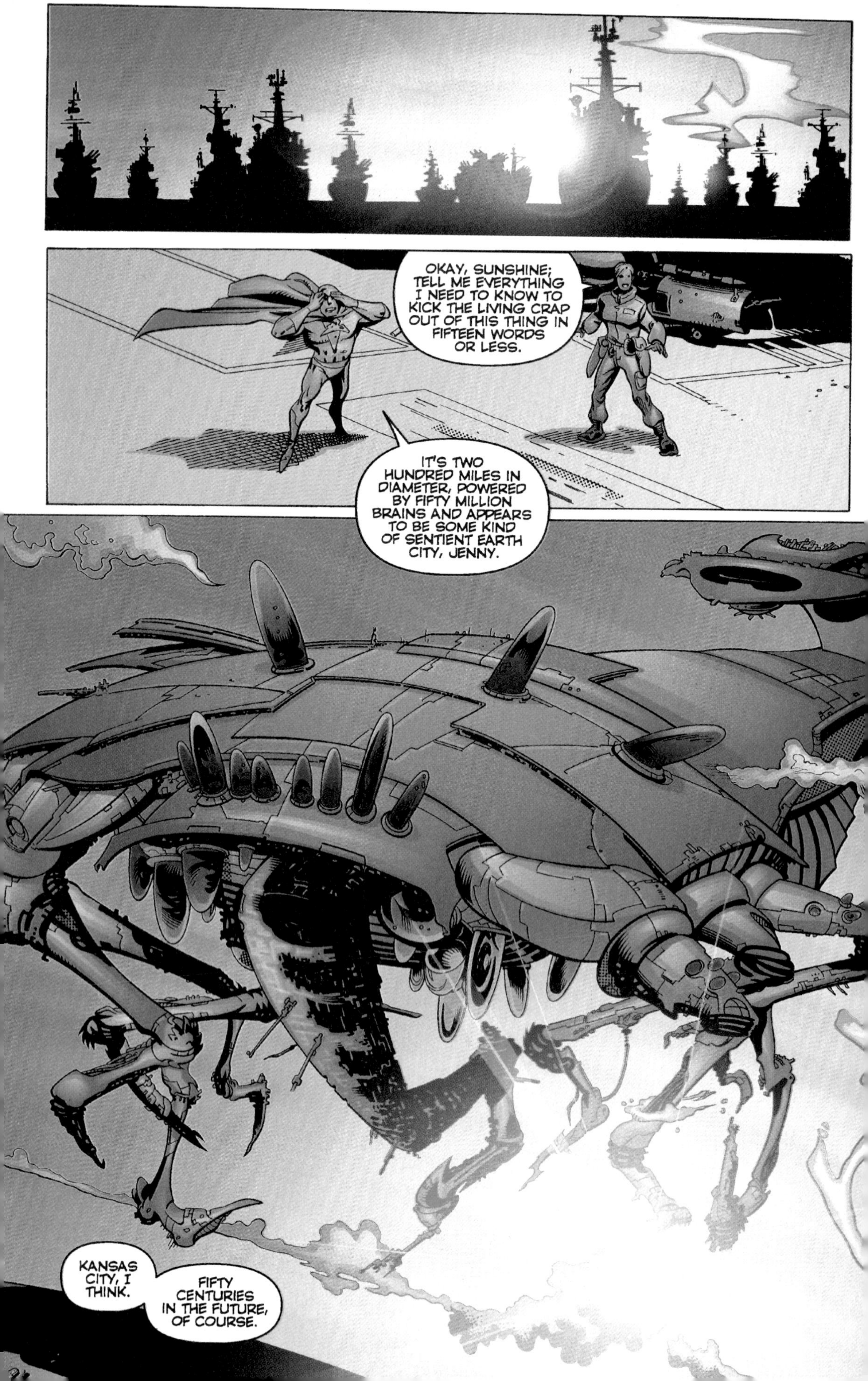
OKAY, SUNSHINE; TELL ME EVERYTHING I NEED TO KNOW TO KICK THE LIVING CRAP OUT OF THIS THING IN FIFTEEN WORDS OR LESS.
IT'S TWO HUNDRED MILES IN DIAMETER, POWERED BY FIFTY MILLION BRAINS AND APPEARS TO BE SOME KIND OF SENTIENT EARTH CITY, JENNY.
KANSAS CITY, I THINK.
FIFTY CENTURIES IN THE FUTURE, OF COURSE.

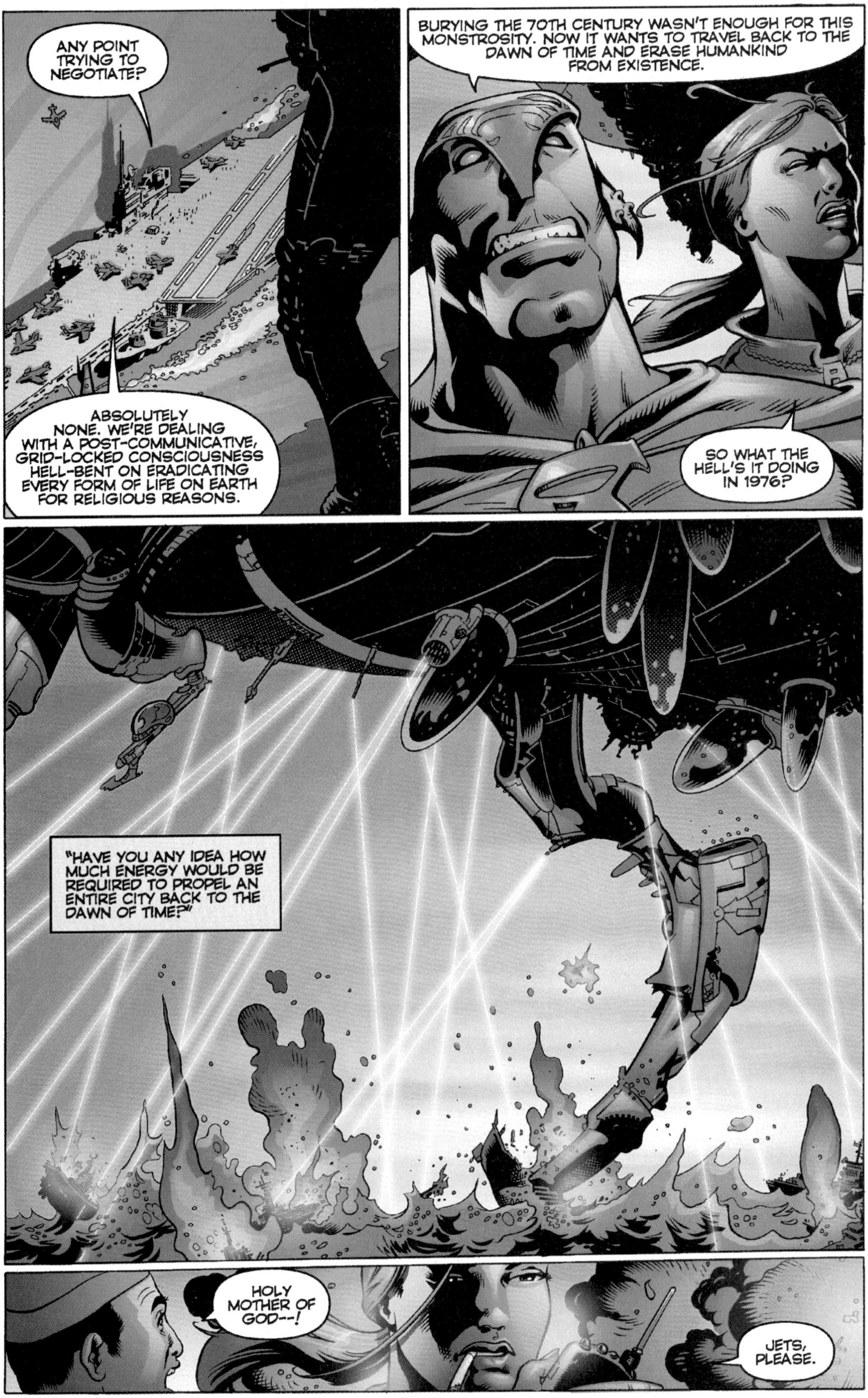
ANY POINT TRYING TO NEGOTIATE?
ABSOLUTELY NONE. WE'RE DEALING WITH A POST-COMMUNICATIVE, GRID-LOCKED CONSCIOUSNESS HELL-BENT ON ERADICATING EVERY FORM OF LIFE ON EARTH FOR RELIGIOUS REASONS.
BURYING THE 70TH CENTURY WASN'T ENOUGH FOR THIS MONSTROSITY. NOW IT WANTS TO TRAVEL BACK TO THE DAWN OF TIME AND ERASE HUMANKIND FROM EXISTENCE.
SO WHAT THE HELL'S IT DOING IN 1976?
"HAVE YOU ANY IDEA HOW MUCH ENERGY WOULD BE REQUIRED TO PROPEL AN ENTIRE CITY BACK TO THE DAWN OF TIME?"
HOLY MOTHER OF GOD--!
JETS, PLEASE.

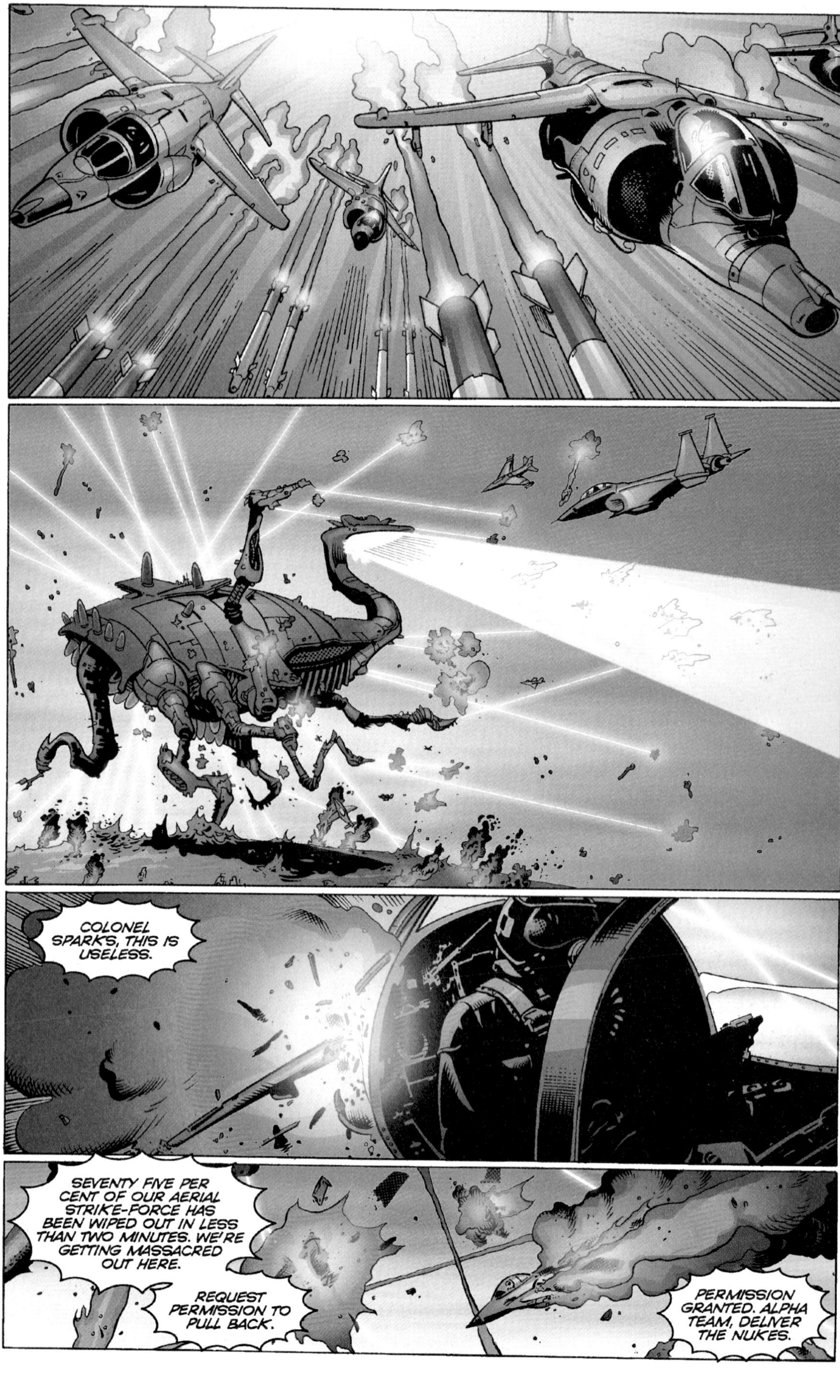
COLONEL SPARKS, THIS IS USELESS.
SEVENTY FIVE PER CENT OF OUR AERIAL STRIKE-FORCE HAS BEEN WIPED OUT IN LESS THAN TWO MINUTES. WE'RE GETTING MASSACRED OUT HERE.
REQUEST PERMISSION TO PULL BACK.
PERMISSION GRANTED. ALPHA TEAM, DELIVER THE NUKES.

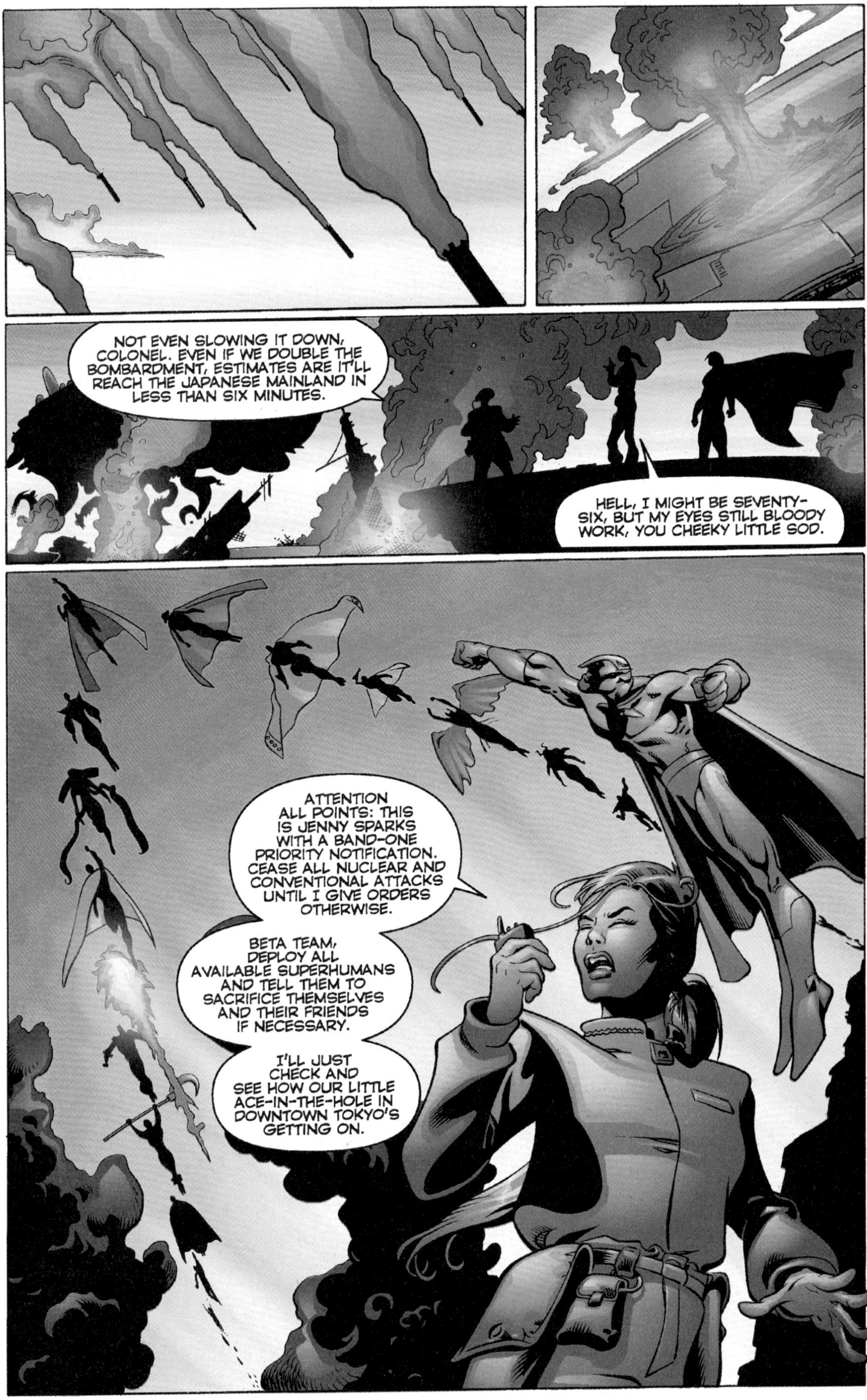
NOT EVEN SLOWING IT DOWN, COLONEL. EVEN IF WE DOUBLE THE BOMBARDMENT, ESTIMATES ARE IT'LL REACH THE JAPANESE MAINLAND IN LESS THAN SIX MINUTES.
HELL, I MIGHT BE SEVENTY-SIX, BUT MY EYES STILL BLOODY WORK, YOU CHEEKY LITTLE SOD.
ATTENTION ALL POINTS: THIS IS JENNY SPARKS WITH A BAND-ONE PRIORITY NOTIFICATION. CEASE ALL NUCLEAR AND CONVENTIONAL ATTACKS UNTIL I GIVE ORDERS OTHERWISE.
BETA TEAM, DEPLOY ALL AVAILABLE SUPERHUMANS AND TELL THEM TO SACRIFICE THEMSELVES AND THEIR FRIENDS IF NECESSARY.
I'LL JUST CHECK AND SEE HOW OUR LITTLE ACE-IN-THE-HOLE IN DOWNTOWN TOKYO'S GETTING ON.

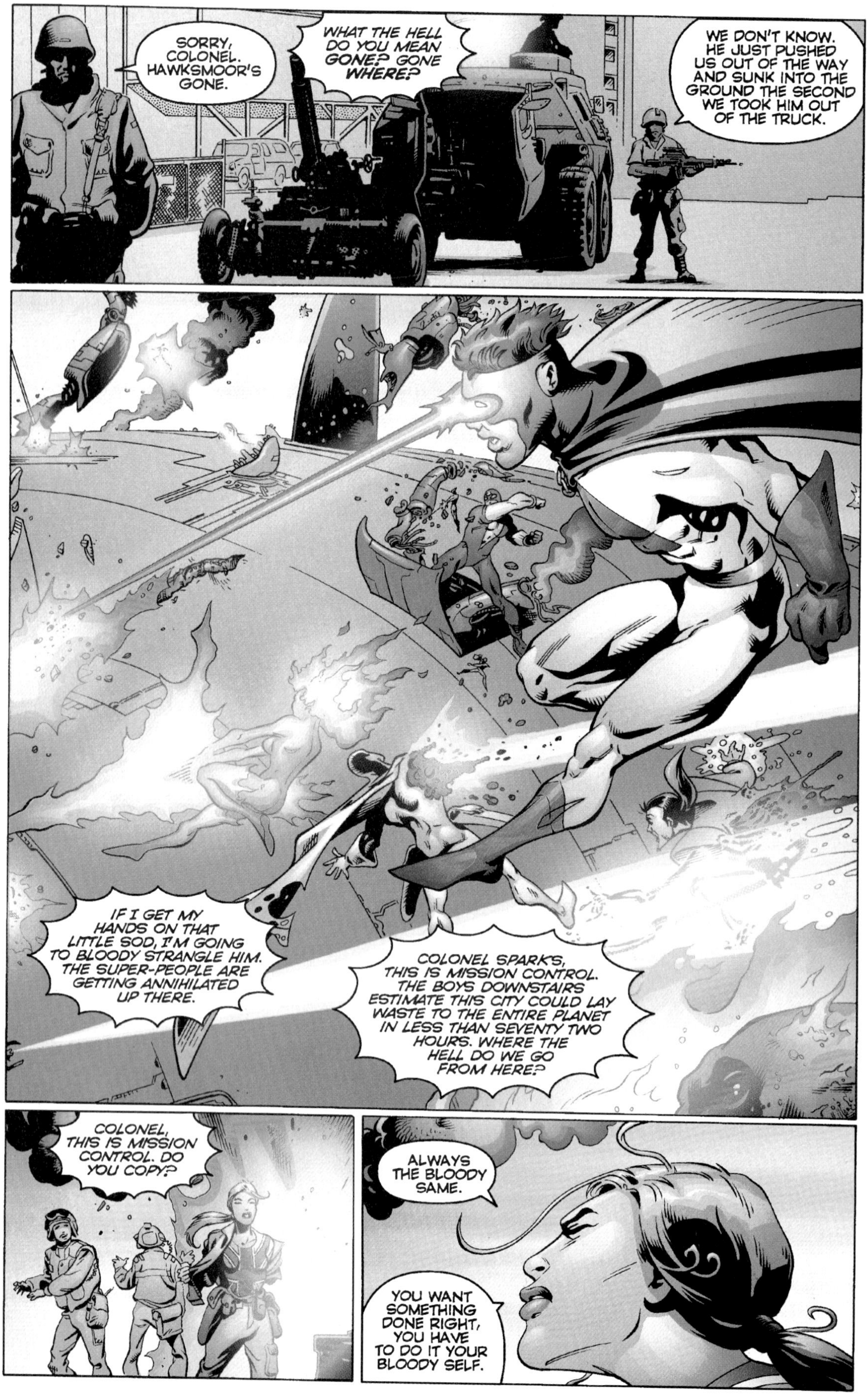
SORRY, COLONEL. HAWKSMOOR'S GONE.
WHAT THE HELL DO YOU MEAN GONE? GONE WHERE?
WE DON'T KNOW. HE JUST PUSHED US OUT OF THE WAY AND SUNK INTO THE GROUND THE SECOND WE TOOK HIM OUT OF THE TRUCK.
IF I GET MY HANDS ON THAT LITTLE SOD, I'M GOING TO BLOODY STRANGLE HIM. THE SUPER-PEOPLE ARE GETTING ANNIHILATED UP THERE.
COLONEL SPARKS, THIS IS MISSION CONTROL. THE BOYS DOWNSTAIRS ESTIMATE THIS CITY COULD LAY WASTE TO THE ENTIRE PLANET IN LESS THAN SEVENTY TWO HOURS. WHERE THE HELL DO WE GO FROM HERE?
COLONEL, THIS IS MISSION CONTROL. DO YOU COPY?
ALWAYS THE BLOODY SAME.
YOU WANT SOMETHING DONE RIGHT, YOU HAVE TO DO IT YOUR BLOODY SELF.

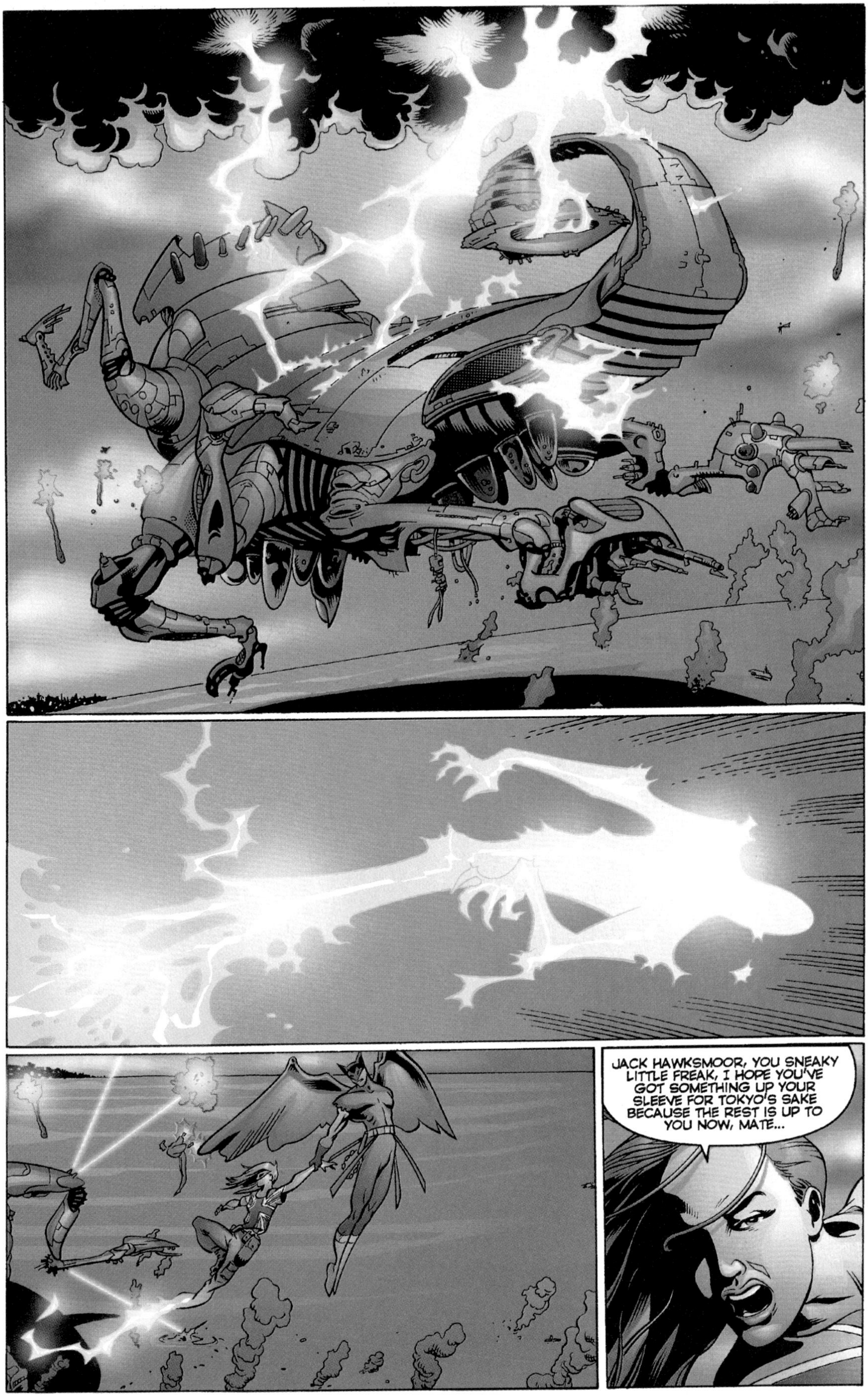
JACK HAWKSMOOR, YOU SNEAKY LITTLE FREAK, I HOPE YOU'VE GOT SOMETHING UP YOUR SLEEVE FOR TOKYO'S SAKE BECAUSE THE REST IS UP TO YOU NOW, MATE...

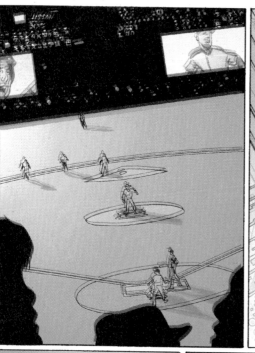

"WELL, BUGGER ME GENTLY...

I SWEAR TO GOD; IF, BY SOME MIRACLE, WE SURVIVE THIS THING, I'M GIVING UP THE WACKY BACCY FOR GOOD THIS TIME, MATE.

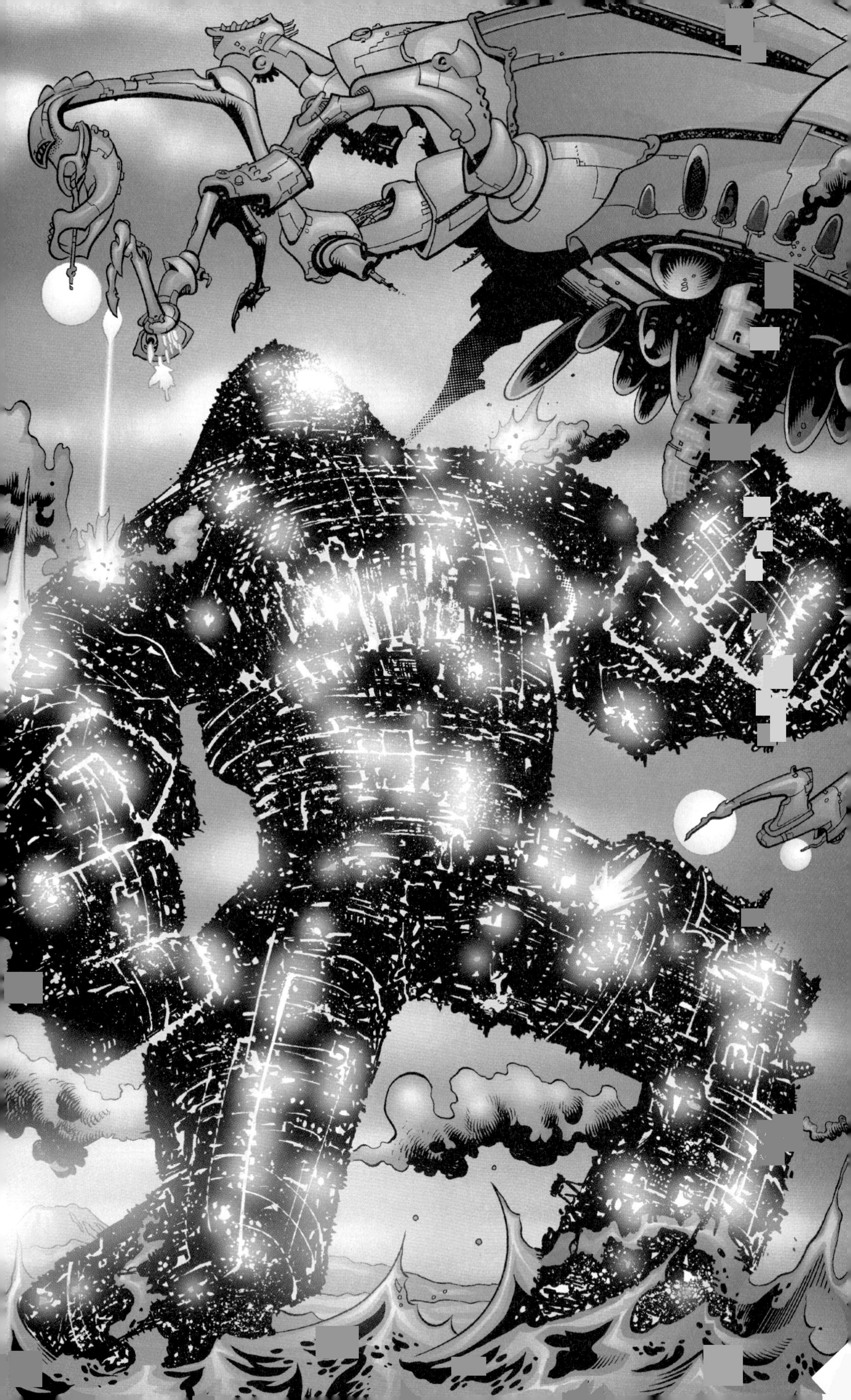

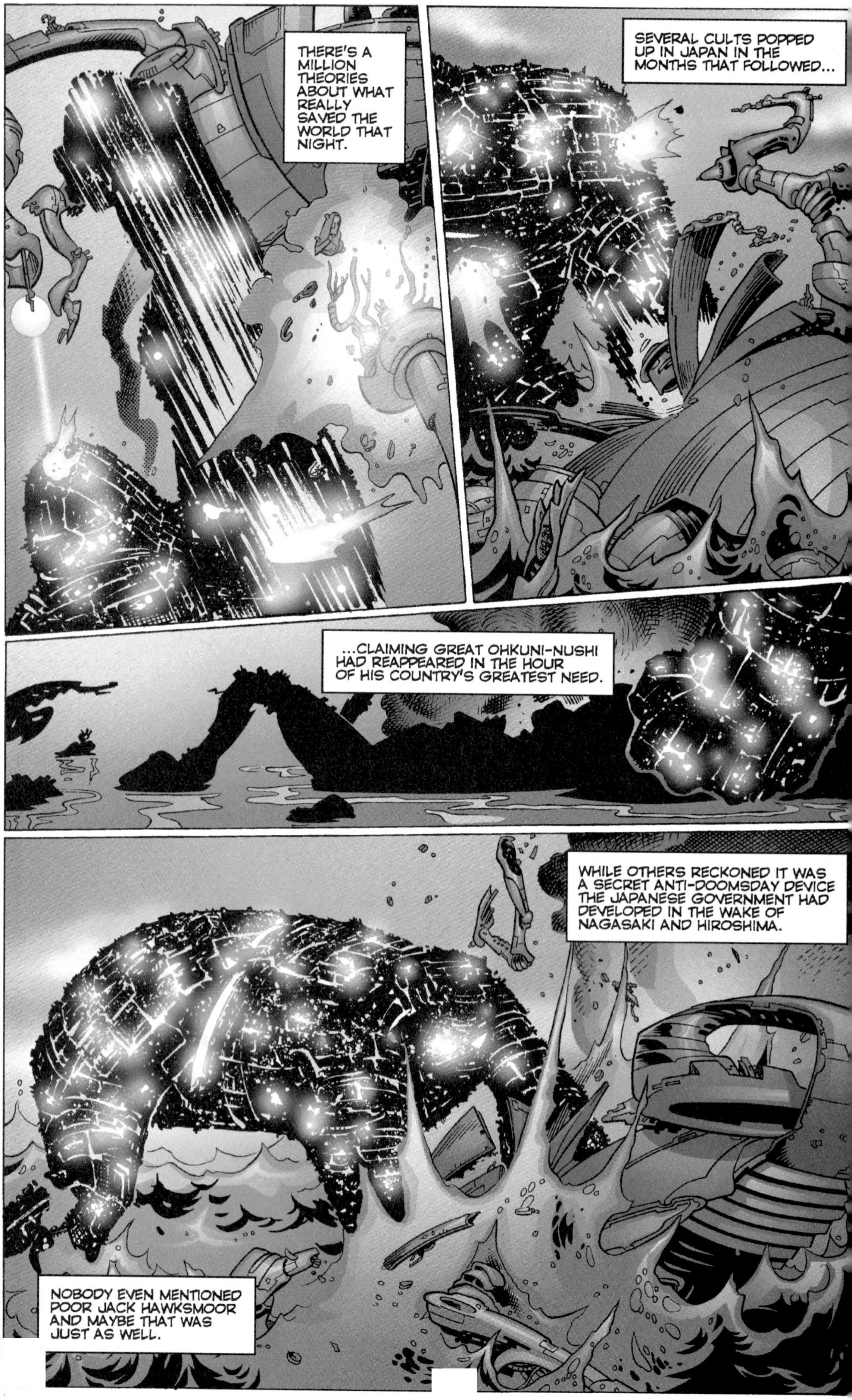
THERE'S A MILLION THEORIES ABOUT WHAT REALLY SAVED THE WORLD THAT NIGHT.
SEVERAL CULTS POPPED UP IN JAPAN IN THE MONTHS THAT FOLLOWED...
...CLAIMING GREAT OHKUNI-NUSHI HAD REAPPEARED IN THE HOUR OF HIS COUNTRY'S GREATEST NEED.
WHILE OTHERS RECKONED IT WAS A SECRET ANTI-DOOMSDAY DEVICE THE JAPANESE GOVERNMENT HAD DEVELOPED IN THE WAKE OF NAGASAKI AND HIROSHIMA.
NOBODY EVEN MENTIONED POOR JACK HAWKSMOOR AND MAYBE THAT WAS JUST AS WELL.

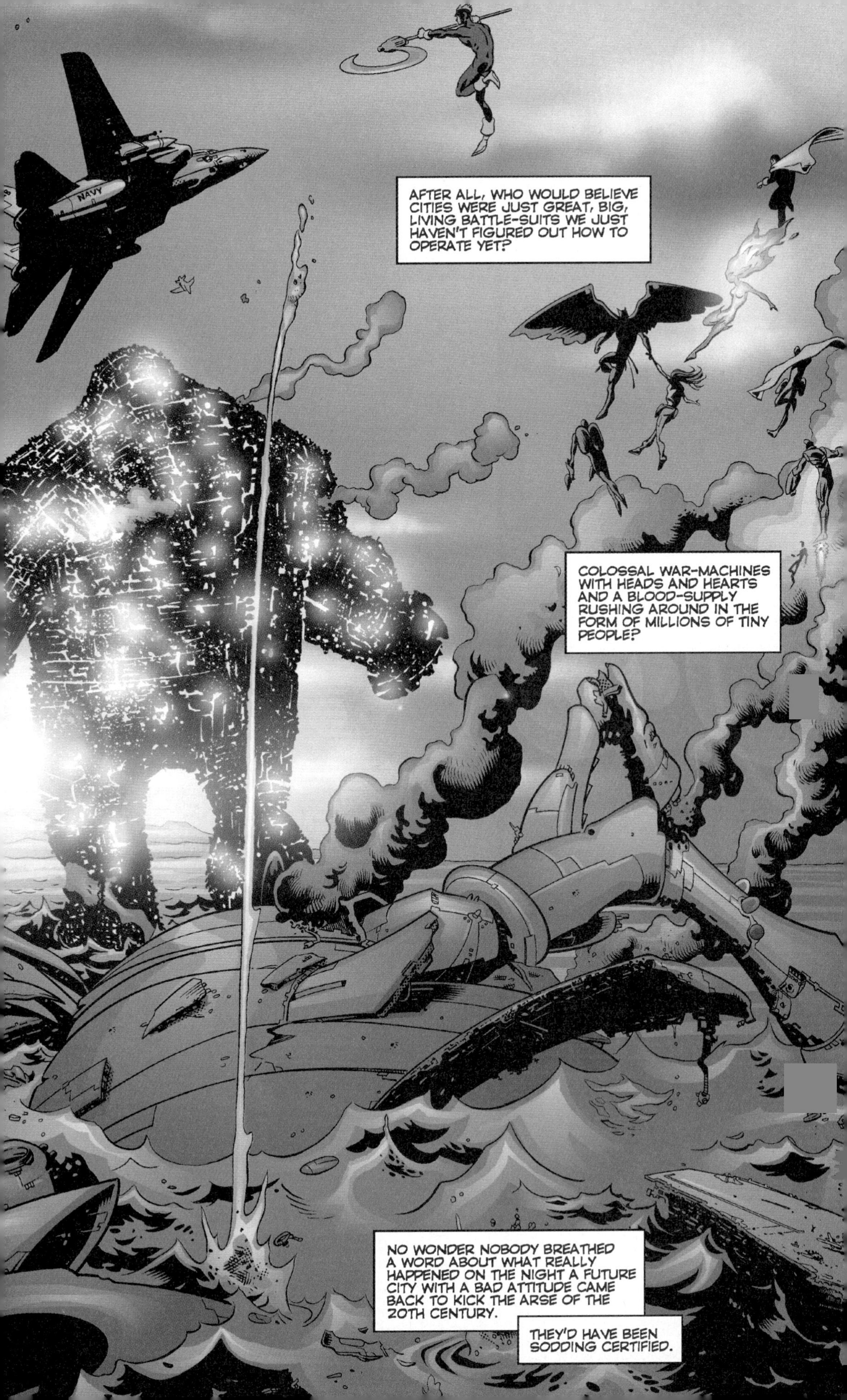
AFTER ALL, WHO WOULD BELIEVE CITIES WERE JUST GREAT, BIG, LIVING BATTLE-SUITS WE JUST HAVEN'T FIGURED OUT HOW TO OPERATE YET?
COLOSSAL WAR-MACHINES WITH HEADS AND HEARTS AND A BLOOD-SUPPLY RUSHING AROUND IN THE FORM OF MILLIONS OF TINY PEOPLE?
NO WONDER NOBODY BREATHED A WORD ABOUT WHAT REALLY HAPPENED ON THE NIGHT A FUTURE CITY WITH A BAD ATTITUDE CAME BACK TO KICK THE ARSE OF THE 20TH CENTURY.
THEY'D HAVE BEEN SODDING CERTIFIED.

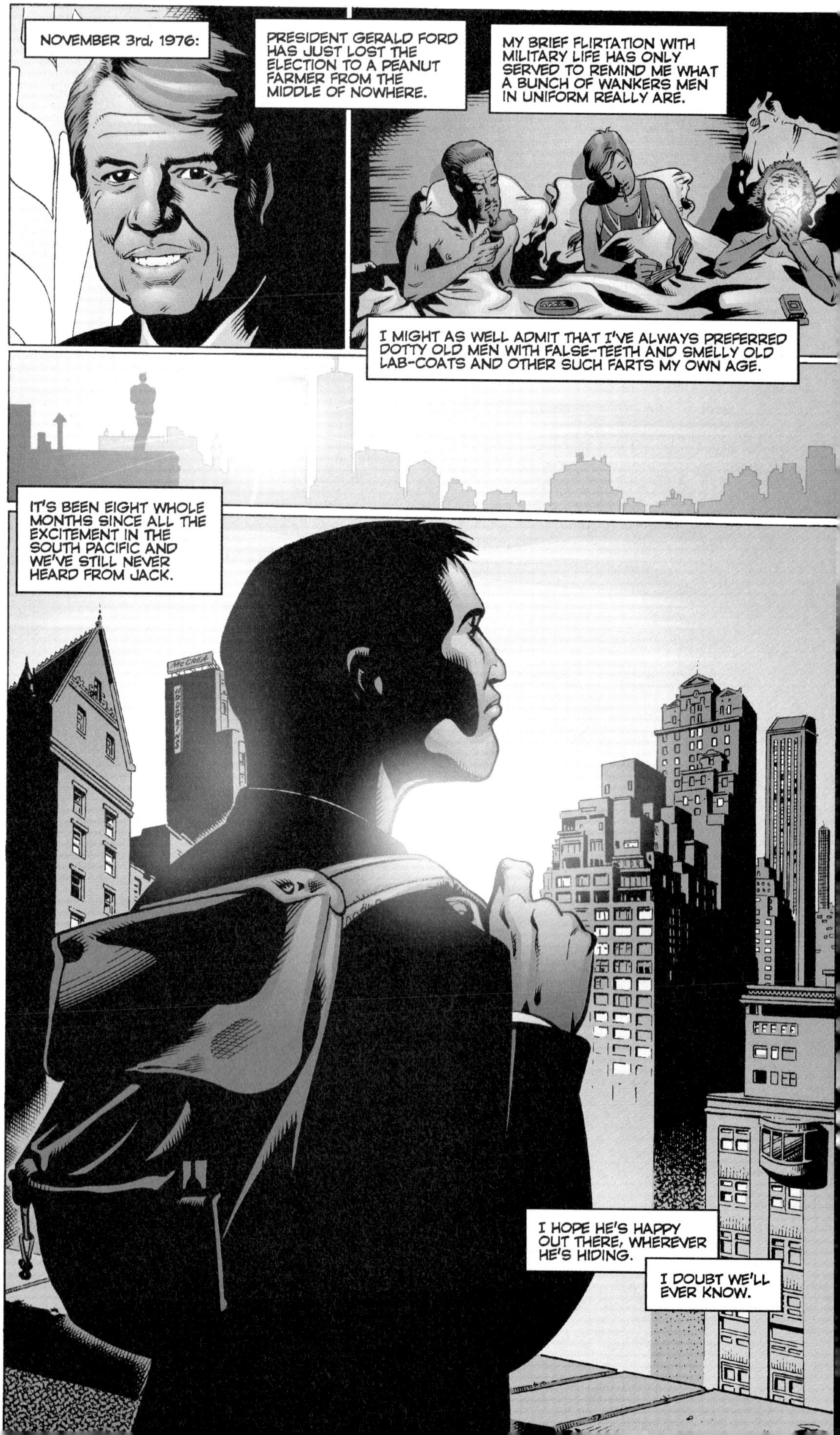
NOVEMBER 3rd, 1976:
PRESIDENT GERALD FORD HAS JUST LOST THE ELECTION TO A PEANUT FARMER FROM THE MIDDLE OF NOWHERE.
MY BRIEF FLIRTATION WITH MILITARY LIFE HAS ONLY SERVED TO REMIND ME WHAT A BUNCH OF WANKERS MEN IN UNIFORM REALLY ARE.
I MIGHT AS WELL ADMIT THAT I'VE ALWAYS PREFERRED DOTTY OLD MEN WITH FALSE-TEETH AND SMELLY OLD LAB-COATS AND OTHER SUCH FARTS MY OWN AGE.
IT'S BEEN EIGHT WHOLE MONTHS SINCE ALL THE EXCITEMENT IN THE SOUTH PACIFIC AND WE'VE STILL NEVER HEARD FROM JACK.
McCREA
I HOPE HE'S HAPPY OUT THERE, WHEREVER HE'S HIDING.
I DOUBT WE'LL EVER KNOW.

Chapter Fou
Many Happy Returns

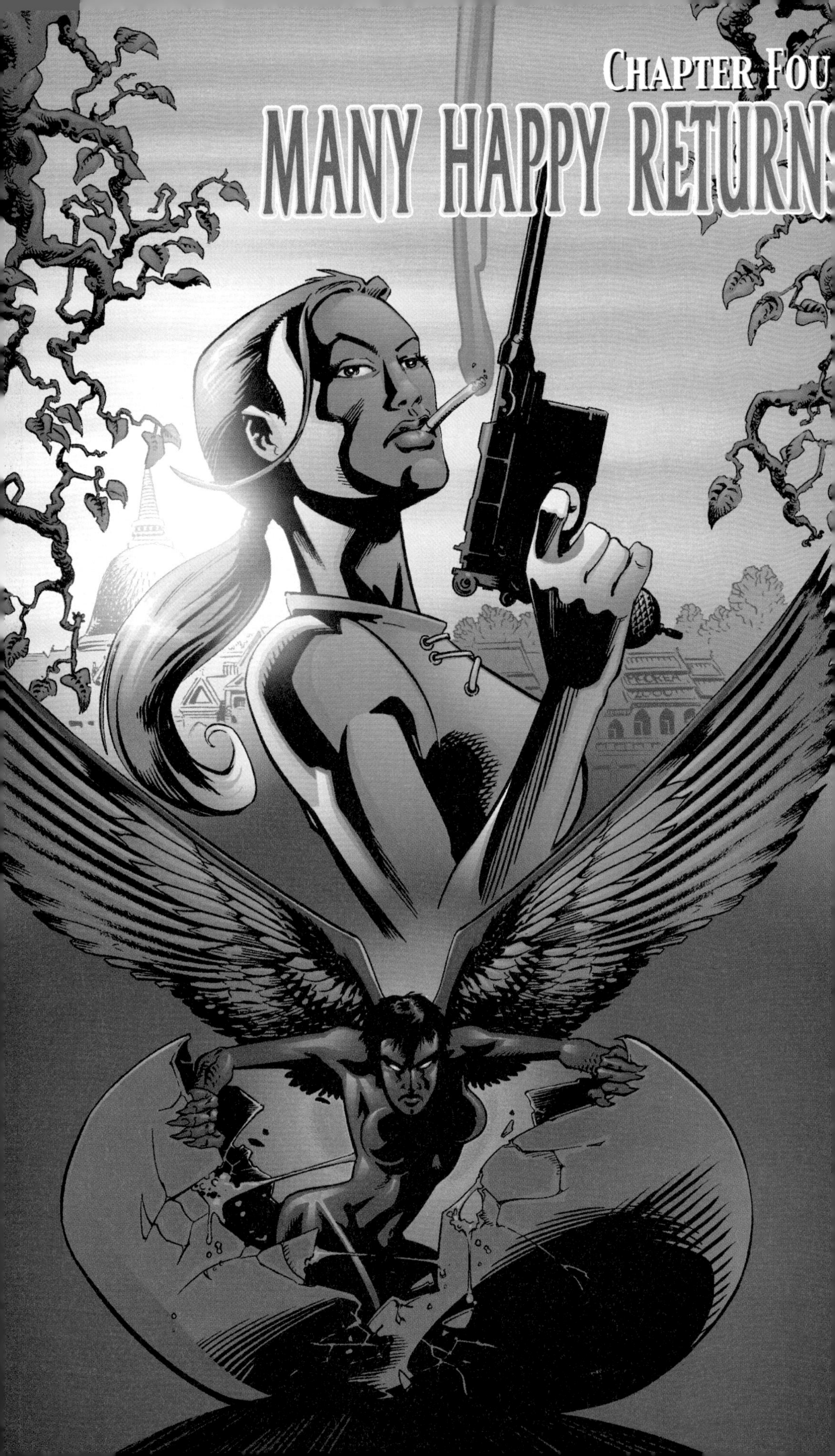

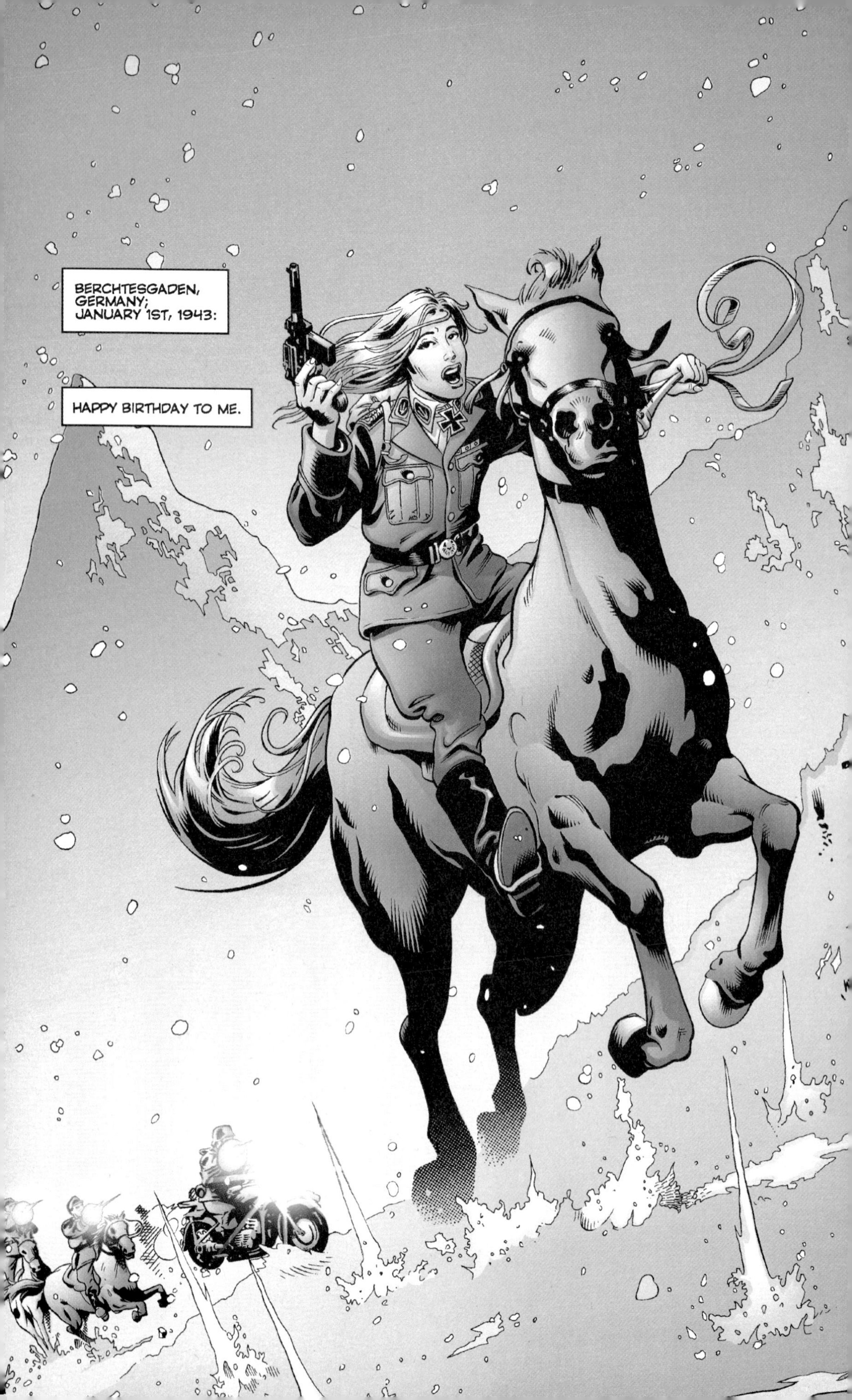
BERCHTESGADEN, GERMANY; JANUARY 1ST, 1943:
HAPPY BIRTHDAY TO ME.

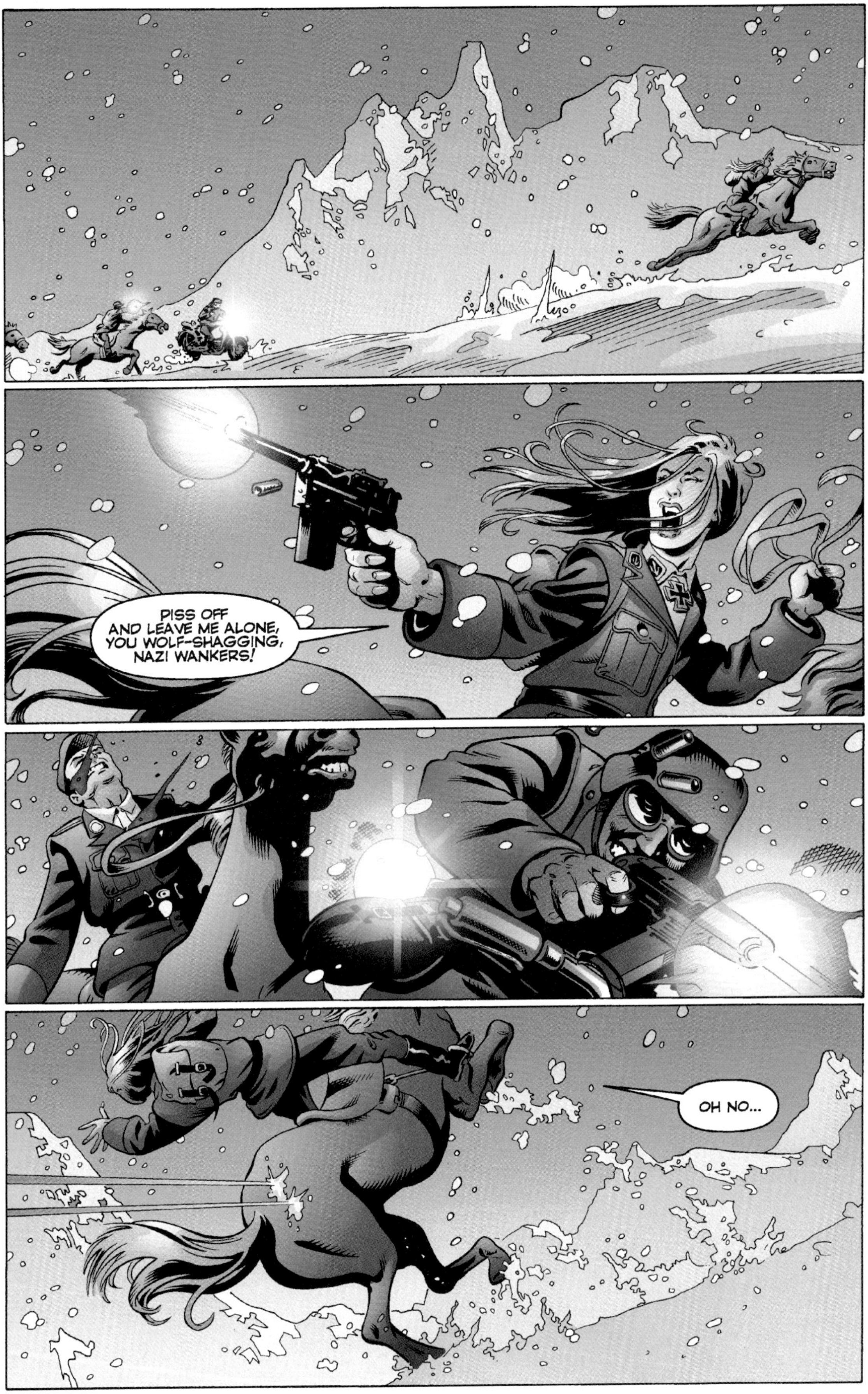
PISS OFF AND LEAVE ME ALONE, YOU WOLF-SHAGGING, NAZI WANKERS!
OH NO...

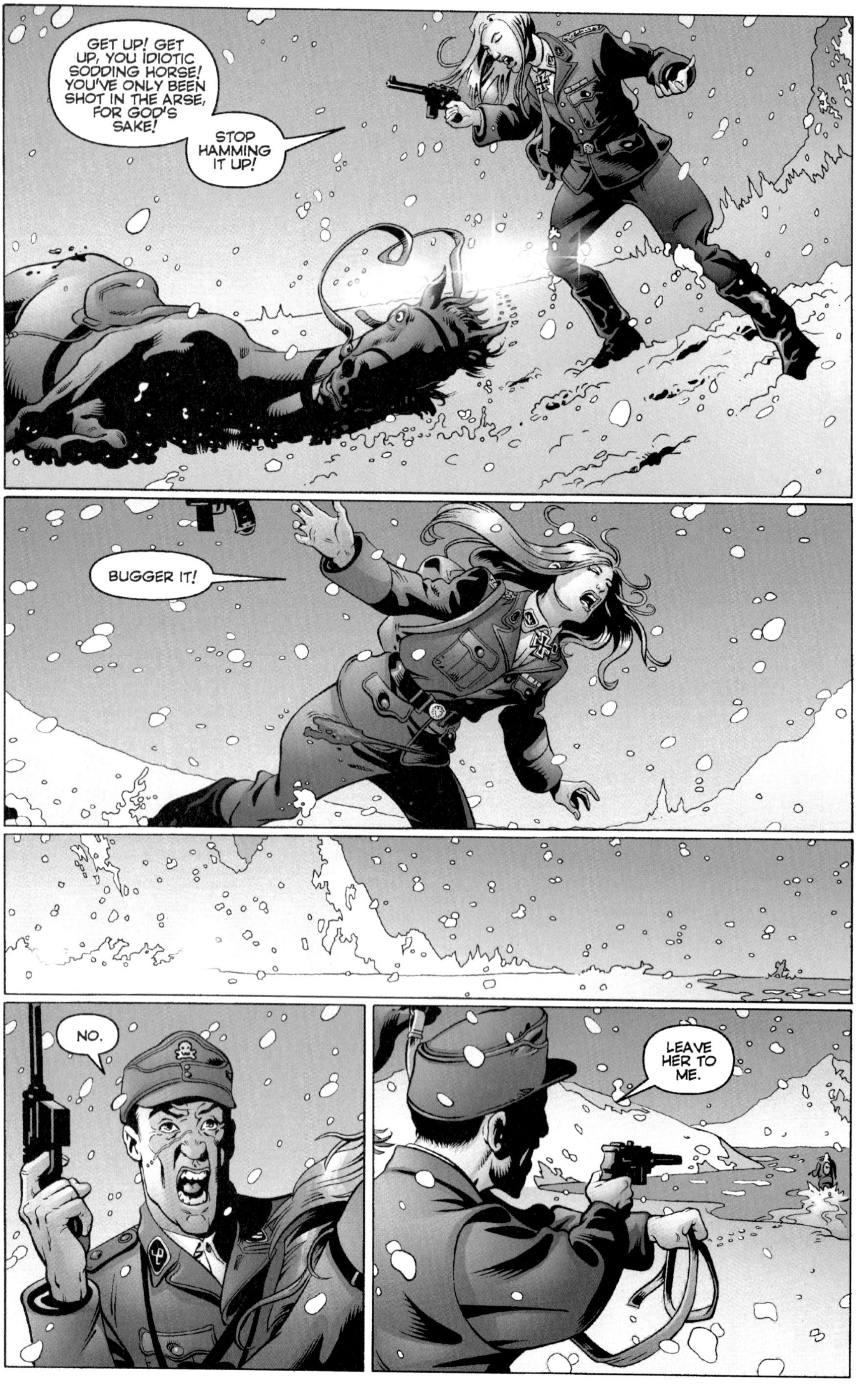
GET UP! GET UP, YOU IDIOTIC SODDING HORSE! YOU'VE ONLY BEEN SHOT IN THE ARSE, FOR GOD'S SAKE!
STOP HAMMING IT UP!
BUGGER IT!
NO.
LEAVE HER TO ME.

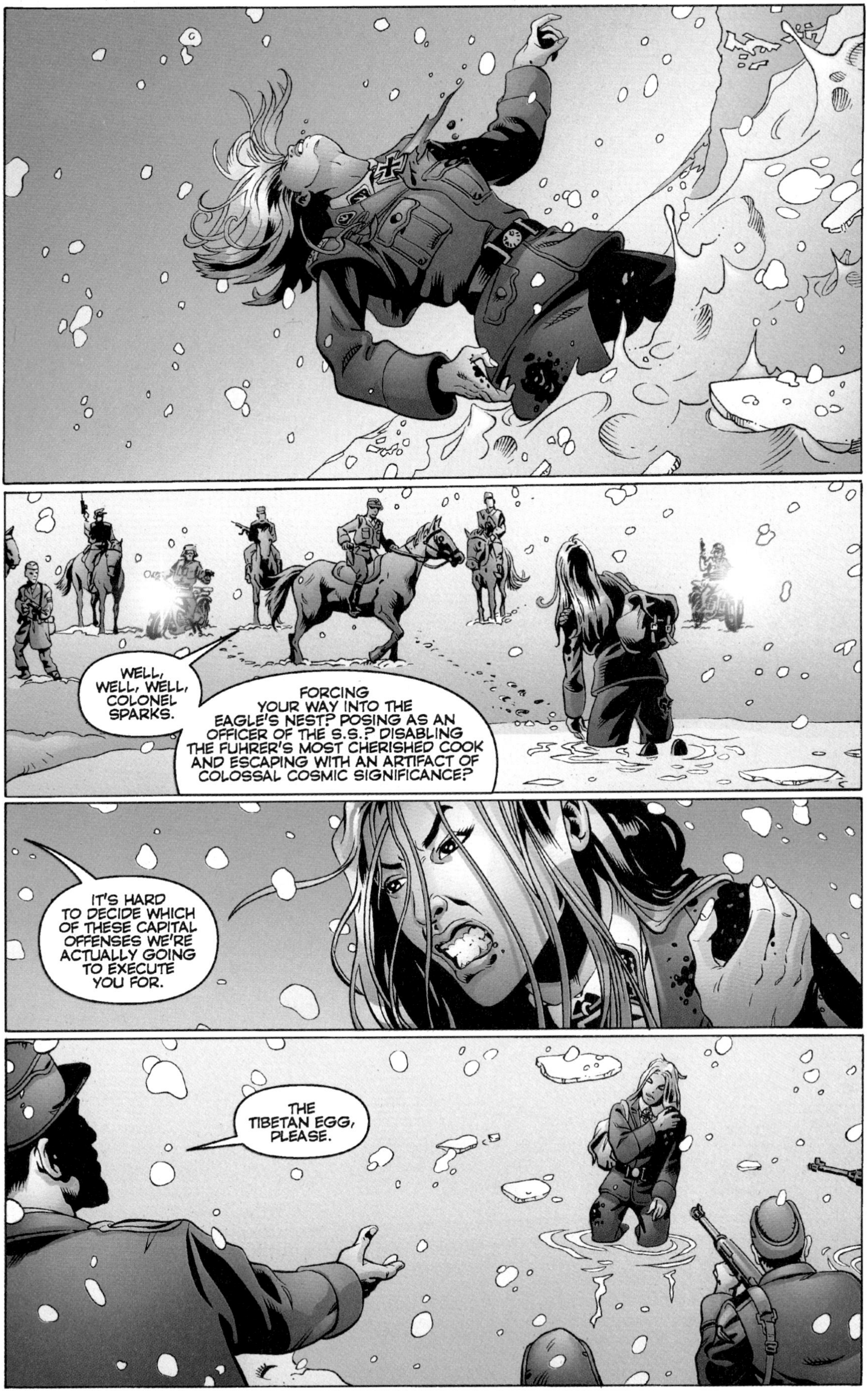
WELL, WELL, WELL, COLONEL SPARKS.
FORCING YOUR WAY INTO THE EAGLE'S NEST? POSING AS AN OFFICER OF THE S.S.? DISABLING THE FUHRER'S MOST CHERISHED COOK AND ESCAPING WITH AN ARTIFACT OF COLOSSAL COSMIC SIGNIFICANCE?
IT'S HARD TO DECIDE WHICH OF THESE CAPITAL OFFENSES WE'RE ACTUALLY GOING TO EXECUTE YOU FOR.
THE TIBETAN EGG, PLEASE.

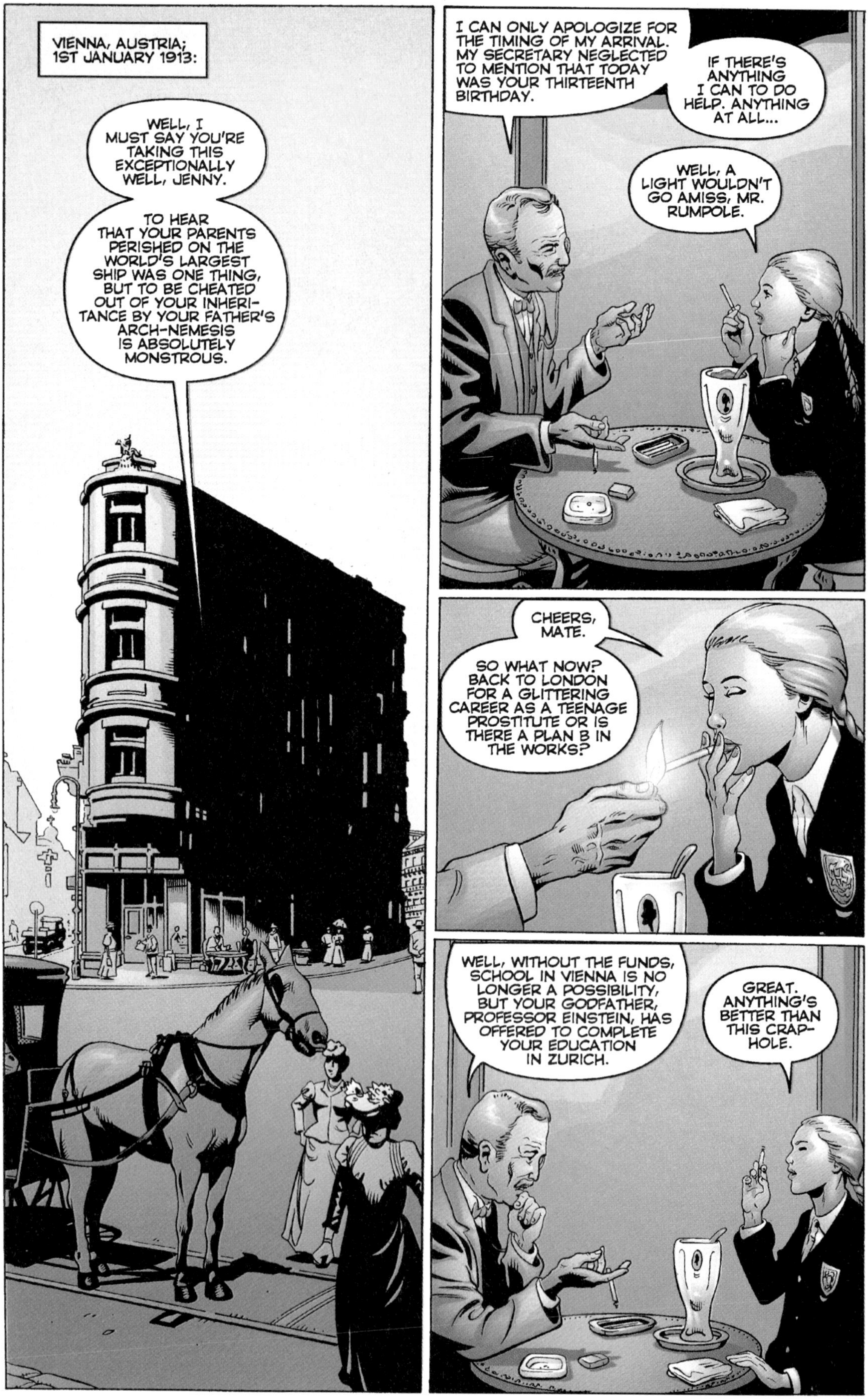
VIENNA, AUSTRIA; 1ST JANUARY 1913:
WELL, I MUST SAY YOU'RE TAKING THIS EXCEPTIONALLY WELL, JENNY.
TO HEAR THAT YOUR PARENTS PERISHED ON THE WORLD'S LARGEST SHIP WAS ONE THING, BUT TO BE CHEATED OUT OF YOUR INHERI-TANCE BY YOUR FATHER'S ARCH-NEMESIS IS ABSOLUTELY MONSTROUS.
I CAN ONLY APOLOGIZE FOR THE TIMING OF MY ARRIVAL. MY SECRETARY NEGLECTED TO MENTION THAT TODAY WAS YOUR THIRTEENTH BIRTHDAY.
IF THERE'S ANYTHING I CAN TO DO HELP. ANYTHING AT ALL...
WELL, A LIGHT WOULDN'T GO AMISS, MR. RUMPOLE.
CHEERS, MATE.
SO WHAT NOW? BACK TO LONDON FOR A GLITTERING CAREER AS A TEENAGE PROSTITUTE OR IS THERE A PLAN B IN THE WORKS?
WELL, WITHOUT THE FUNDS, SCHOOL IN VIENNA IS NO LONGER A POSSIBILITY, BUT YOUR GODFATHER, PROFESSOR EINSTEIN, HAS OFFERED TO COMPLETE YOUR EDUCATION IN ZURICH.
GREAT. ANYTHING'S BETTER THAN THIS CRAP-HOLE.

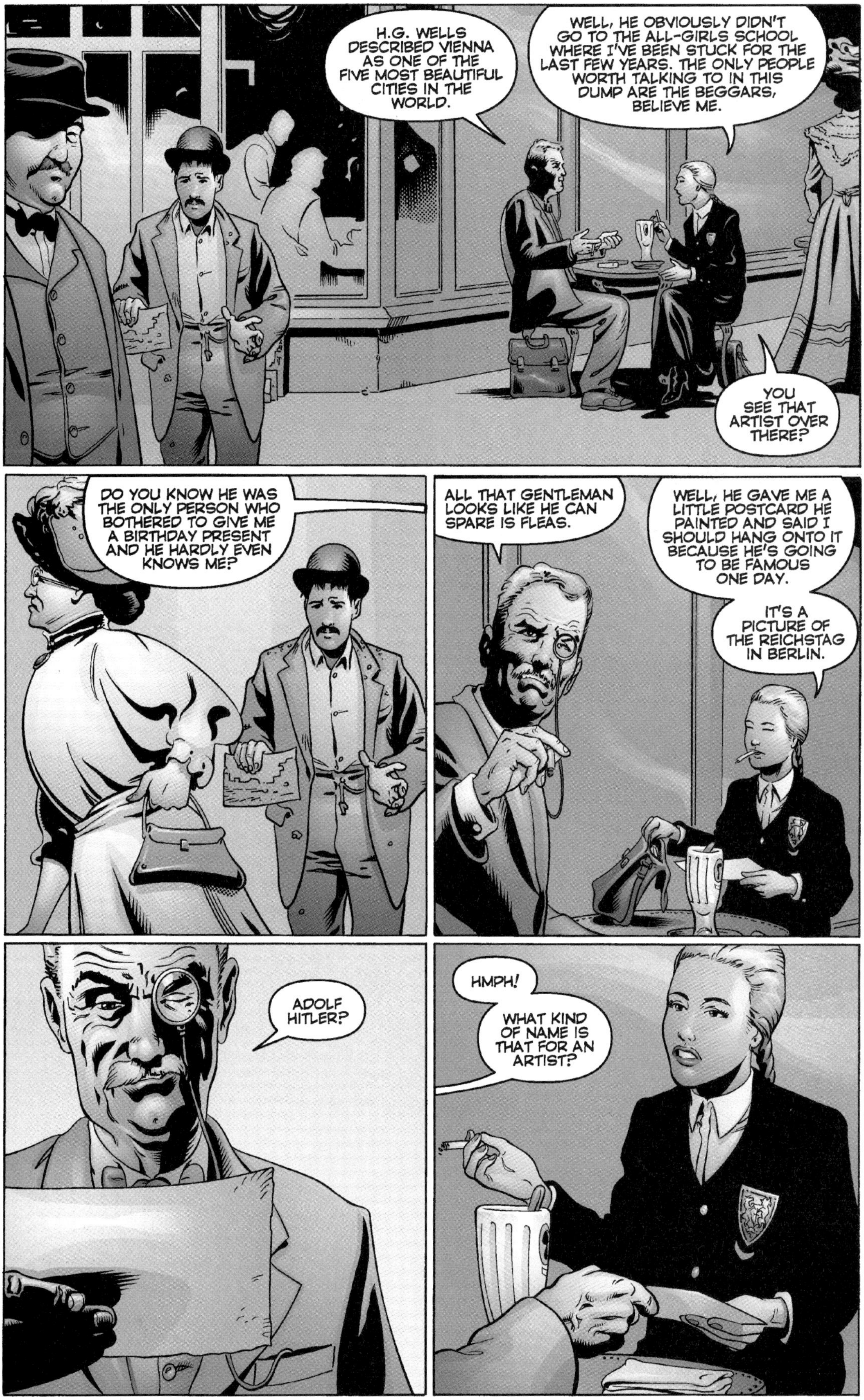
H.G. WELLS DESCRIBED VIENNA AS ONE OF THE FIVE MOST BEAUTIFUL CITIES IN THE WORLD.
WELL, HE OBVIOUSLY DIDN'T GO TO THE ALL-GIRLS SCHOOL WHERE I'VE BEEN STUCK FOR THE LAST FEW YEARS. THE ONLY PEOPLE WORTH TALKING TO IN THIS DUMP ARE THE BEGGARS, BELIEVE ME.
YOU SEE THAT ARTIST OVER THERE?
DO YOU KNOW HE WAS THE ONLY PERSON WHO BOTHERED TO GIVE ME A BIRTHDAY PRESENT AND HE HARDLY EVEN KNOWS ME?
ALL THAT GENTLEMAN LOOKS LIKE HE CAN SPARE IS FLEAS.
WELL, HE GAVE ME A LITTLE POSTCARD HE PAINTED AND SAID I SHOULD HANG ONTO IT BECAUSE HE'S GOING TO BE FAMOUS ONE DAY.
IT'S A PICTURE OF THE REICHSTAG IN BERLIN.
ADOLF HITLER?
HMPH!
WHAT KIND OF NAME IS THAT FOR AN ARTIST?

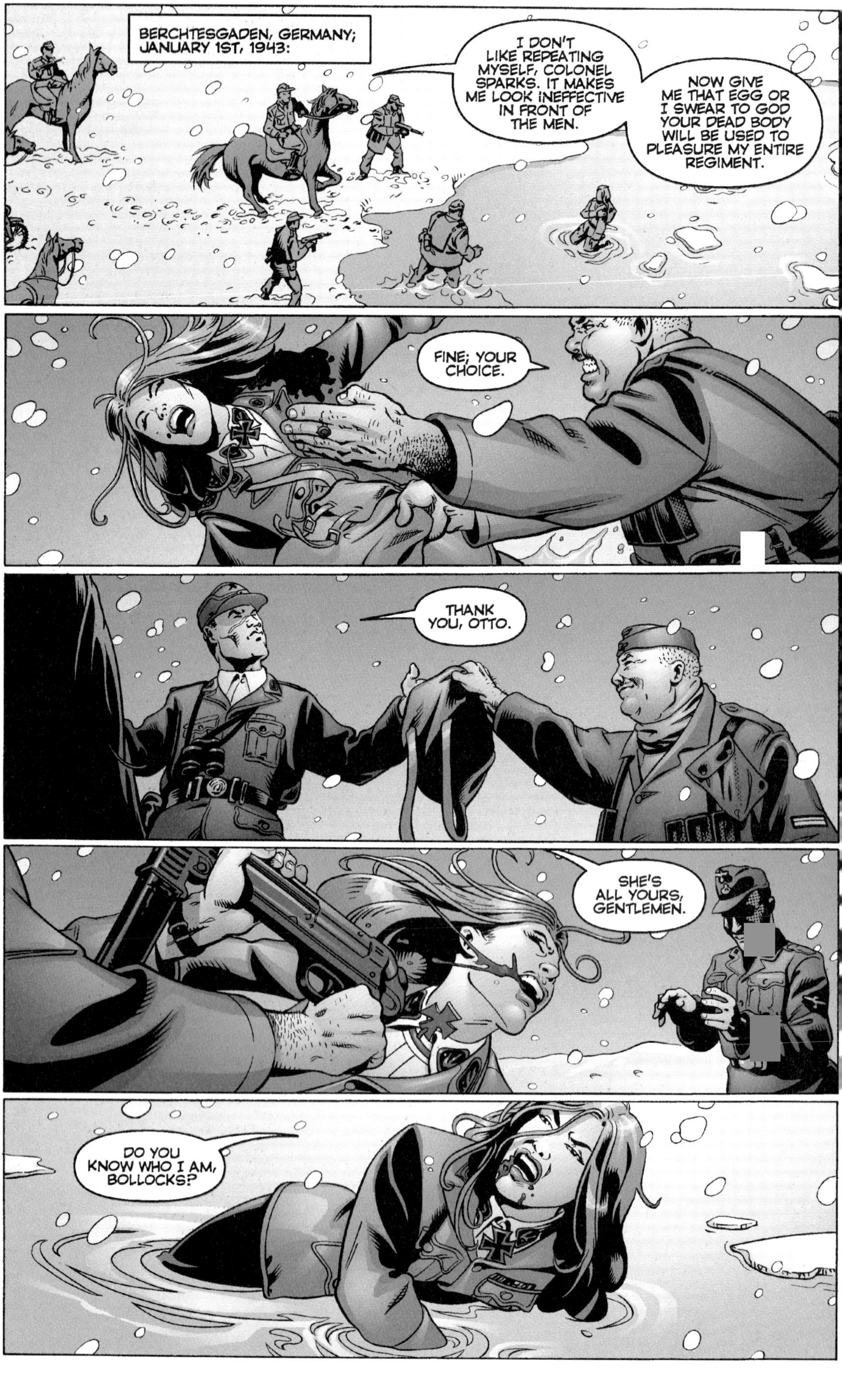
BERCHTESGADEN, GERMANY; JANUARY 1ST, 1943:
I DON'T LIKE REPEATING MYSELF, COLONEL SPARKS. IT MAKES ME LOOK INEFFECTIVE IN FRONT OF THE MEN.
NOW GIVE ME THAT EGG OR I SWEAR TO GOD YOUR DEAD BODY WILL BE USED TO PLEASURE MY ENTIRE REGIMENT.
FINE; YOUR CHOICE.
THANK YOU, OTTO.
SHE'S ALL YOURS, GENTLEMEN.
DO YOU KNOW WHO I AM, BOLLOCKS?

EXCUSE ME?

I SAID, DO YOU HAVE ANY IDEA WHAT THE HELL YOU'RE ACTUALLY DEALING WITH HERE, YOU STUPID, GOOSE-STEPPING TWIT?

YOU MEAN BESIDES AN OVER-PROMOTED LITTLE ALLIED AGENT WHO'S ABOUT TO BE RAPED TO DEATH BECAUSE SHE VOLUNTEERED FOR A MISSION SHE PROBABLY DOESN'T EVEN UNDERSTAND?

NO, COLONEL SPARKS. I'M AFRAID I DON'T KNOW WHAT I'M DEALING WITH HERE.

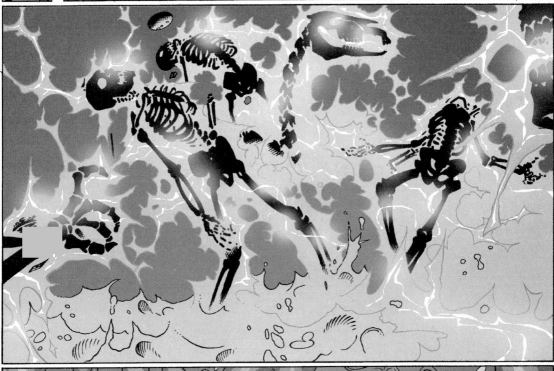

THOUGHT SO.

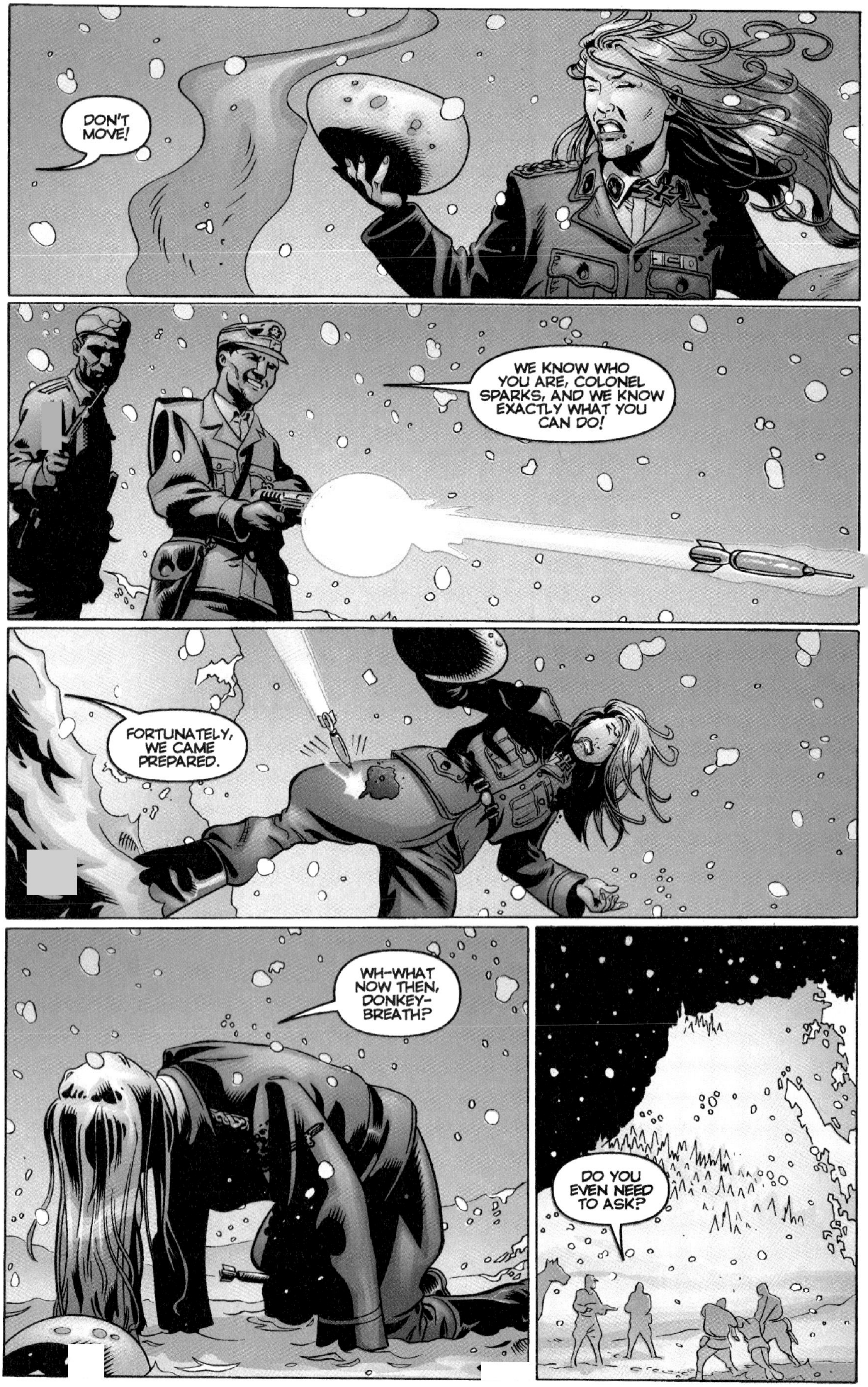
DON'T MOVE!
WE KNOW WHO YOU ARE, COLONEL SPARKS, AND WE KNOW EXACTLY WHAT YOU CAN DO!
FORTUNATELY, WE CAME PREPARED.
WH-WHAT NOW THEN, DONKEY-BREATH?
DO YOU EVEN NEED TO ASK?

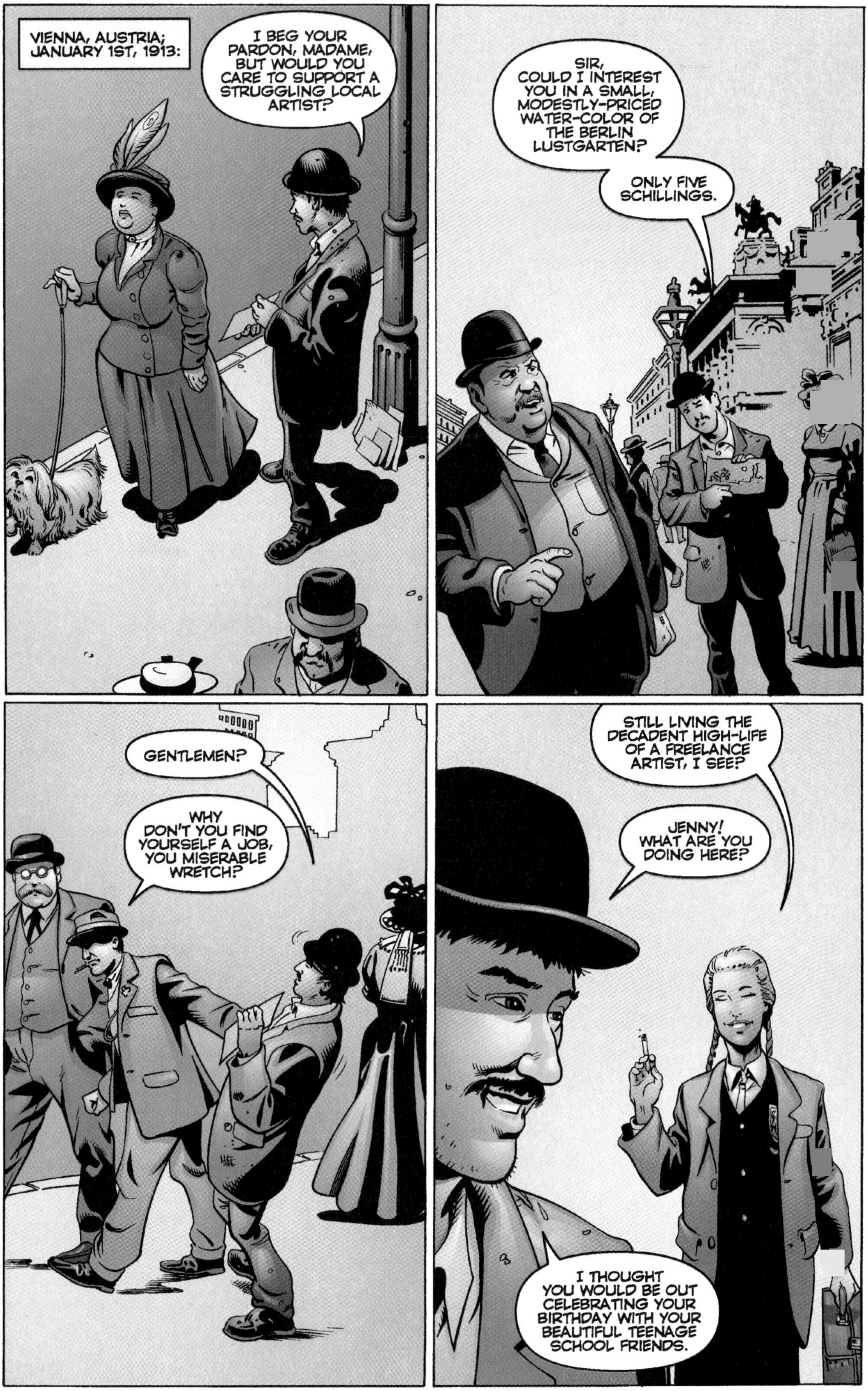
VIENNA, AUSTRIA; JANUARY 1ST, 1913:
I BEG YOUR PARDON, MADAME, BUT WOULD YOU CARE TO SUPPORT A STRUGGLING LOCAL ARTIST?
SIR, COULD I INTEREST YOU IN A SMALL, MODESTLY-PRICED WATER-COLOR OF THE BERLIN LUSTGARTEN?
ONLY FIVE SCHILLINGS.
GENTLEMEN?
WHY DON'T YOU FIND YOURSELF A JOB, YOU MISERABLE WRETCH?
STILL LIVING THE DECADENT HIGH-LIFE OF A FREELANCE ARTIST, I SEE?
JENNY! WHAT ARE YOU DOING HERE?
I THOUGHT YOU WOULD BE OUT CELEBRATING YOUR BIRTHDAY WITH YOUR BEAUTIFUL TEENAGE SCHOOL FRIENDS.

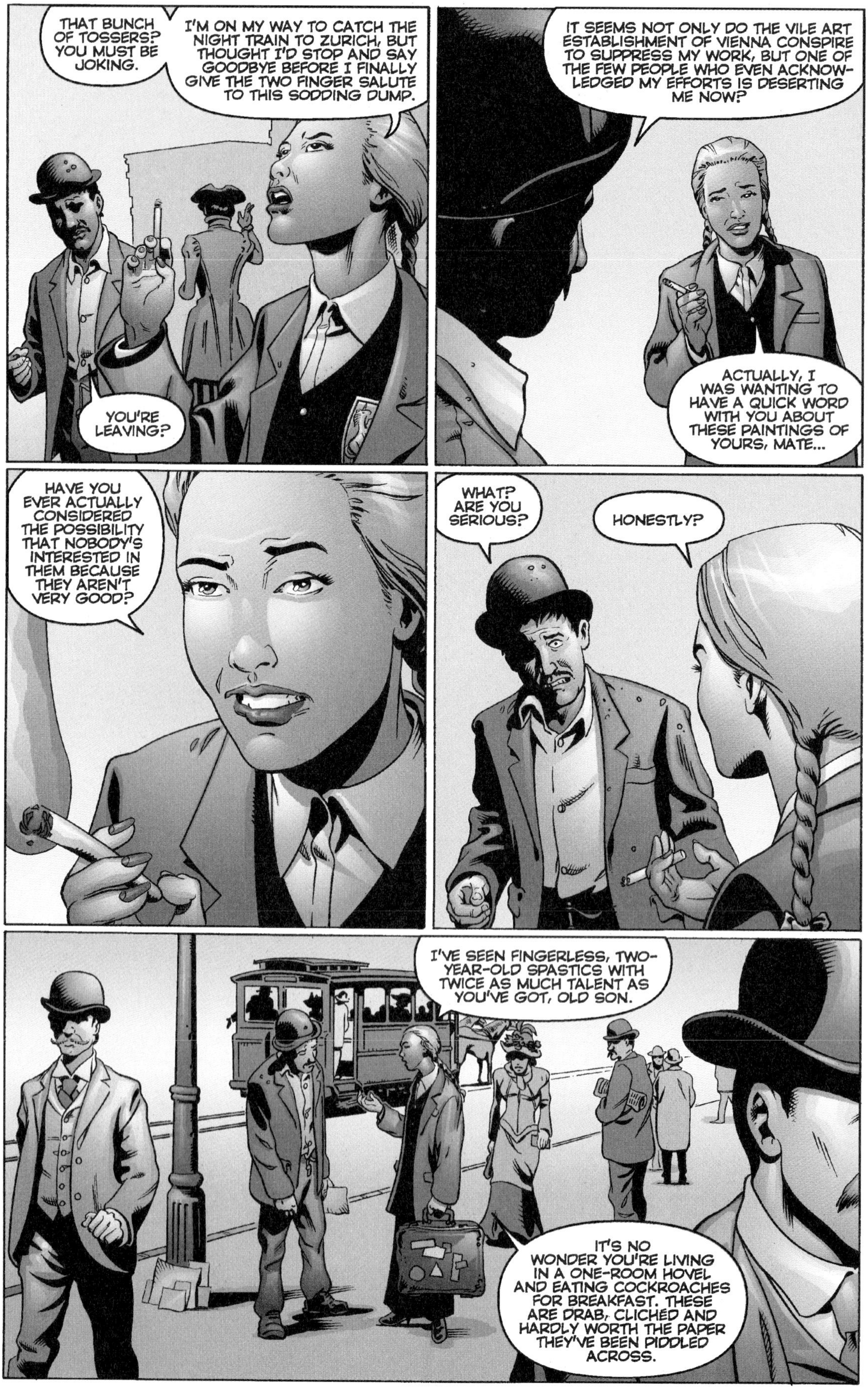
THAT BUNCH OF TOSSERS? YOU MUST BE JOKING.
I'M ON MY WAY TO CATCH THE NIGHT TRAIN TO ZURICH, BUT THOUGHT I'D STOP AND SAY GOODBYE BEFORE I FINALLY GIVE THE TWO FINGER SALUTE TO THIS SODDING DUMP.
YOU'RE LEAVING?
IT SEEMS NOT ONLY DO THE VILE ART ESTABLISHMENT OF VIENNA CONSPIRE TO SUPPRESS MY WORK, BUT ONE OF THE FEW PEOPLE WHO EVEN ACKNOWLEDGED MY EFFORTS IS DESERTING ME NOW?
ACTUALLY, I WAS WANTING TO HAVE A QUICK WORD WITH YOU ABOUT THESE PAINTINGS OF YOURS, MATE...
HAVE YOU EVER ACTUALLY CONSIDERED THE POSSIBILITY THAT NOBODY'S INTERESTED IN THEM BECAUSE THEY AREN'T VERY GOOD?
WHAT? ARE YOU SERIOUS?
HONESTLY?
I'VE SEEN FINGERLESS, TWO-YEAR-OLD SPASTICS WITH TWICE AS MUCH TALENT AS YOU'VE GOT, OLD SON.
IT'S NO WONDER YOU'RE LIVING IN A ONE-ROOM HOVEL AND EATING COCKROACHES FOR BREAKFAST. THESE ARE DRAB, CLICHED AND HARDLY WORTH THE PAPER THEY'VE BEEN PIDDLED ACROSS.

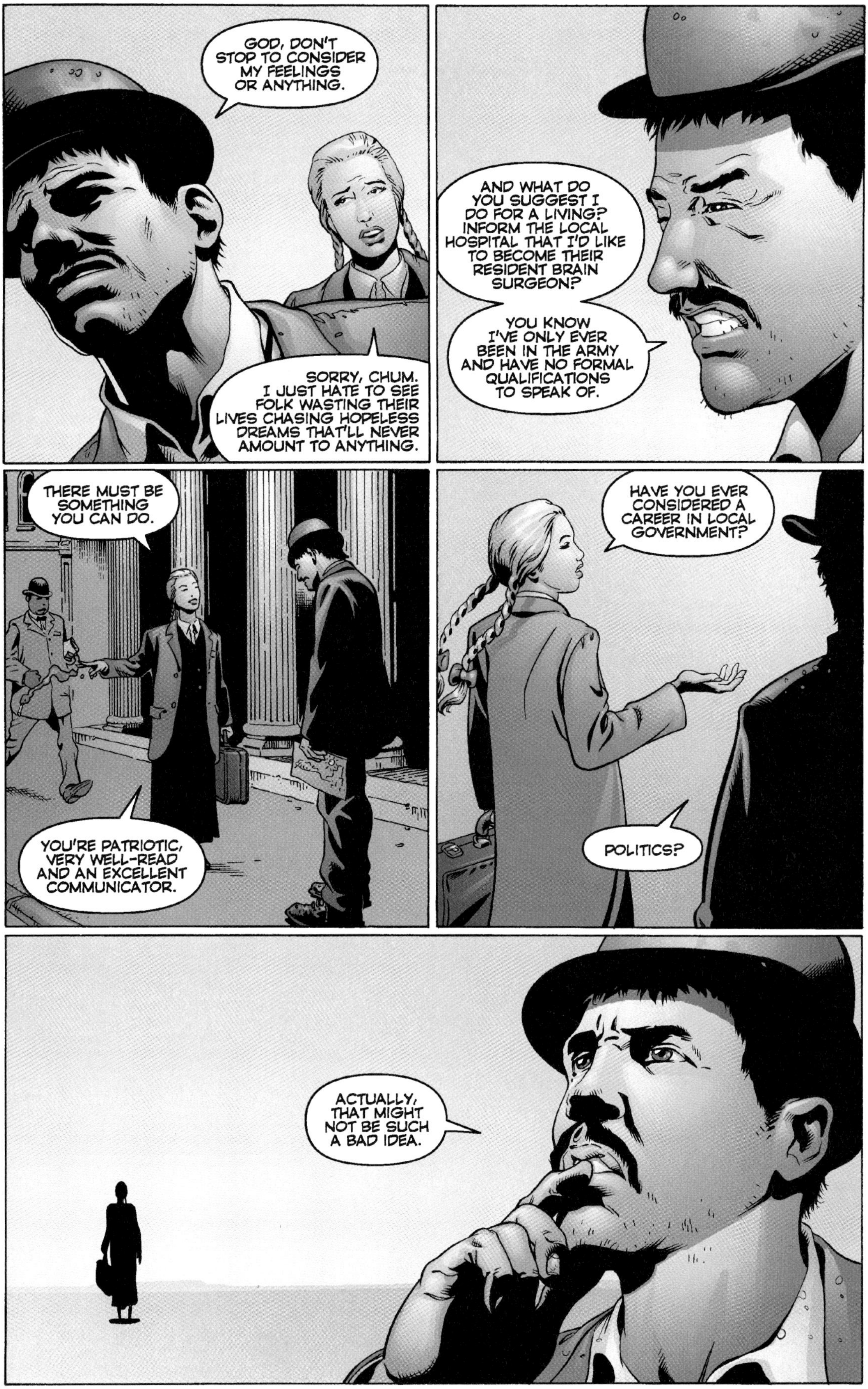
GOD, DON'T STOP TO CONSIDER MY FEELINGS OR ANYTHING.
SORRY, CHUM. I JUST HATE TO SEE FOLK WASTING THEIR LIVES CHASING HOPELESS DREAMS THAT'LL NEVER AMOUNT TO ANYTHING.
AND WHAT DO YOU SUGGEST I DO FOR A LIVING? INFORM THE LOCAL HOSPITAL THAT I'D LIKE TO BECOME THEIR RESIDENT BRAIN SURGEON?
YOU KNOW I'VE ONLY EVER BEEN IN THE ARMY AND HAVE NO FORMAL QUALIFICATIONS TO SPEAK OF.
THERE MUST BE SOMETHING YOU CAN DO.
YOU'RE PATRIOTIC, VERY WELL-READ AND AN EXCELLENT COMMUNICATOR.
HAVE YOU EVER CONSIDERED A CAREER IN LOCAL GOVERNMENT?
POLITICS?
ACTUALLY, THAT MIGHT NOT BE SUCH A BAD IDEA.

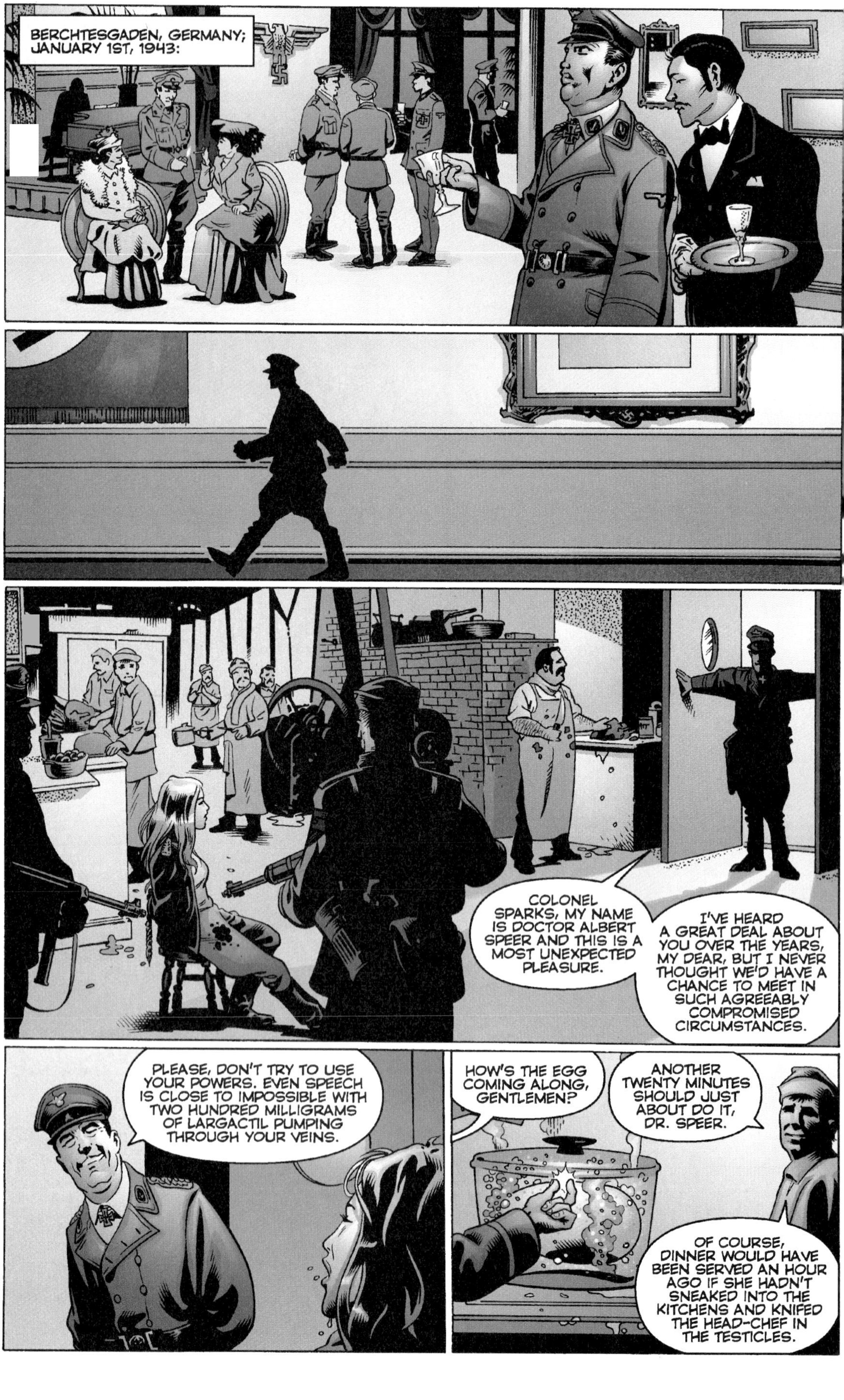
BERCHTESGADEN, GERMANY; JANUARY 1ST, 1943:
COLONEL SPARKS, MY NAME IS DOCTOR ALBERT SPEER AND THIS IS A MOST UNEXPECTED PLEASURE.
I'VE HEARD A GREAT DEAL ABOUT YOU OVER THE YEARS, MY DEAR, BUT I NEVER THOUGHT WE'D HAVE A CHANCE TO MEET IN SUCH AGREEABLY COMPROMISED CIRCUMSTANCES.
PLEASE, DON'T TRY TO USE YOUR POWERS. EVEN SPEECH IS CLOSE TO IMPOSSIBLE WITH TWO HUNDRED MILLIGRAMS OF LARGACTIL PUMPING THROUGH YOUR VEINS.
HOW'S THE EGG COMING ALONG, GENTLEMEN?
ANOTHER TWENTY MINUTES SHOULD JUST ABOUT DO IT, DR. SPEER.
OF COURSE, DINNER WOULD HAVE BEEN SERVED AN HOUR AGO IF SHE HADN'T SNEAKED INTO THE KITCHENS AND KNIFED THE HEAD-CHEF IN THE TESTICLES.

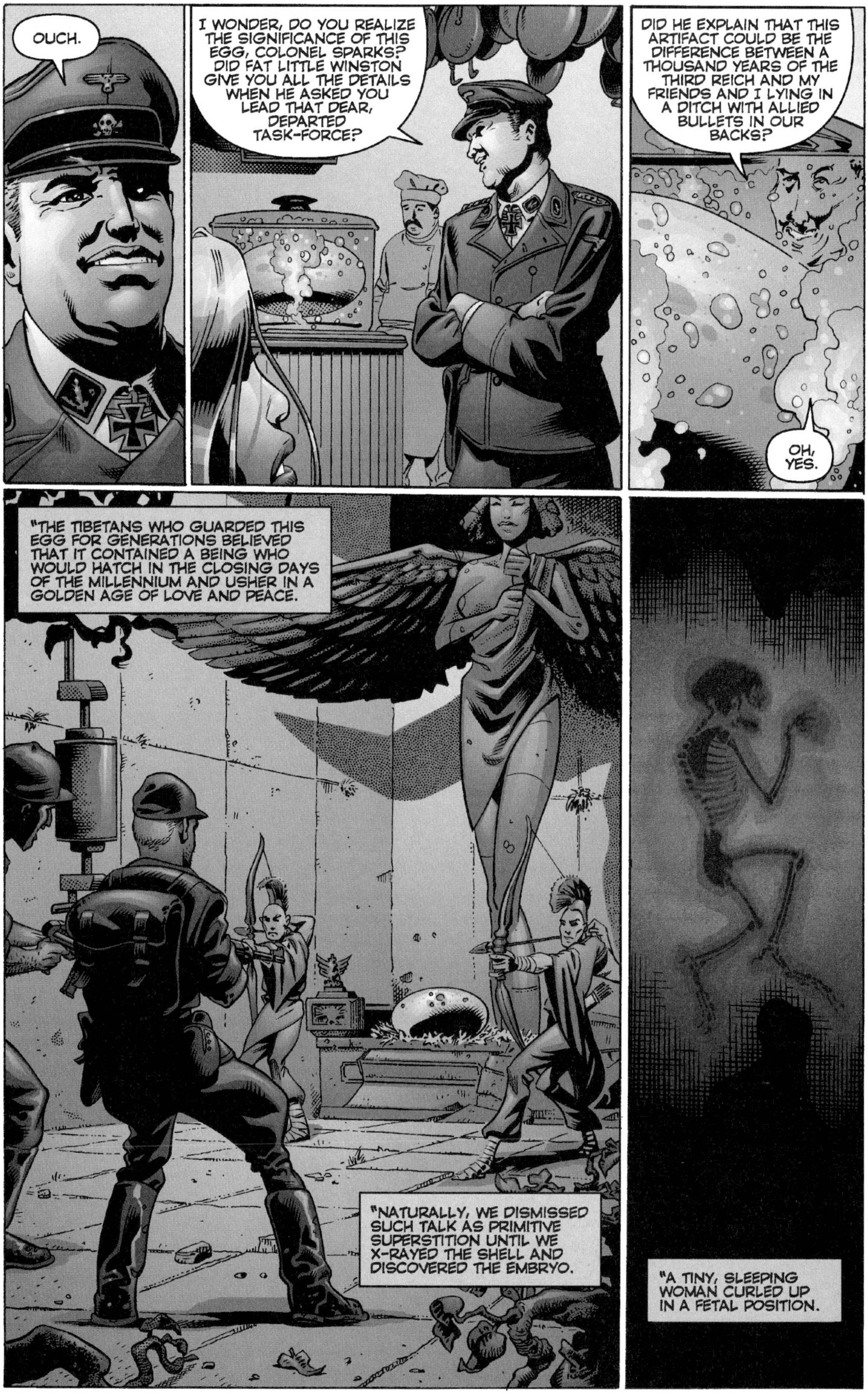
OUCH.
I WONDER, DO YOU REALIZE THE SIGNIFICANCE OF THIS EGG, COLONEL SPARKS? DID FAT LITTLE WINSTON GIVE YOU ALL THE DETAILS WHEN HE ASKED YOU LEAD THAT DEAR, DEPARTED TASK-FORCE?
DID HE EXPLAIN THAT THIS ARTIFACT COULD BE THE DIFFERENCE BETWEEN A THOUSAND YEARS OF THE THIRD REICH AND MY FRIENDS AND I LYING IN A DITCH WITH ALLIED BULLETS IN OUR BACKS?
OH, YES.
"THE TIBETANS WHO GUARDED THIS EGG FOR GENERATIONS BELIEVED THAT IT CONTAINED A BEING WHO WOULD HATCH IN THE CLOSING DAYS OF THE MILLENNIUM AND USHER IN A GOLDEN AGE OF LOVE AND PEACE.
"NATURALLY, WE DISMISSED SUCH TALK AS PRIMITIVE SUPERSTITION UNTIL WE X-RAYED THE SHELL AND DISCOVERED THE EMBRYO.
"A TINY, SLEEPING WOMAN CURLED UP IN A FETAL POSITION.

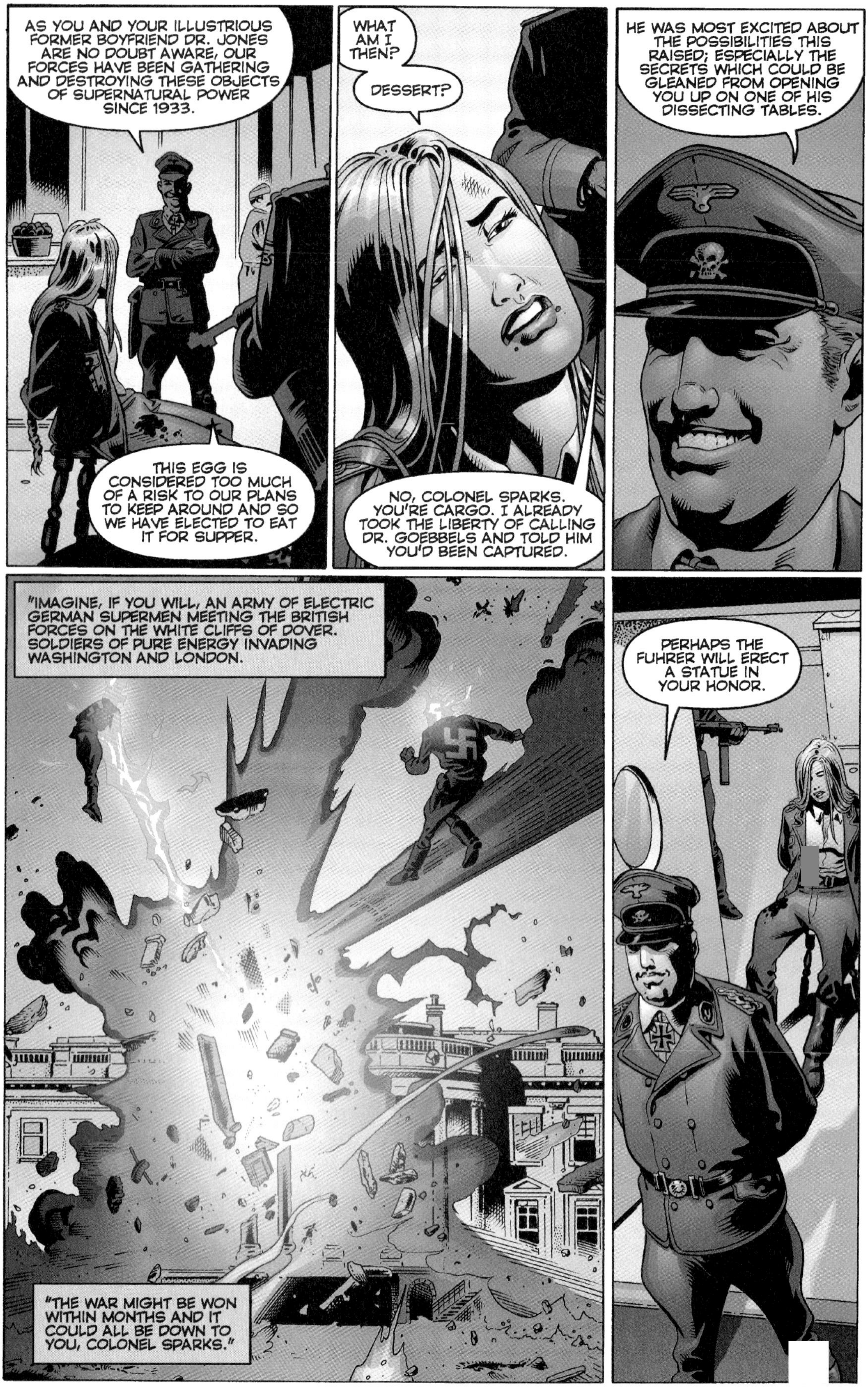
AS YOU AND YOUR ILLUSTRIOUS FORMER BOYFRIEND DR. JONES ARE NO DOUBT AWARE, OUR FORCES HAVE BEEN GATHERING AND DESTROYING THESE OBJECTS OF SUPERNATURAL POWER SINCE 1933.
THIS EGG IS CONSIDERED TOO MUCH OF A RISK TO OUR PLANS TO KEEP AROUND AND SO WE HAVE ELECTED TO EAT IT FOR SUPPER.
WHAT AM I THEN?
DESSERT?
NO, COLONEL SPARKS. YOU'RE CARGO. I ALREADY TOOK THE LIBERTY OF CALLING DR. GOEBBELS AND TOLD HIM YOU'D BEEN CAPTURED.
HE WAS MOST EXCITED ABOUT THE POSSIBILITIES THIS RAISED; ESPECIALLY THE SECRETS WHICH COULD BE GLEANED FROM OPENING YOU UP ON ONE OF HIS DISSECTING TABLES.
"IMAGINE, IF YOU WILL, AN ARMY OF ELECTRIC GERMAN SUPERMEN MEETING THE BRITISH FORCES ON THE WHITE CLIFFS OF DOVER. SOLDIERS OF PURE ENERGY INVADING WASHINGTON AND LONDON.
"THE WAR MIGHT BE WON WITHIN MONTHS AND IT COULD ALL BE DOWN TO YOU, COLONEL SPARKS."
PERHAPS THE FUHRER WILL ERECT A STATUE IN YOUR HONOR.

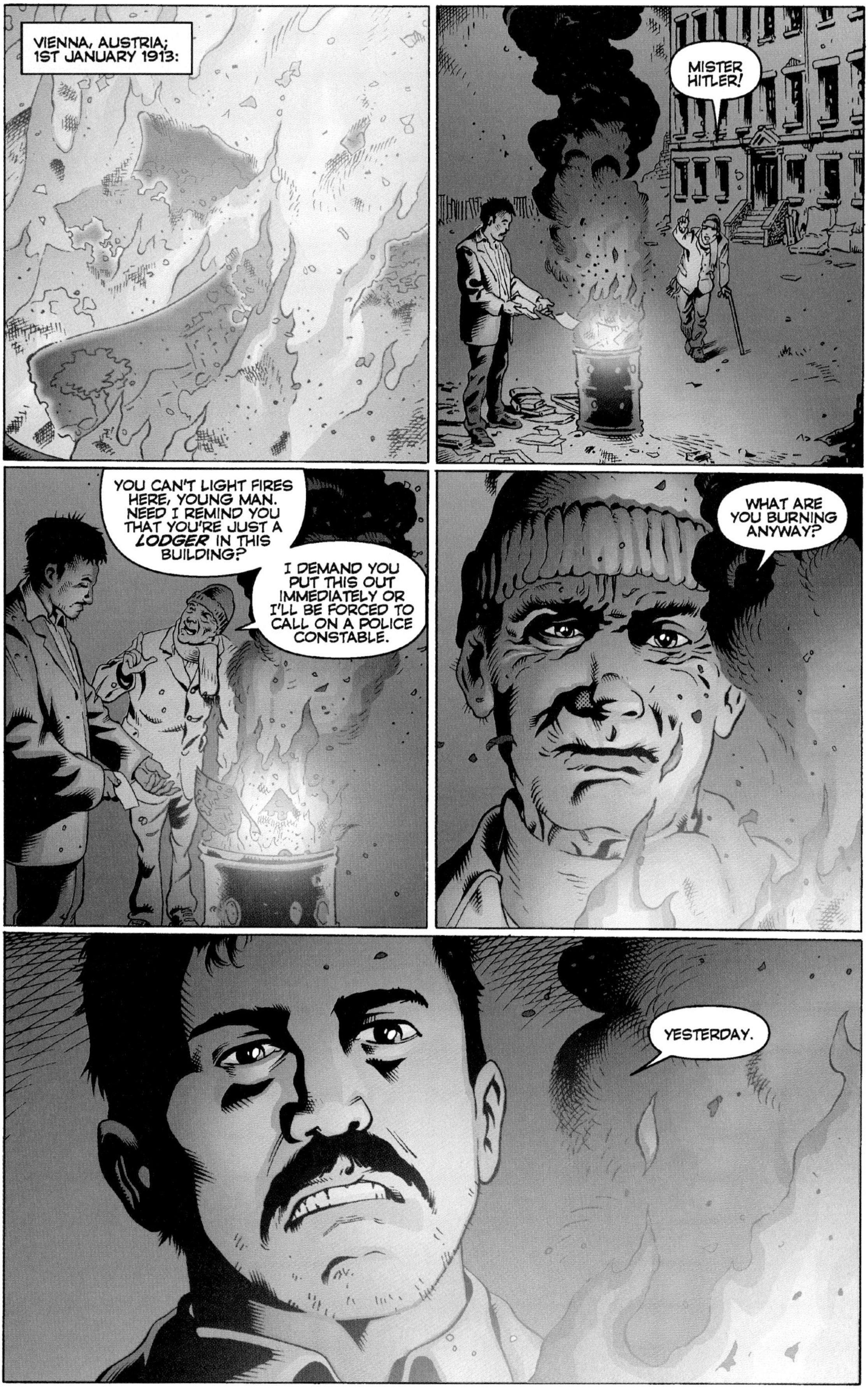
VIENNA, AUSTRIA; 1ST JANUARY 1913:
MISTER HITLER!
YOU CAN'T LIGHT FIRES HERE, YOUNG MAN. NEED I REMIND YOU THAT YOU'RE JUST A *LODGER* IN THIS BUILDING?
I DEMAND YOU PUT THIS OUT IMMEDIATELY OR I'LL BE FORCED TO CALL ON A POLICE CONSTABLE.
WHAT ARE YOU BURNING ANYWAY?
YESTERDAY.

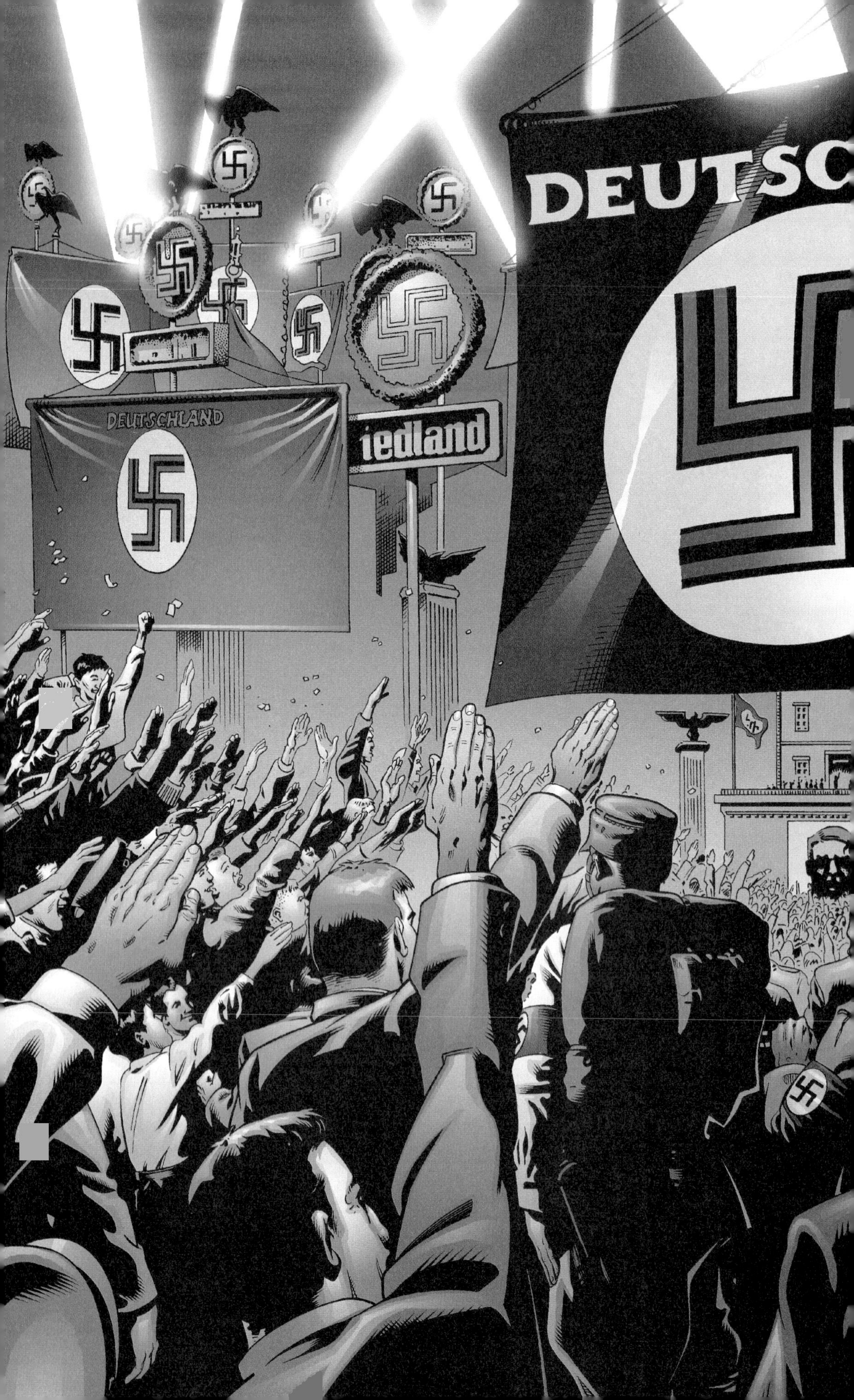
DEUTSC
DEUTSCHLAND
iedland

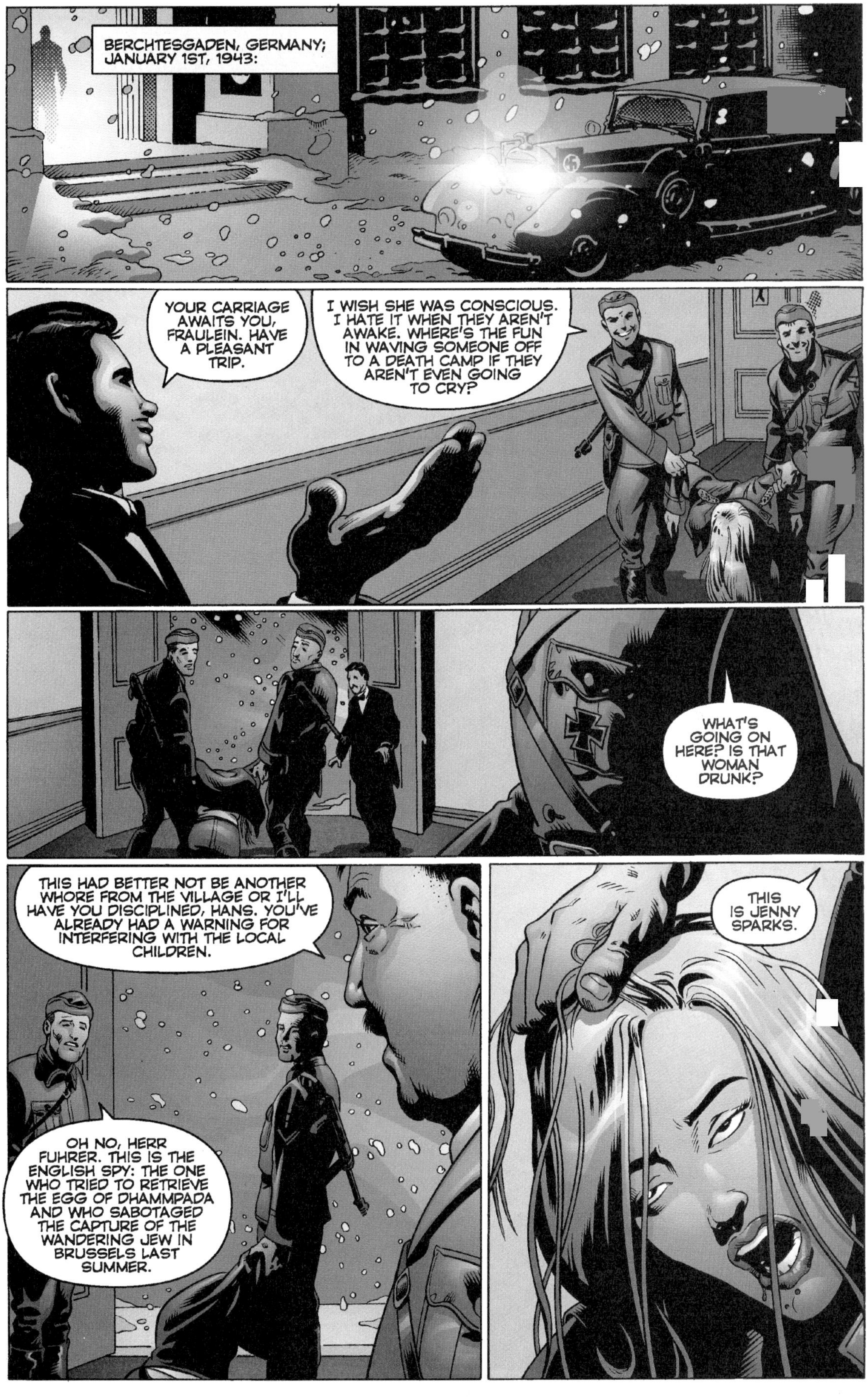
BERCHTESGADEN, GERMANY; JANUARY 1ST, 1943:
YOUR CARRIAGE AWAITS YOU, FRAULEIN. HAVE A PLEASANT TRIP.
I WISH SHE WAS CONSCIOUS. I HATE IT WHEN THEY AREN'T AWAKE. WHERE'S THE FUN IN WAVING SOMEONE OFF TO A DEATH CAMP IF THEY AREN'T EVEN GOING TO CRY?
WHAT'S GOING ON HERE? IS THAT WOMAN DRUNK?
THIS HAD BETTER NOT BE ANOTHER WHORE FROM THE VILLAGE OR I'LL HAVE YOU DISCIPLINED, HANS. YOU'VE ALREADY HAD A WARNING FOR INTERFERING WITH THE LOCAL CHILDREN.
OH NO, HERR FUHRER. THIS IS THE ENGLISH SPY: THE ONE WHO TRIED TO RETRIEVE THE EGG OF DHAMMPADA AND WHO SABOTAGED THE CAPTURE OF THE WANDERING JEW IN BRUSSELS LAST SUMMER.
THIS IS JENNY SPARKS.

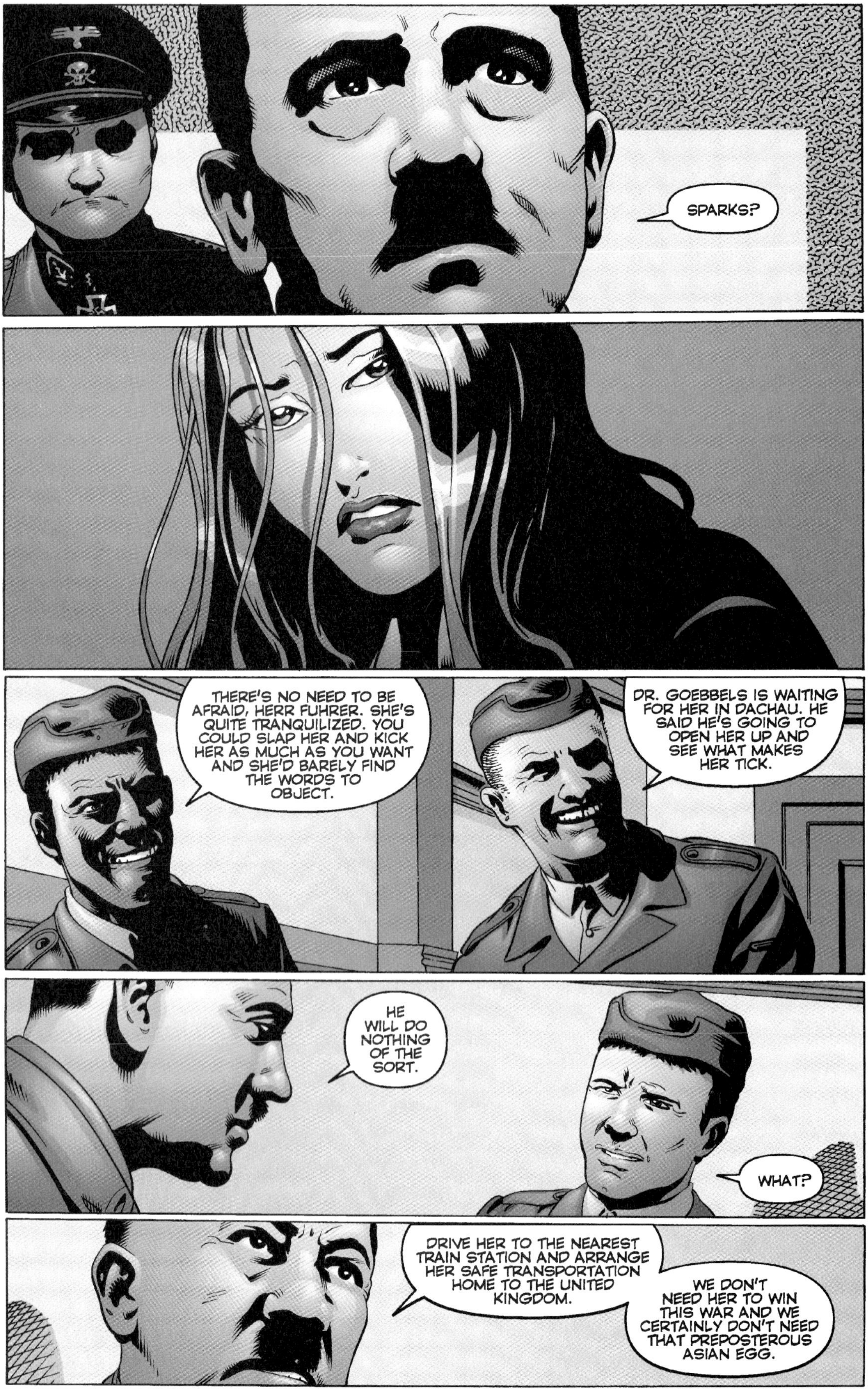
SPARKS?
THERE'S NO NEED TO BE AFRAID, HERR FUHRER. SHE'S QUITE TRANQUILIZED. YOU COULD SLAP HER AND KICK HER AS MUCH AS YOU WANT AND SHE'D BARELY FIND THE WORDS TO OBJECT.
DR. GOEBBELS IS WAITING FOR HER IN DACHAU. HE SAID HE'S GOING TO OPEN HER UP AND SEE WHAT MAKES HER TICK.
HE WILL DO NOTHING OF THE SORT.
WHAT?
DRIVE HER TO THE NEAREST TRAIN STATION AND ARRANGE HER SAFE TRANSPORTATION HOME TO THE UNITED KINGDOM.
WE DON'T NEED HER TO WIN THIS WAR AND WE CERTAINLY DON'T NEED THAT PREPOSTEROUS ASIAN EGG.

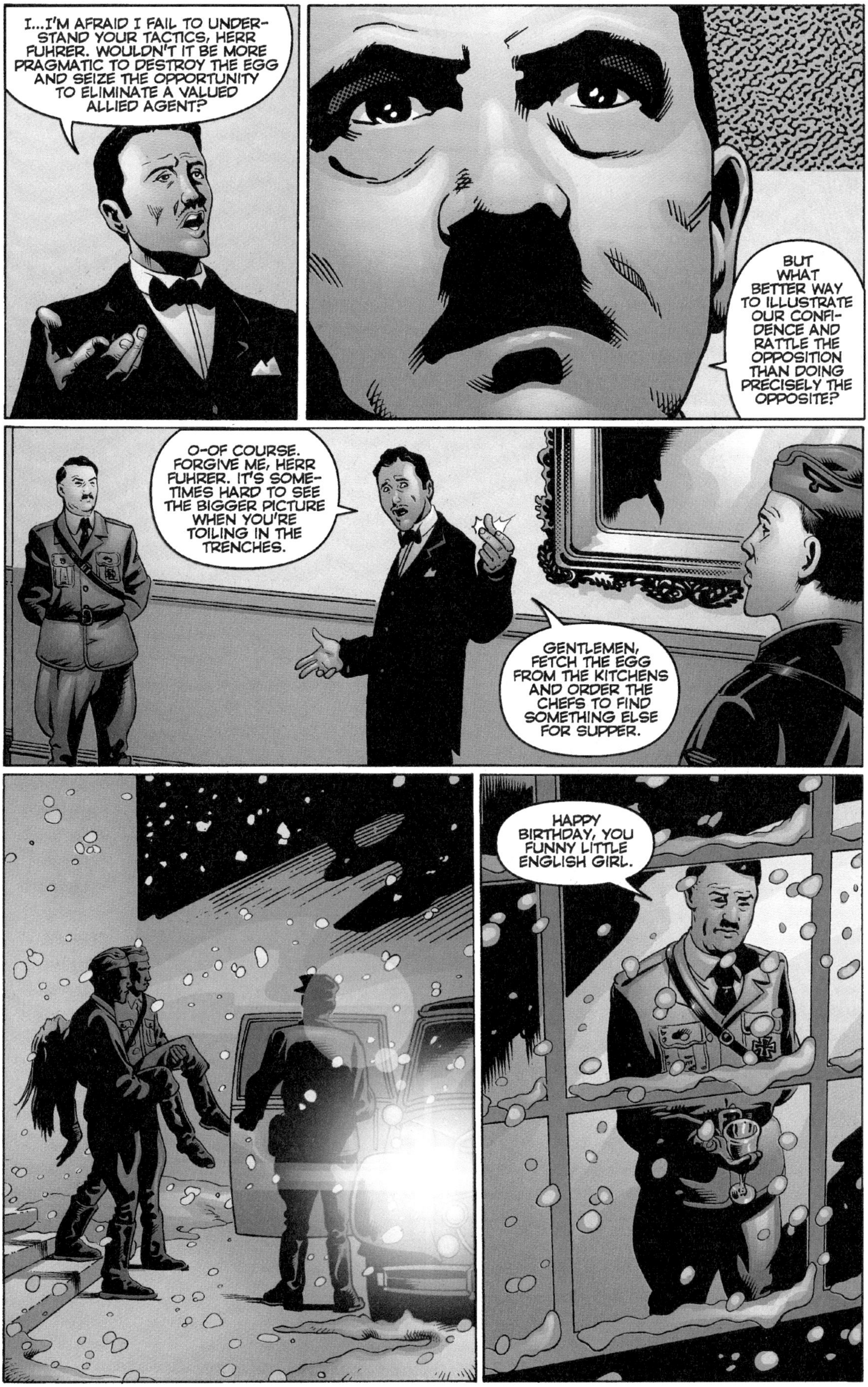
I...I'M AFRAID I FAIL TO UNDERSTAND YOUR TACTICS, HERR FUHRER. WOULDN'T IT BE MORE PRAGMATIC TO DESTROY THE EGG AND SEIZE THE OPPORTUNITY TO ELIMINATE A VALUED ALLIED AGENT?
BUT WHAT BETTER WAY TO ILLUSTRATE OUR CONFIDENCE AND RATTLE THE OPPOSITION THAN DOING PRECISELY THE OPPOSITE?
O-OF COURSE. FORGIVE ME, HERR FUHRER. IT'S SOMETIMES HARD TO SEE THE BIGGER PICTURE WHEN YOU'RE TOILING IN THE TRENCHES.
GENTLEMEN, FETCH THE EGG FROM THE KITCHENS AND ORDER THE CHEFS TO FIND SOMETHING ELSE FOR SUPPER.
HAPPY BIRTHDAY, YOU FUNNY LITTLE ENGLISH GIRL.

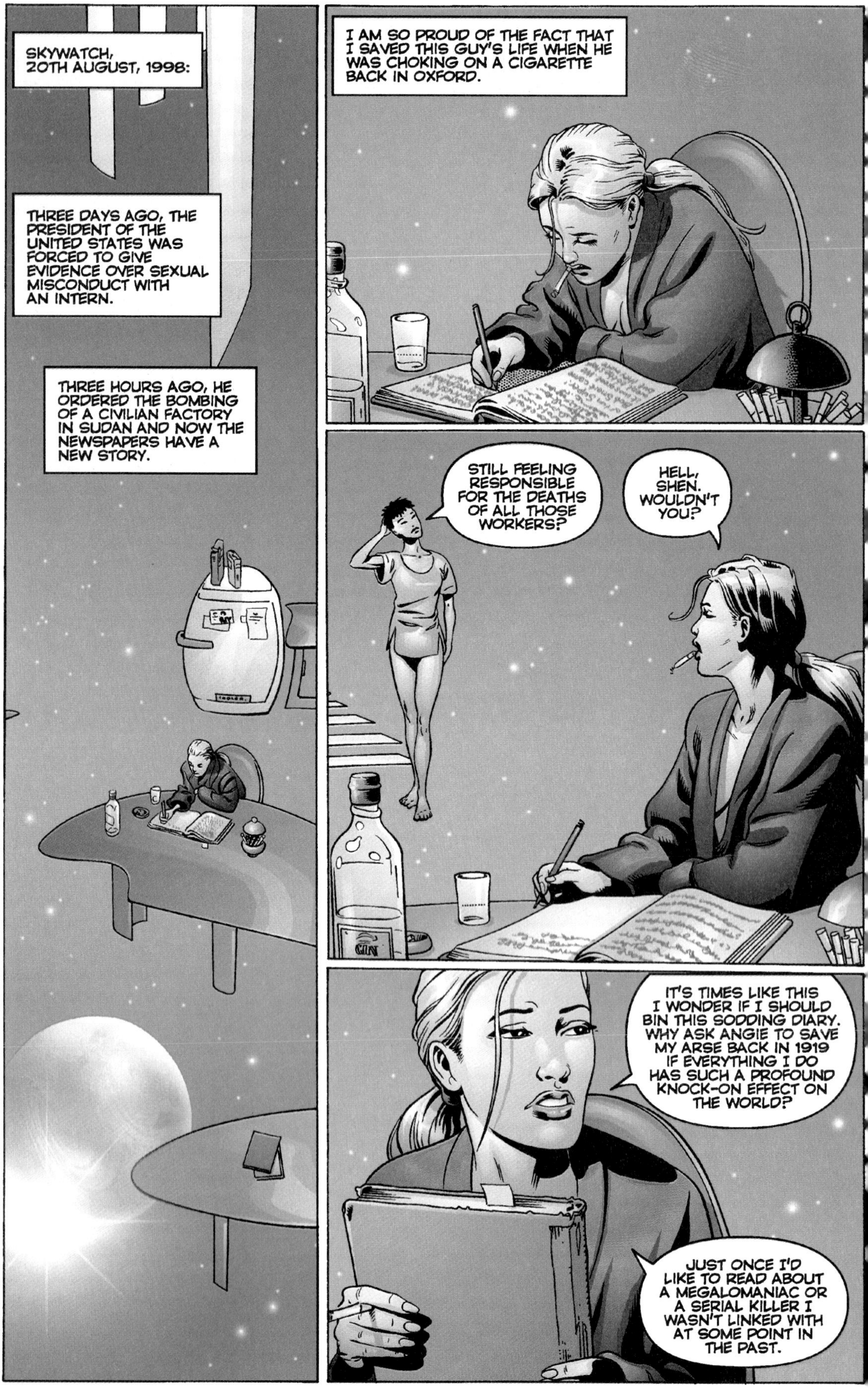
SKYWATCH,
20TH AUGUST, 1998:
THREE DAYS AGO, THE PRESIDENT OF THE UNITED STATES WAS FORCED TO GIVE EVIDENCE OVER SEXUAL MISCONDUCT WITH AN INTERN.
THREE HOURS AGO, HE ORDERED THE BOMBING OF A CIVILIAN FACTORY IN SUDAN AND NOW THE NEWSPAPERS HAVE A NEW STORY.
I AM SO PROUD OF THE FACT THAT I SAVED THIS GUY'S LIFE WHEN HE WAS CHOKING ON A CIGARETTE BACK IN OXFORD.
STILL FEELING RESPONSIBLE FOR THE DEATHS OF ALL THOSE WORKERS?
HELL, SHEN. WOULDN'T YOU?
GIN
IT'S TIMES LIKE THIS I WONDER IF I SHOULD BIN THIS SODDING DIARY. WHY ASK ANGIE TO SAVE MY ARSE BACK IN 1919 IF EVERYTHING I DO HAS SUCH A PROFOUND KNOCK-ON EFFECT ON THE WORLD?
JUST ONCE I'D LIKE TO READ ABOUT A MEGALOMANIAC OR A SERIAL KILLER I WASN'T LINKED WITH AT SOME POINT IN THE PAST.

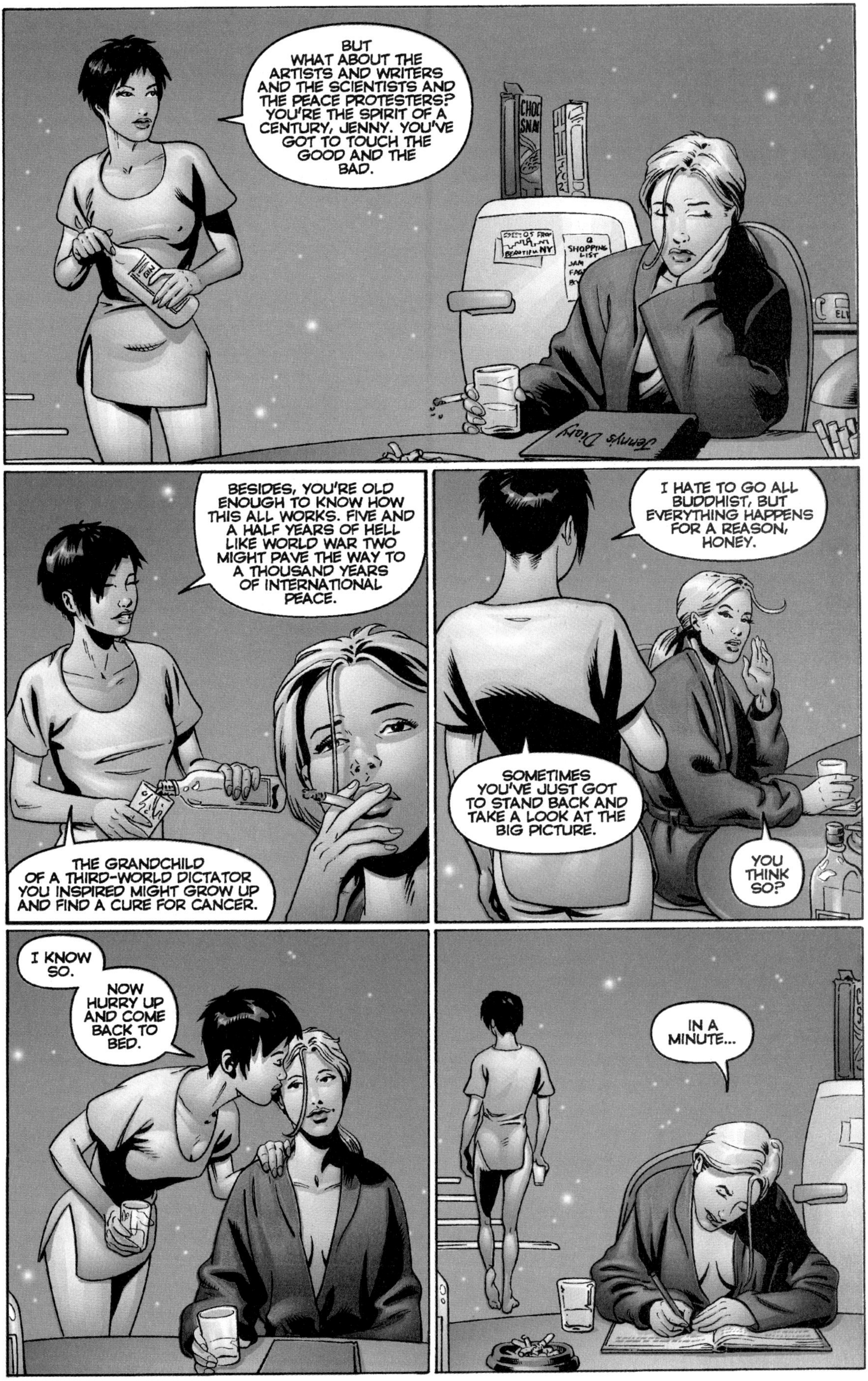
BUT WHAT ABOUT THE ARTISTS AND WRITERS AND THE SCIENTISTS AND THE PEACE PROTESTERS? YOU'RE THE SPIRIT OF A CENTURY, JENNY. YOU'VE GOT TO TOUCH THE GOOD AND THE BAD.
CHOC
SHOPPING LIST
Jenny's Diary
BESIDES, YOU'RE OLD ENOUGH TO KNOW HOW THIS ALL WORKS. FIVE AND A HALF YEARS OF HELL LIKE WORLD WAR TWO MIGHT PAVE THE WAY TO A THOUSAND YEARS OF INTERNATIONAL PEACE.
THE GRANDCHILD OF A THIRD-WORLD DICTATOR YOU INSPIRED MIGHT GROW UP AND FIND A CURE FOR CANCER.
I HATE TO GO ALL BUDDHIST, BUT EVERYTHING HAPPENS FOR A REASON, HONEY.
SOMETIMES YOU'VE JUST GOT TO STAND BACK AND TAKE A LOOK AT THE BIG PICTURE.
YOU THINK SO?
I KNOW SO.
NOW HURRY UP AND COME BACK TO BED.
IN A MINUTE...

Chapter Five
There's Nothing I Haven't Sung About

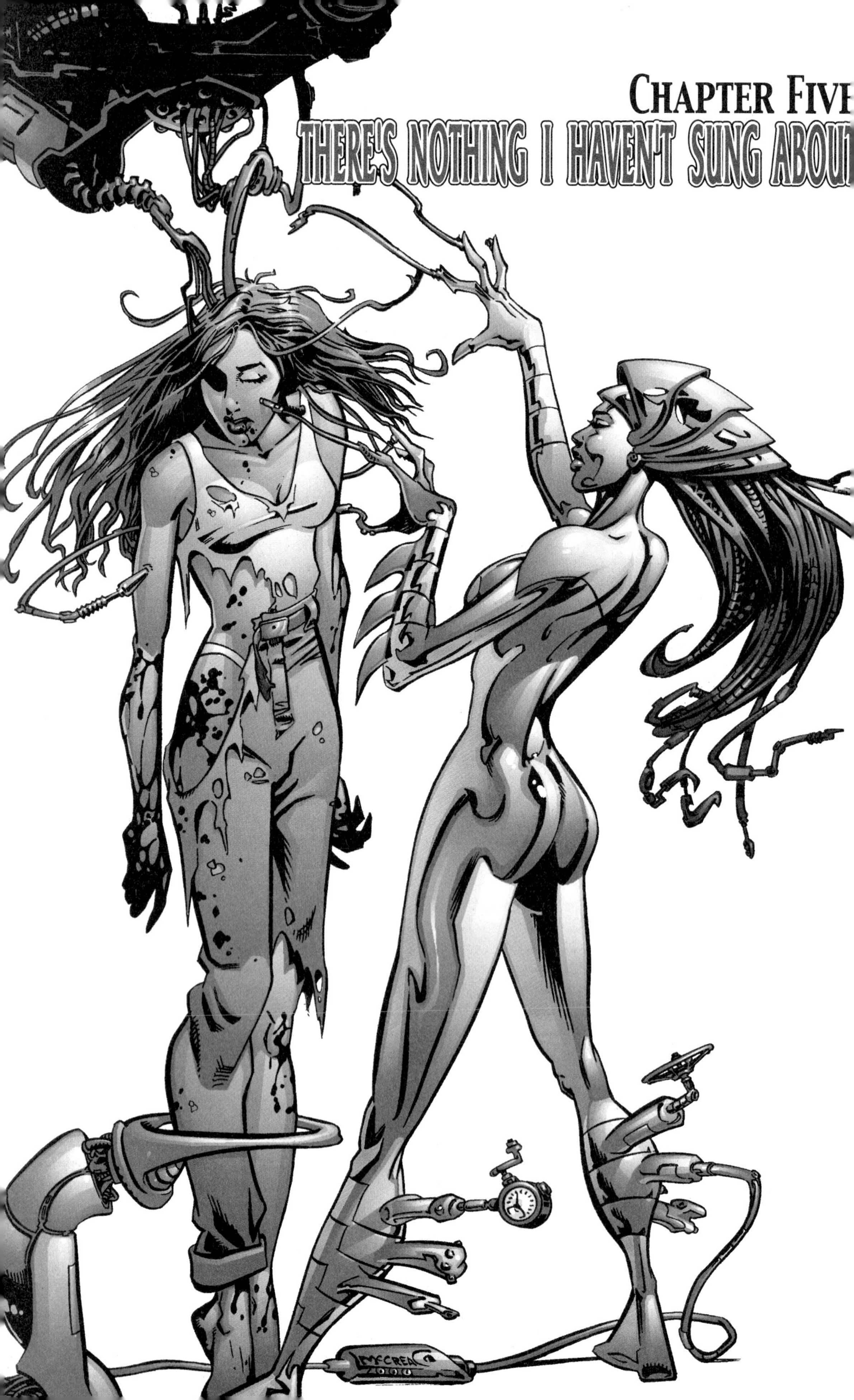

FROM THE JOURNAL OF COLONEL JENNIFER SPARKS:

WESTMINSTER ABBEY; SLIDING ALBION, DECEMBER 28TH, 1919:

DO YOU LORENZO ANTONIO SLZFI -- PRINCE OF BRYGGEN AND CHANCELLOR FOR THE DUCHY OF LANCASTER--

-- FREELY AND WILLINGLY TAKE JENNIFER SPARKS AS YOUR LAWFUL WEDDED WIFE ACCORDING TO THE LAWS OF GOD AND OF HOLY MOTHER CHURCH?

I DO.

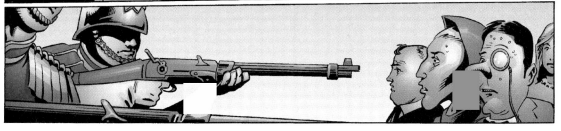

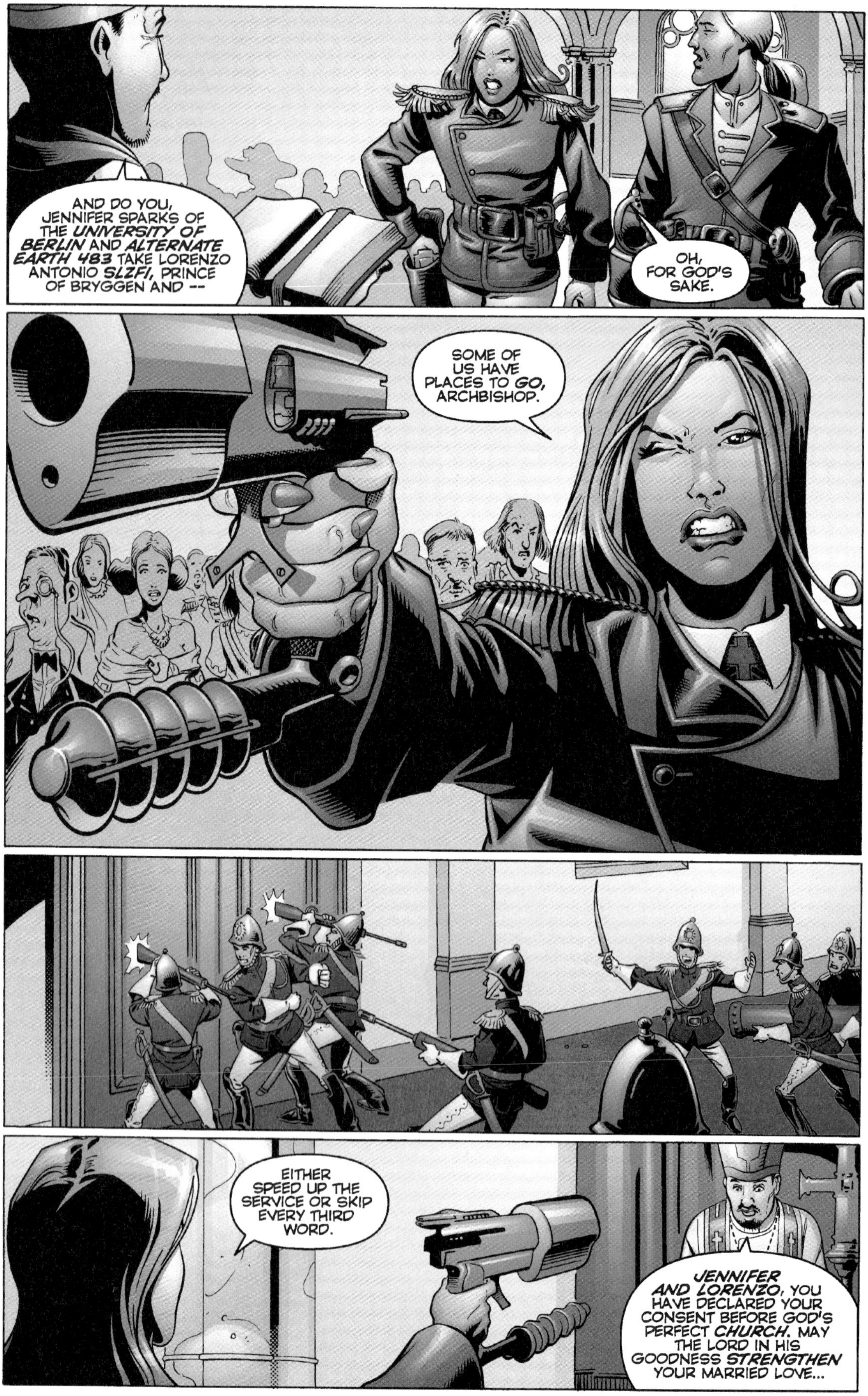
AND DO YOU, JENNIFER SPARKS OF THE UNIVERSITY OF BERLIN AND ALTERNATE EARTH 483 TAKE LORENZO ANTONIO SLZFI, PRINCE OF BRYGGEN AND --
OH, FOR GOD'S SAKE.
SOME OF US HAVE PLACES TO GO, ARCHBISHOP.
EITHER SPEED UP THE SERVICE OR SKIP EVERY THIRD WORD.
JENNIFER AND LORENZO, YOU HAVE DECLARED YOUR CONSENT BEFORE GOD'S PERFECT CHURCH. MAY THE LORD IN HIS GOODNESS STRENGTHEN YOUR MARRIED LOVE...

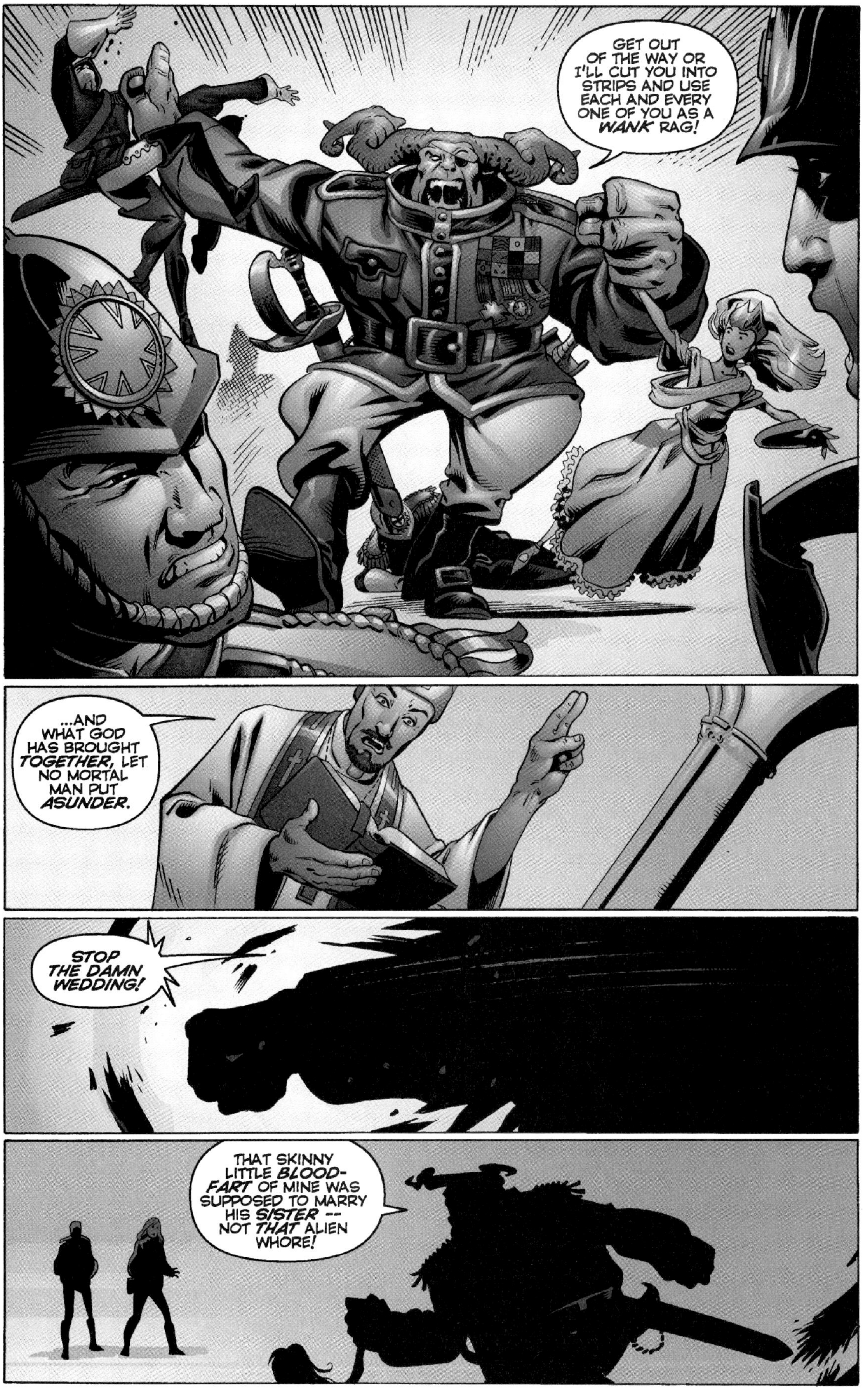
GET OUT OF THE WAY OR I'LL CUT YOU INTO STRIPS AND USE EACH AND EVERY ONE OF YOU AS A WANK RAG!
...AND WHAT GOD HAS BROUGHT TOGETHER, LET NO MORTAL MAN PUT ASUNDER.
STOP THE DAMN WEDDING!
THAT SKINNY LITTLE BLOOD-FART OF MINE WAS SUPPOSED TO MARRY HIS SISTER -- NOT THAT ALIEN WHORE!

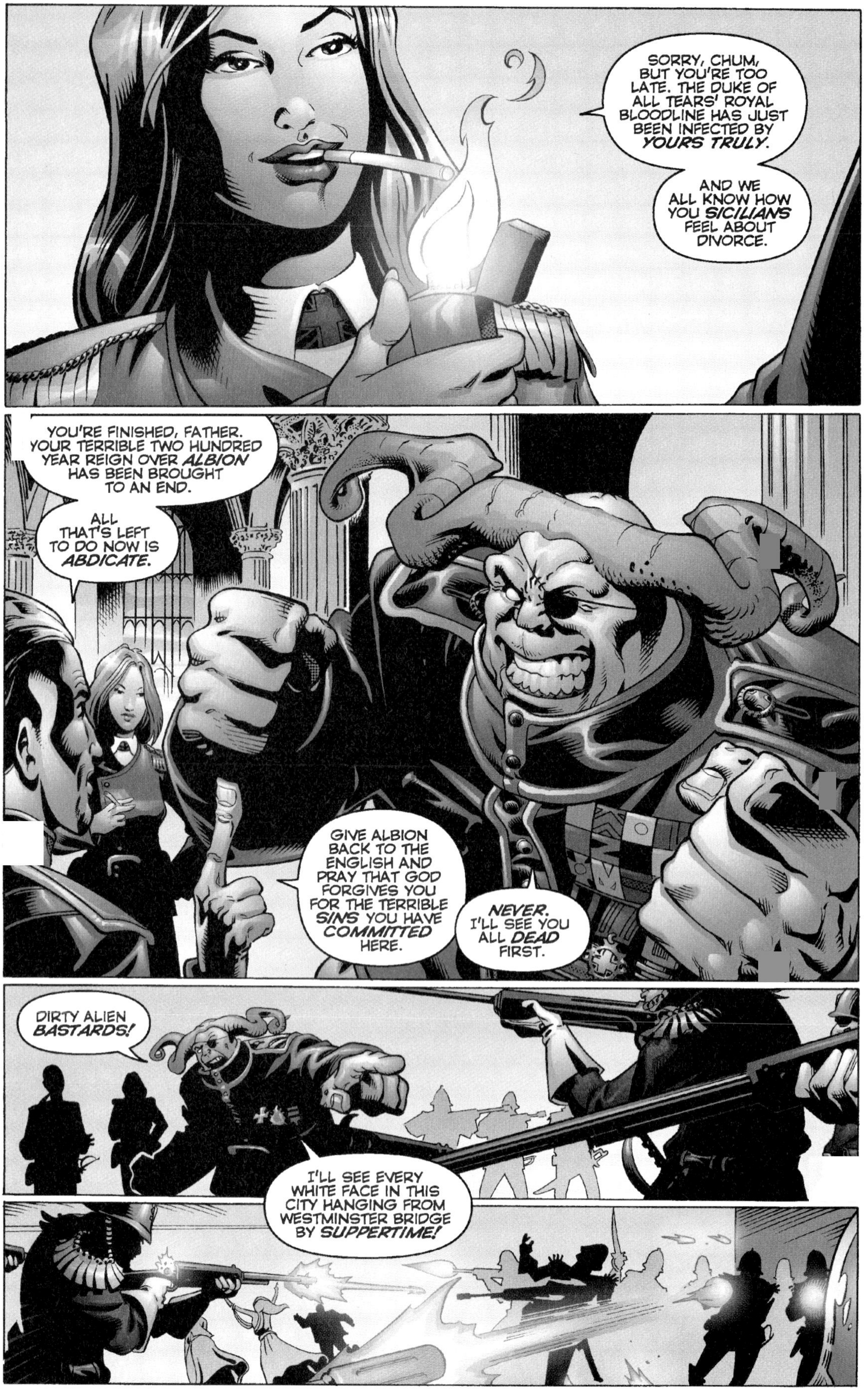
SORRY, CHUM, BUT YOU'RE TOO LATE. THE DUKE OF ALL TEARS' ROYAL BLOODLINE HAS JUST BEEN INFECTED BY YOURS TRULY.
AND WE ALL KNOW HOW YOU SICILIANS FEEL ABOUT DIVORCE.
YOU'RE FINISHED, FATHER. YOUR TERRIBLE TWO HUNDRED YEAR REIGN OVER ALBION HAS BEEN BROUGHT TO AN END.
ALL THAT'S LEFT TO DO NOW IS ABDICATE.
GIVE ALBION BACK TO THE ENGLISH AND PRAY THAT GOD FORGIVES YOU FOR THE TERRIBLE SINS YOU HAVE COMMITTED HERE.
NEVER. I'LL SEE YOU ALL DEAD FIRST.
DIRTY ALIEN BASTARDS!
I'LL SEE EVERY WHITE FACE IN THIS CITY HANGING FROM WESTMINSTER BRIDGE BY SUPPERTIME!

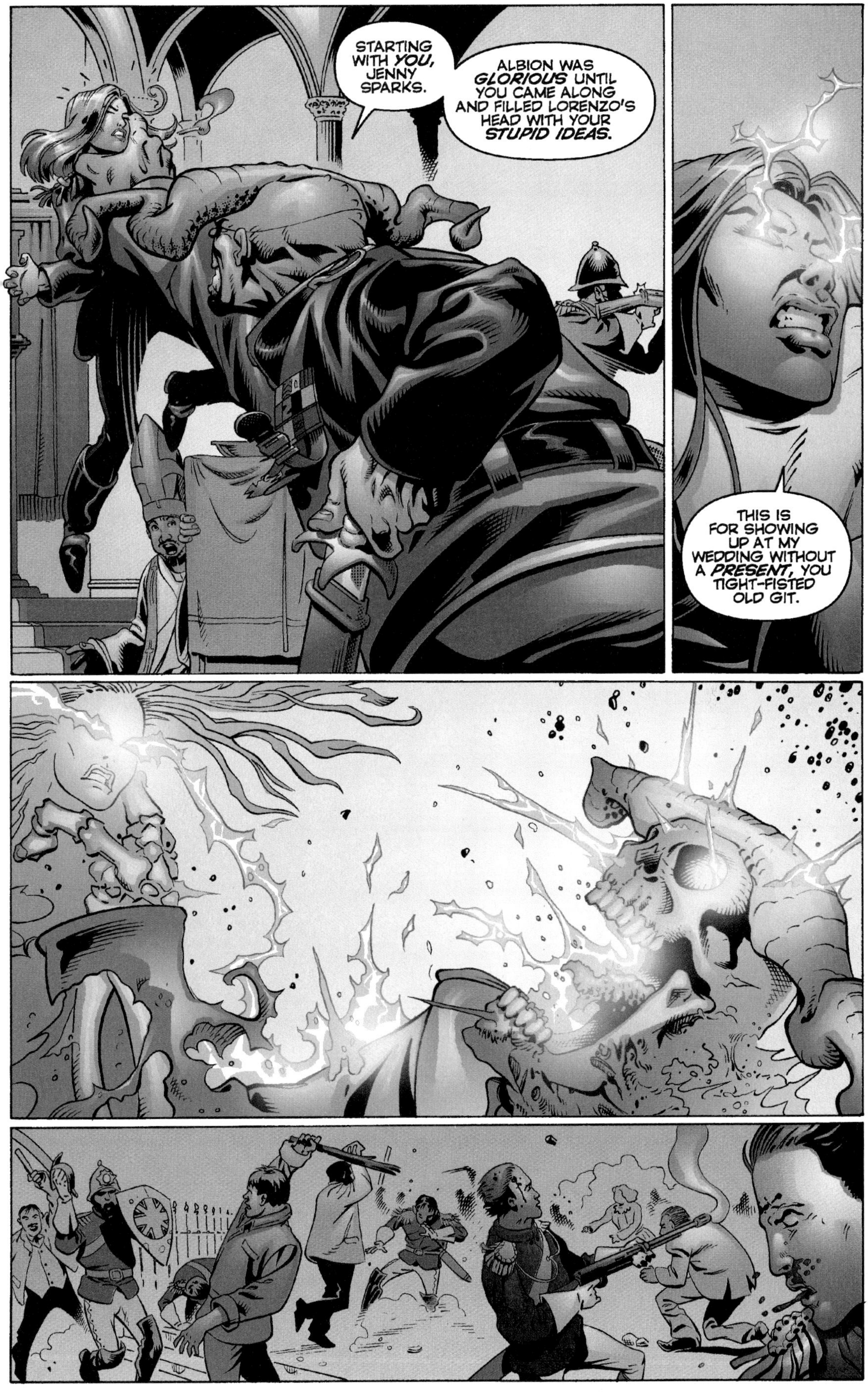
STARTING WITH *YOU,* JENNY SPARKS.
ALBION WAS *GLORIOUS* UNTIL YOU CAME ALONG AND FILLED LORENZO'S HEAD WITH YOUR *STUPID IDEAS.*
THIS IS FOR SHOWING UP AT MY WEDDING WITHOUT A *PRESENT,* YOU TIGHT-FISTED OLD GIT.

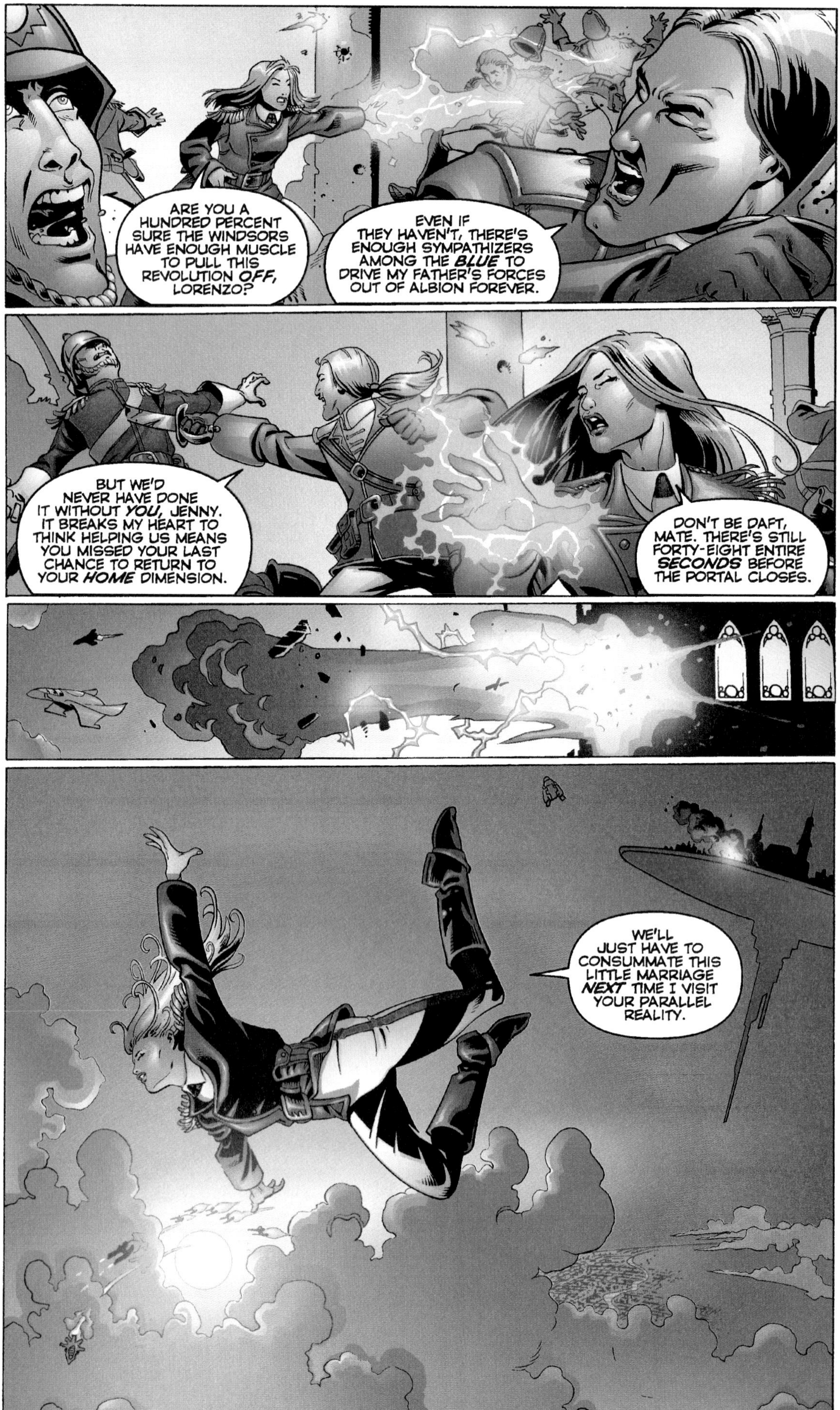
ARE YOU A HUNDRED PERCENT SURE THE WINDSORS HAVE ENOUGH MUSCLE TO PULL THIS REVOLUTION *OFF,* LORENZO?
EVEN IF THEY HAVEN'T, THERE'S ENOUGH SYMPATHIZERS AMONG THE *BLUE* TO DRIVE MY FATHER'S FORCES OUT OF ALBION FOREVER.
BUT WE'D NEVER HAVE DONE IT WITHOUT *YOU,* JENNY. IT BREAKS MY HEART TO THINK HELPING US MEANS YOU MISSED YOUR LAST CHANCE TO RETURN TO YOUR *HOME* DIMENSION.
DON'T BE DAFT, MATE. THERE'S STILL FORTY-EIGHT ENTIRE *SECONDS* BEFORE THE PORTAL CLOSES.
WE'LL JUST HAVE TO CONSUMMATE THIS LITTLE MARRIAGE *NEXT* TIME I VISIT YOUR PARALLEL REALITY.

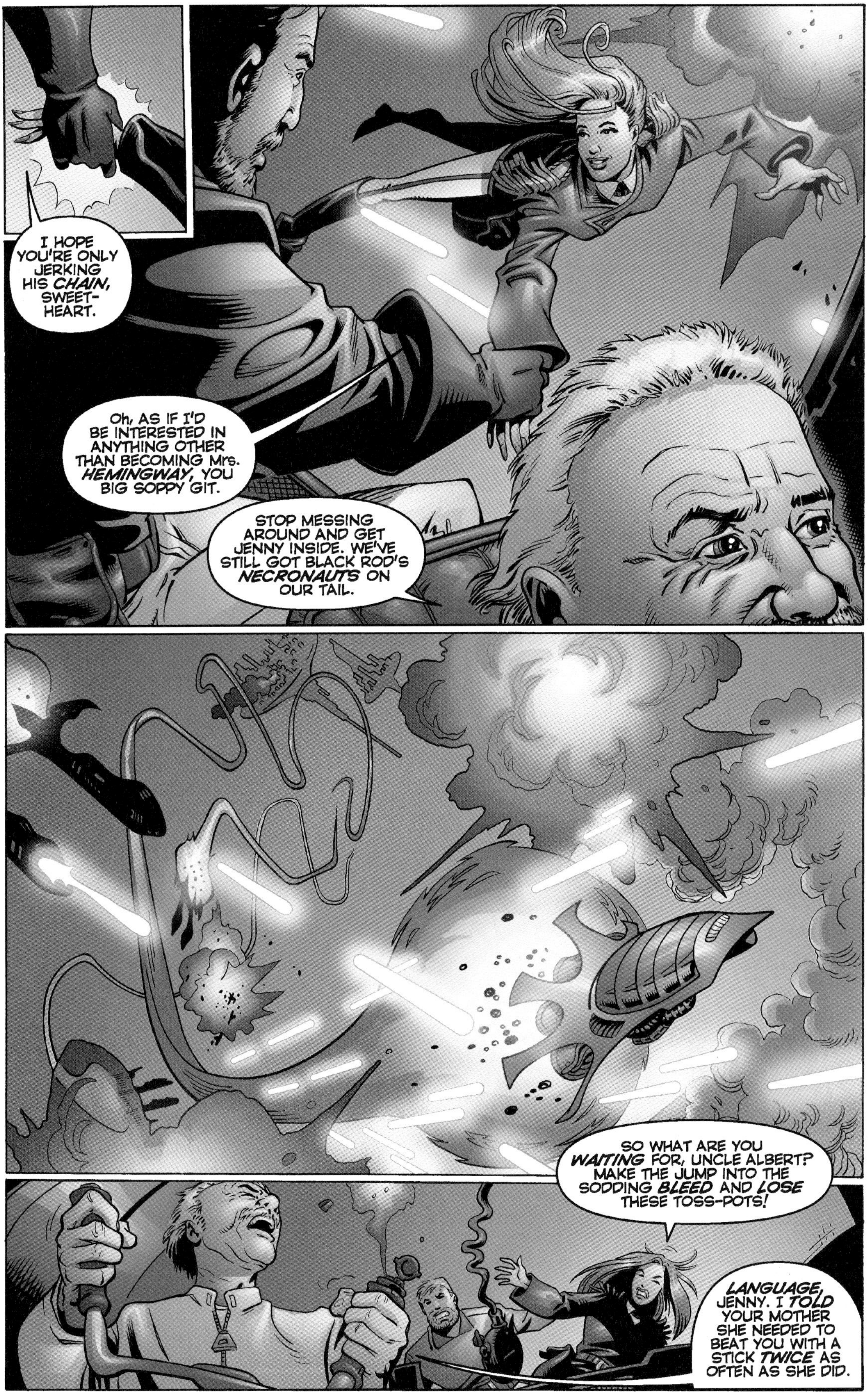
I HOPE YOU'RE ONLY JERKING HIS *CHAIN,* SWEET-HEART.
Oh, AS IF I'D BE INTERESTED IN ANYTHING OTHER THAN BECOMING Mrs. *HEMINGWAY,* YOU BIG SOPPY GIT.
STOP MESSING AROUND AND GET JENNY INSIDE. WE'VE STILL GOT BLACK ROD'S *NECRONAUTS* ON OUR TAIL.
SO WHAT ARE YOU *WAITING* FOR, UNCLE ALBERT? MAKE THE JUMP INTO THE SODDING *BLEED* AND *LOSE* THESE TOSS-POTS!
LANGUAGE, JENNY. I *TOLD* YOUR MOTHER SHE NEEDED TO BEAT YOU WITH A STICK *TWICE* AS OFTEN AS SHE DID.

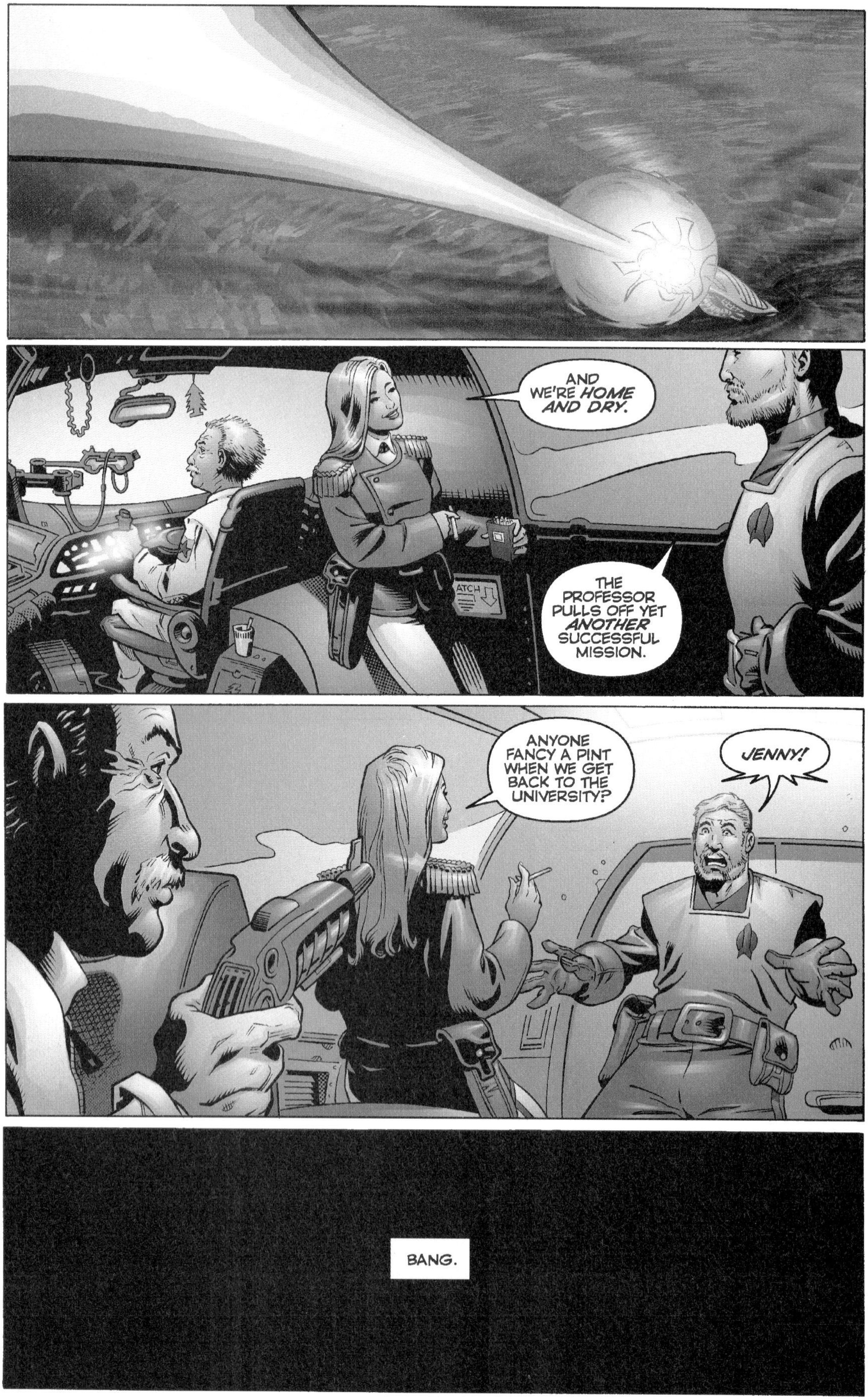
AND WE'RE *HOME AND DRY.*
THE PROFESSOR PULLS OFF YET *ANOTHER* SUCCESSFUL MISSION.
ANYONE FANCY A PINT WHEN WE GET BACK TO THE UNIVERSITY?
JENNY!
BANG.

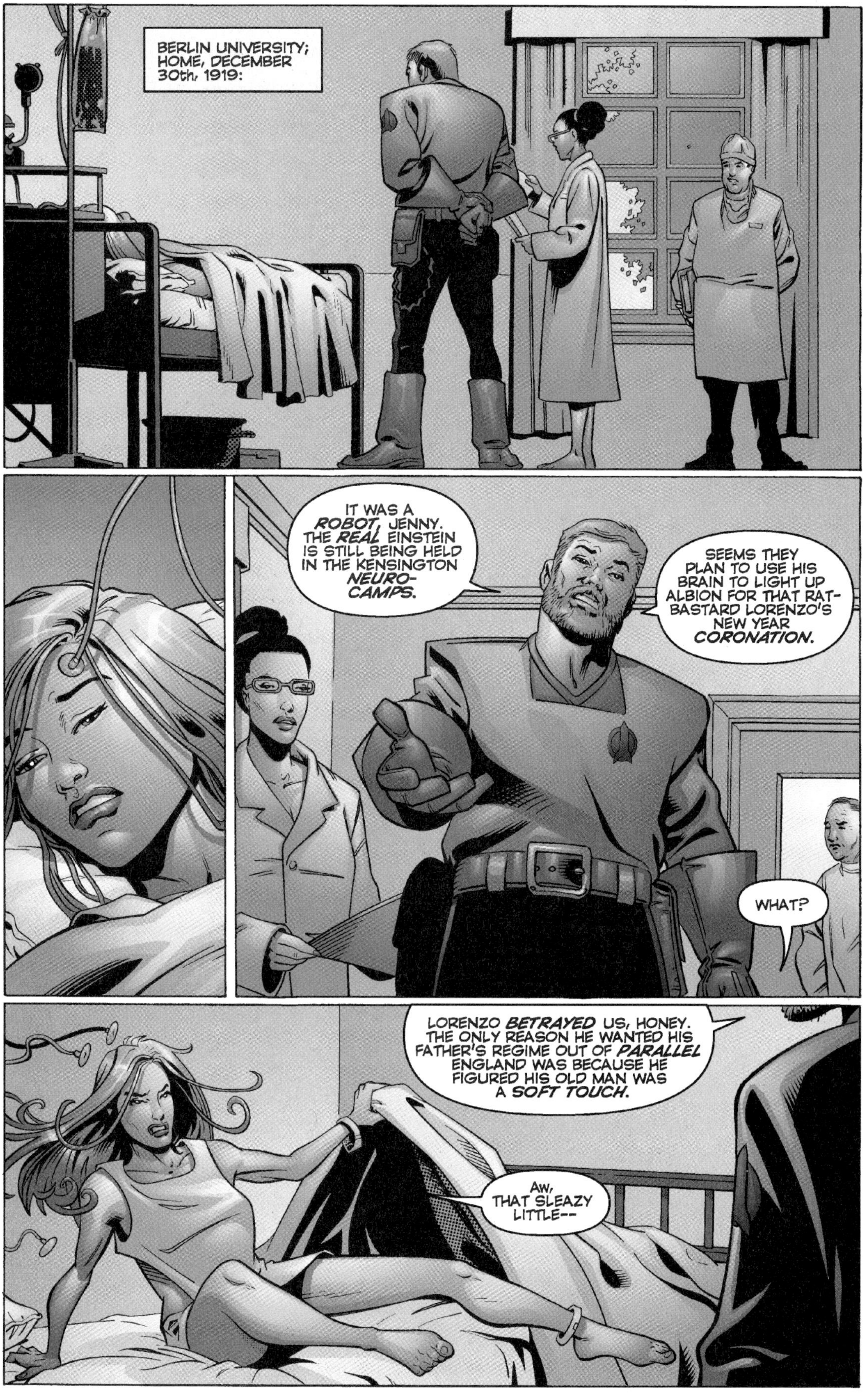
BERLIN UNIVERSITY; HOME, DECEMBER 30th, 1919:
IT WAS A ROBOT, JENNY. THE REAL EINSTEIN IS STILL BEING HELD IN THE KENSINGTON NEURO-CAMPS.
SEEMS THEY PLAN TO USE HIS BRAIN TO LIGHT UP ALBION FOR THAT RAT-BASTARD LORENZO'S NEW YEAR CORONATION.
WHAT?
LORENZO BETRAYED US, HONEY. THE ONLY REASON HE WANTED HIS FATHER'S REGIME OUT OF PARALLEL ENGLAND WAS BECAUSE HE FIGURED HIS OLD MAN WAS A SOFT TOUCH.
AW, THAT SLEAZY LITTLE--

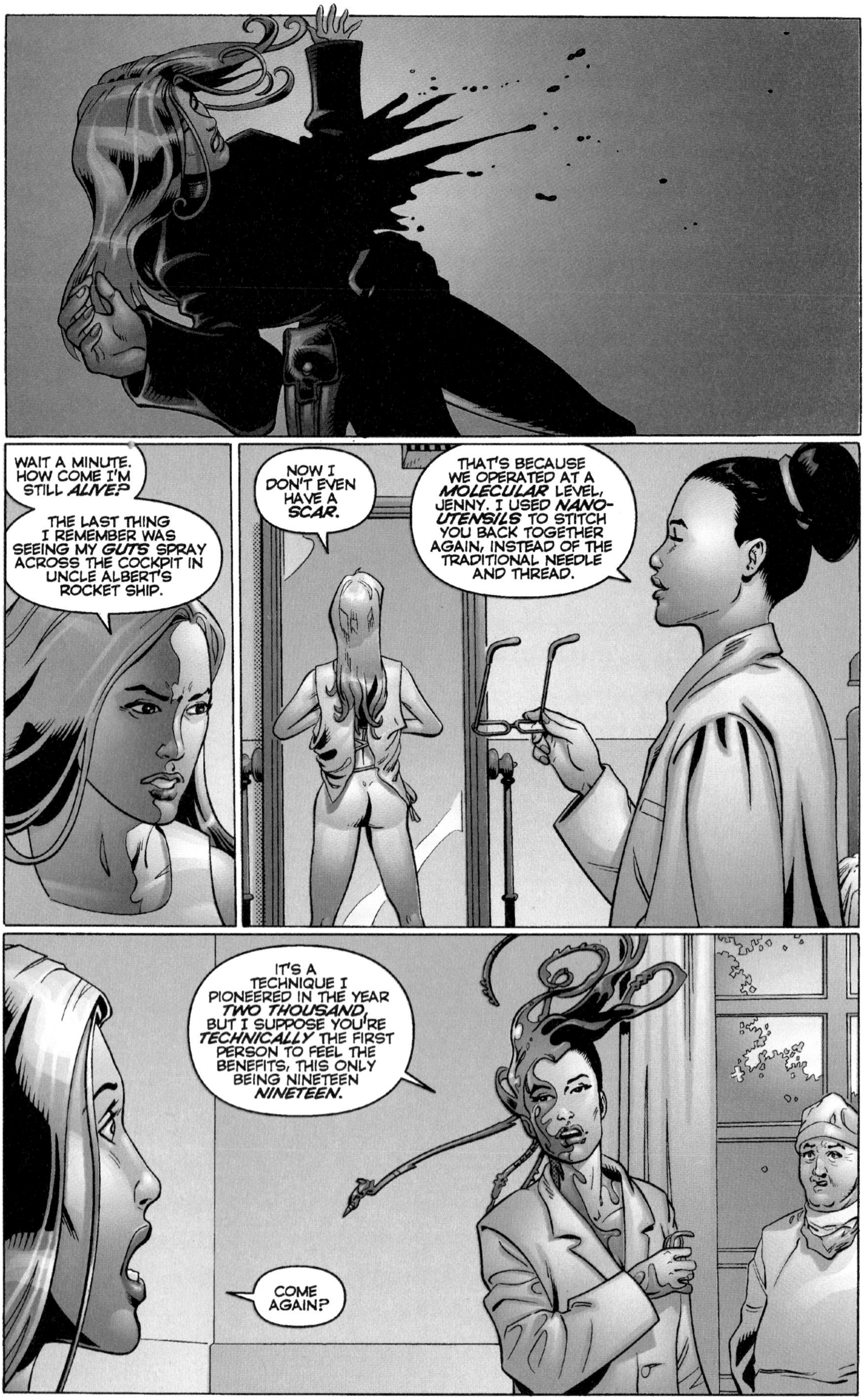
WAIT A MINUTE. HOW COME I'M STILL *ALIVE?*
THE LAST THING I REMEMBER WAS SEEING MY *GUTS* SPRAY ACROSS THE COCKPIT IN UNCLE ALBERT'S ROCKET SHIP.
NOW I DON'T EVEN HAVE A *SCAR*.
THAT'S BECAUSE WE OPERATED AT A *MOLECULAR* LEVEL, JENNY. I USED *NANO-UTENSILS* TO STITCH YOU BACK TOGETHER AGAIN, INSTEAD OF THE TRADITIONAL NEEDLE AND THREAD.
IT'S A TECHNIQUE I PIONEERED IN THE YEAR *TWO THOUSAND*, BUT I SUPPOSE YOU'RE *TECHNICALLY* THE FIRST PERSON TO FEEL THE BENEFITS, THIS ONLY BEING NINETEEN *NINETEEN*.
COME AGAIN?

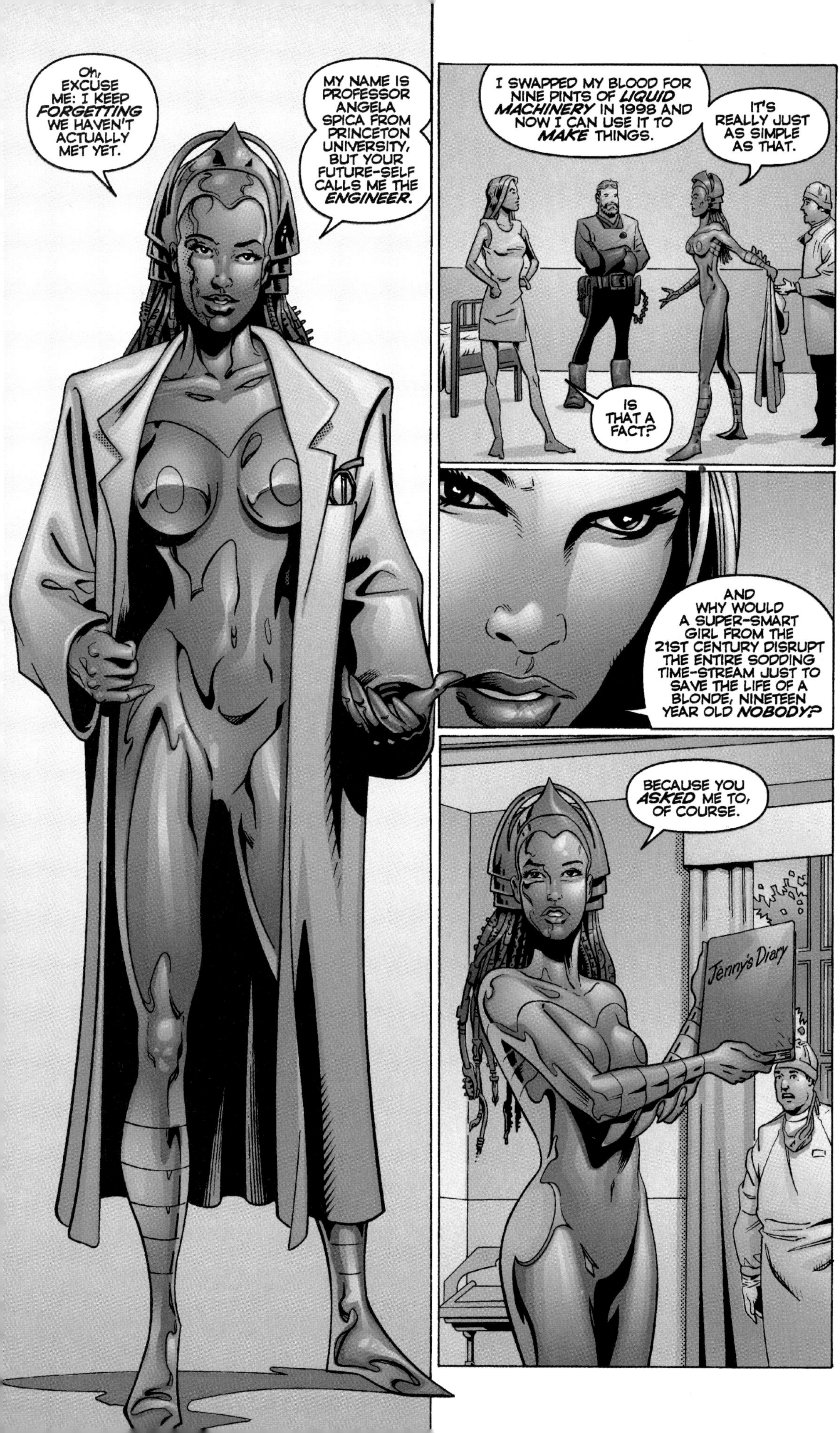
Oh, EXCUSE ME: I KEEP FORGETTING WE HAVEN'T ACTUALLY MET YET.
MY NAME IS PROFESSOR ANGELA SPICA FROM PRINCETON UNIVERSITY, BUT YOUR FUTURE-SELF CALLS ME THE ENGINEER.
I SWAPPED MY BLOOD FOR NINE PINTS OF LIQUID MACHINERY IN 1998 AND NOW I CAN USE IT TO MAKE THINGS.
IT'S REALLY JUST AS SIMPLE AS THAT.
IS THAT A FACT?
AND WHY WOULD A SUPER-SMART GIRL FROM THE 21ST CENTURY DISRUPT THE ENTIRE SODDING TIME-STREAM JUST TO SAVE THE LIFE OF A BLONDE, NINETEEN YEAR OLD NOBODY?
BECAUSE YOU ASKED ME TO, OF COURSE.
Jenny's Diary

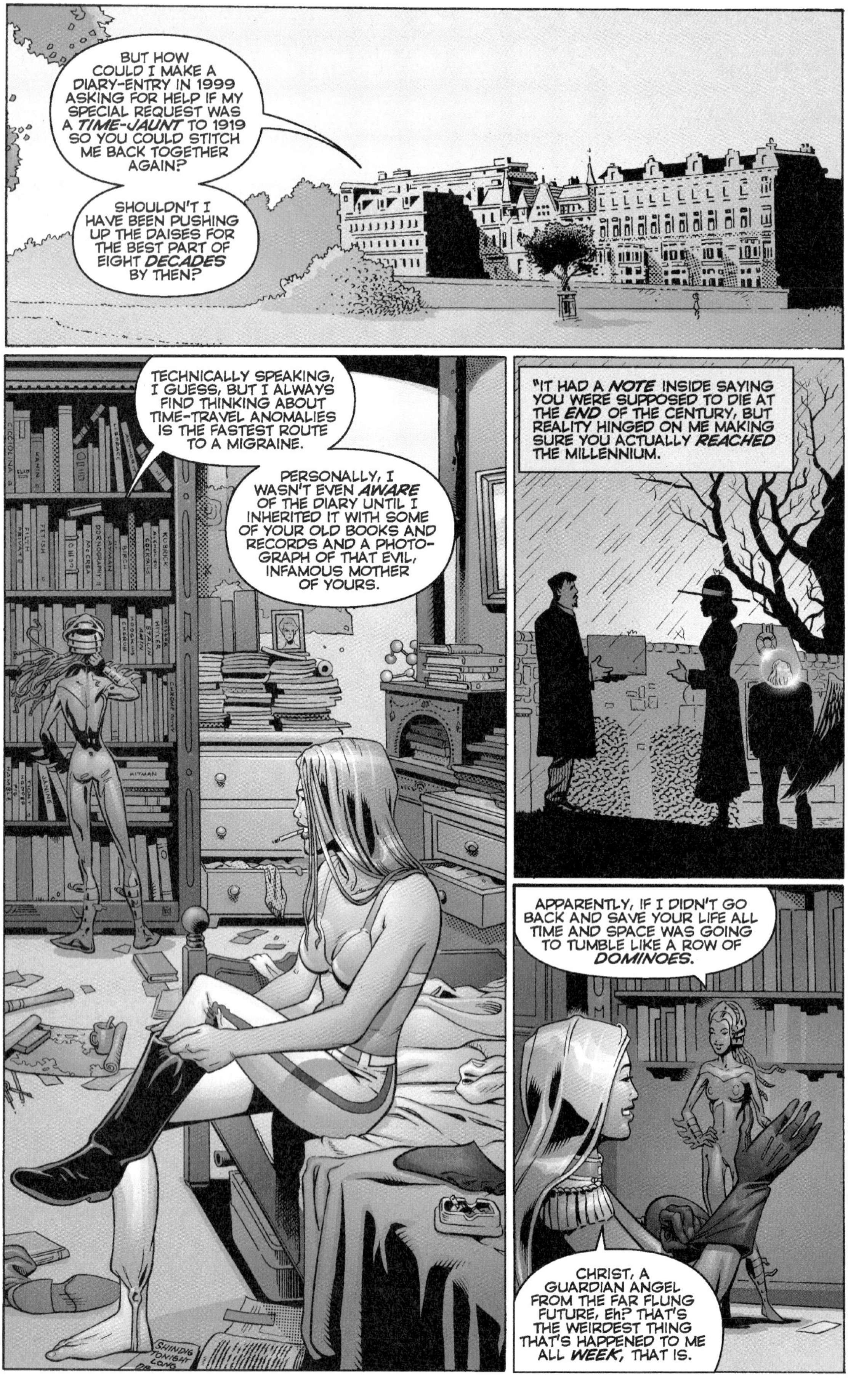
BUT HOW COULD I MAKE A DIARY-ENTRY IN 1999 ASKING FOR HELP IF MY SPECIAL REQUEST WAS A TIME-JAUNT TO 1919 SO YOU COULD STITCH ME BACK TOGETHER AGAIN?
SHOULDN'T I HAVE BEEN PUSHING UP THE DAISES FOR THE BEST PART OF EIGHT DECADES BY THEN?
TECHNICALLY SPEAKING, I GUESS, BUT I ALWAYS FIND THINKING ABOUT TIME-TRAVEL ANOMALIES IS THE FASTEST ROUTE TO A MIGRAINE.
PERSONALLY, I WASN'T EVEN AWARE OF THE DIARY UNTIL I INHERITED IT WITH SOME OF YOUR OLD BOOKS AND RECORDS AND A PHOTOGRAPH OF THAT EVIL, INFAMOUS MOTHER OF YOURS.
"IT HAD A NOTE INSIDE SAYING YOU WERE SUPPOSED TO DIE AT THE END OF THE CENTURY, BUT REALITY HINGED ON ME MAKING SURE YOU ACTUALLY REACHED THE MILLENNIUM.
APPARENTLY, IF I DIDN'T GO BACK AND SAVE YOUR LIFE ALL TIME AND SPACE WAS GOING TO TUMBLE LIKE A ROW OF DOMINOES.
CHRIST, A GUARDIAN ANGEL FROM THE FAR FLUNG FUTURE, EH? THAT'S THE WEIRDEST THING THAT'S HAPPENED TO ME ALL WEEK, THAT IS.

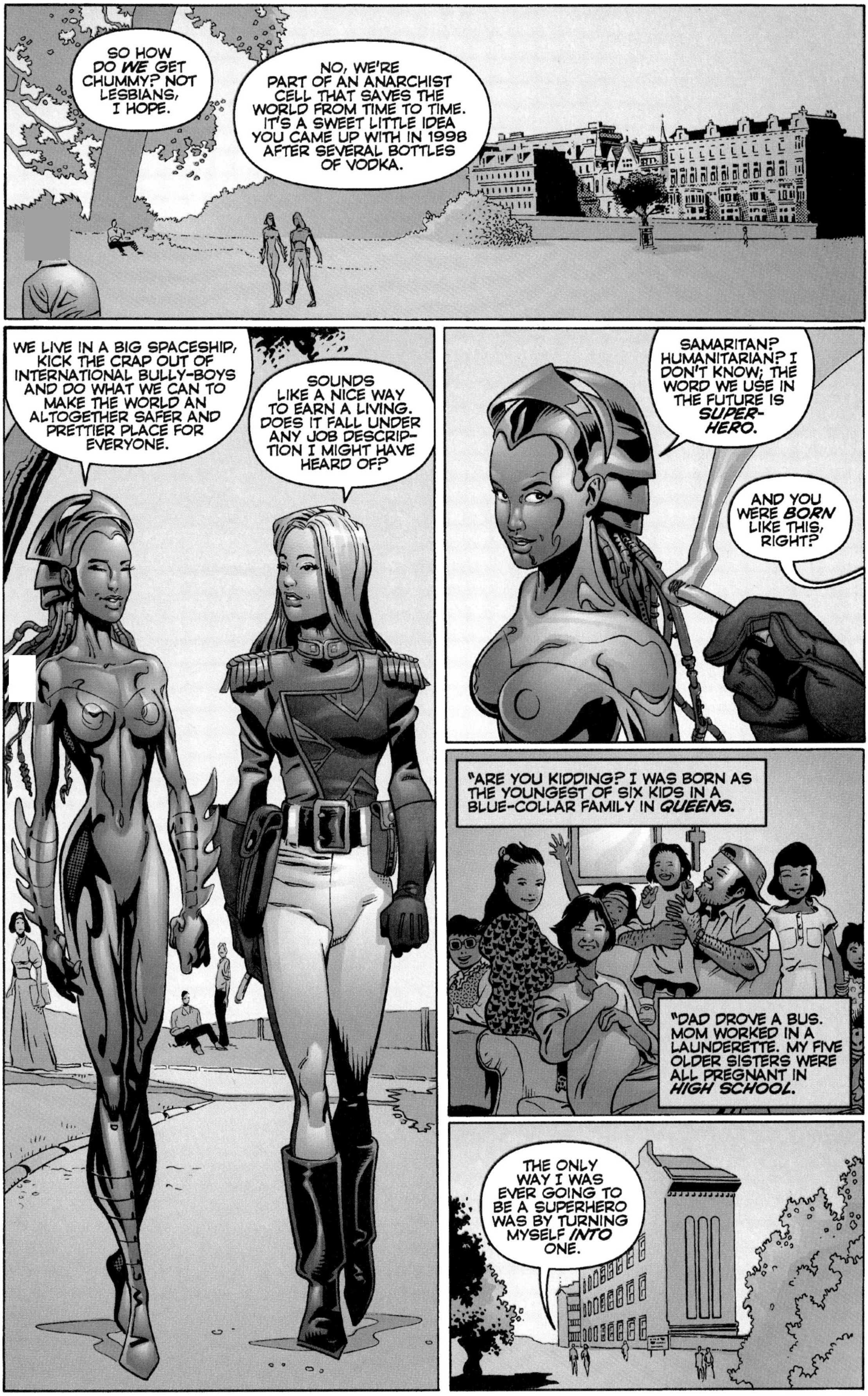
SO HOW DO *WE* GET CHUMMY? NOT LESBIANS, I HOPE.
NO, WE'RE PART OF AN ANARCHIST CELL THAT SAVES THE WORLD FROM TIME TO TIME. IT'S A SWEET LITTLE IDEA YOU CAME UP WITH IN 1998 AFTER SEVERAL BOTTLES OF VODKA.
WE LIVE IN A BIG SPACESHIP, KICK THE CRAP OUT OF INTERNATIONAL BULLY-BOYS AND DO WHAT WE CAN TO MAKE THE WORLD AN ALTOGETHER SAFER AND PRETTIER PLACE FOR EVERYONE.
SOUNDS LIKE A NICE WAY TO EARN A LIVING. DOES IT FALL UNDER ANY JOB DESCRIPTION I MIGHT HAVE HEARD OF?
SAMARITAN? HUMANITARIAN? I DON'T KNOW; THE WORD WE USE IN THE FUTURE IS *SUPER-HERO.*
AND YOU WERE *BORN* LIKE THIS, RIGHT?
"ARE YOU KIDDING? I WAS BORN AS THE YOUNGEST OF SIX KIDS IN A BLUE-COLLAR FAMILY IN *QUEENS.*
"DAD DROVE A BUS. MOM WORKED IN A LAUNDERETTE. MY FIVE OLDER SISTERS WERE ALL PREGNANT IN *HIGH SCHOOL.*
THE ONLY WAY I WAS EVER GOING TO BE A SUPERHERO WAS BY TURNING MYSELF *INTO* ONE.

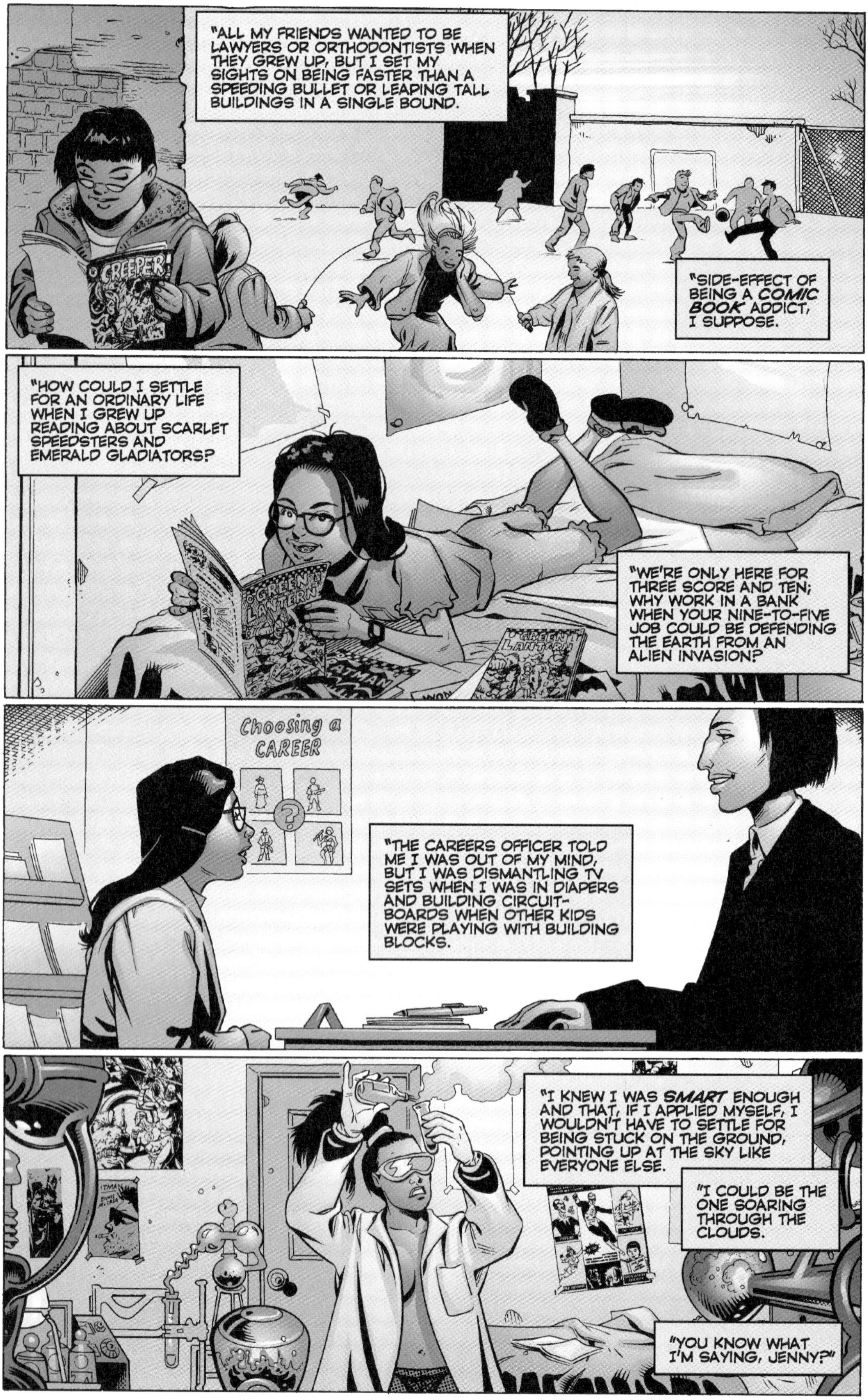
"ALL MY FRIENDS WANTED TO BE LAWYERS OR ORTHODONTISTS WHEN THEY GREW UP, BUT I SET MY SIGHTS ON BEING FASTER THAN A SPEEDING BULLET OR LEAPING TALL BUILDINGS IN A SINGLE BOUND.
CREEPER
"SIDE-EFFECT OF BEING A *COMIC BOOK* ADDICT, I SUPPOSE.
"HOW COULD I SETTLE FOR AN ORDINARY LIFE WHEN I GREW UP READING ABOUT SCARLET SPEEDSTERS AND EMERALD GLADIATORS?
GREEN LANTERN
GREEN LANTERN
"WE'RE ONLY HERE FOR THREE SCORE AND TEN; WHY WORK IN A BANK WHEN YOUR NINE-TO-FIVE JOB COULD BE DEFENDING THE EARTH FROM AN ALIEN INVASION?
Choosing a CAREER
"THE CAREERS OFFICER TOLD ME I WAS OUT OF MY MIND, BUT I WAS DISMANTLING TV SETS WHEN I WAS IN DIAPERS AND BUILDING CIRCUIT-BOARDS WHEN OTHER KIDS WERE PLAYING WITH BUILDING BLOCKS.
"I KNEW I WAS *SMART* ENOUGH AND THAT, IF I APPLIED MYSELF, I WOULDN'T HAVE TO SETTLE FOR BEING STUCK ON THE GROUND, POINTING UP AT THE SKY LIKE EVERYONE ELSE.
"I COULD BE THE ONE SOARING THROUGH THE CLOUDS.
"YOU KNOW WHAT I'M SAYING, JENNY?"

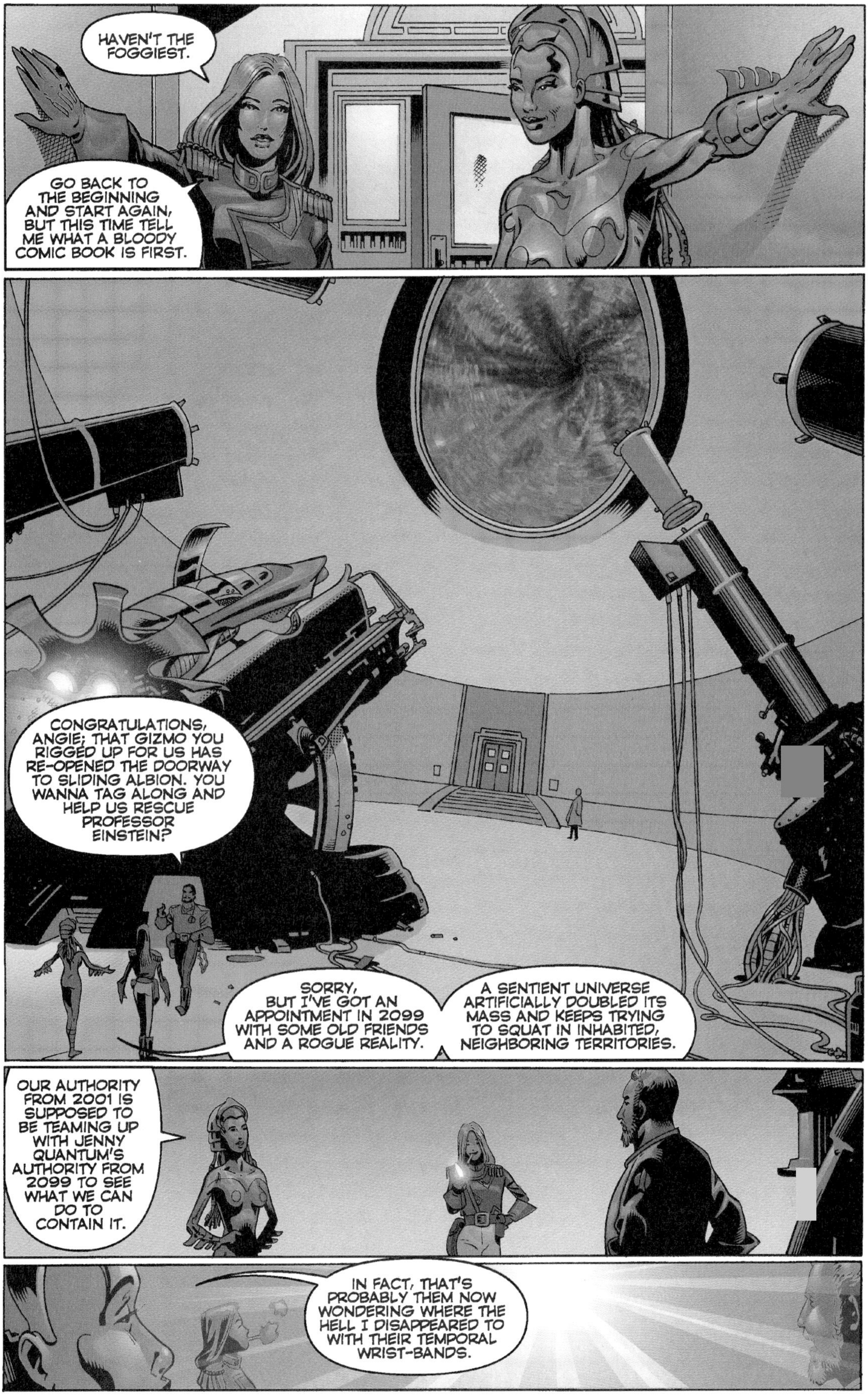
HAVEN'T THE FOGGIEST.
GO BACK TO THE BEGINNING AND START AGAIN, BUT THIS TIME TELL ME WHAT A BLOODY COMIC BOOK IS FIRST.
CONGRATULATIONS, ANGIE; THAT GIZMO YOU RIGGED UP FOR US HAS RE-OPENED THE DOORWAY TO SLIDING ALBION. YOU WANNA TAG ALONG AND HELP US RESCUE PROFESSOR EINSTEIN?
SORRY, BUT I'VE GOT AN APPOINTMENT IN 2099 WITH SOME OLD FRIENDS AND A ROGUE REALITY.
A SENTIENT UNIVERSE ARTIFICIALLY DOUBLED ITS MASS AND KEEPS TRYING TO SQUAT IN INHABITED, NEIGHBORING TERRITORIES.
OUR AUTHORITY FROM 2001 IS SUPPOSED TO BE TEAMING UP WITH JENNY QUANTUM'S AUTHORITY FROM 2099 TO SEE WHAT WE CAN DO TO CONTAIN IT.
IN FACT, THAT'S PROBABLY THEM NOW WONDERING WHERE THE HELL I DISAPPEARED TO WITH THEIR TEMPORAL WRIST-BANDS.

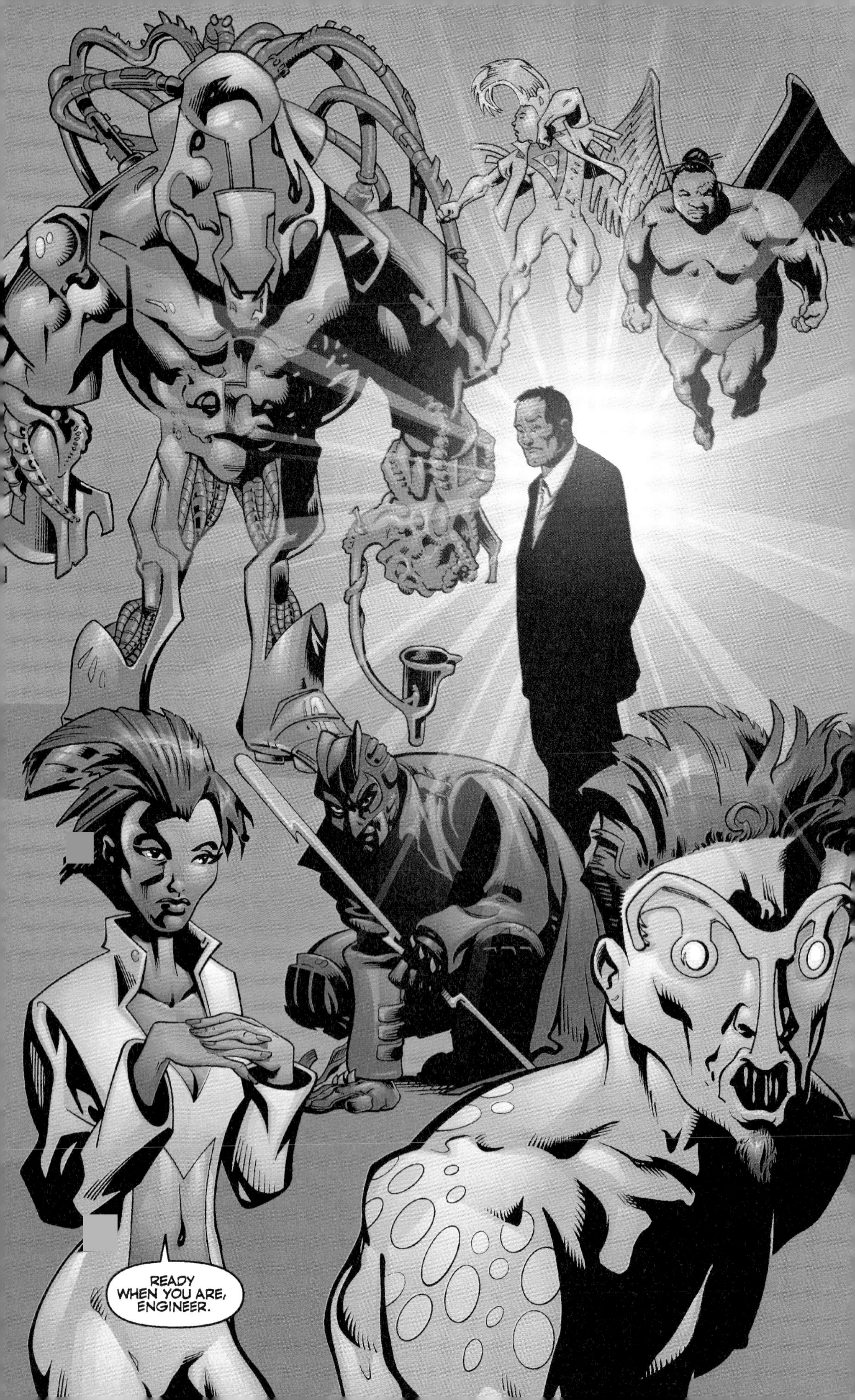
READY WHEN YOU ARE, ENGINEER.

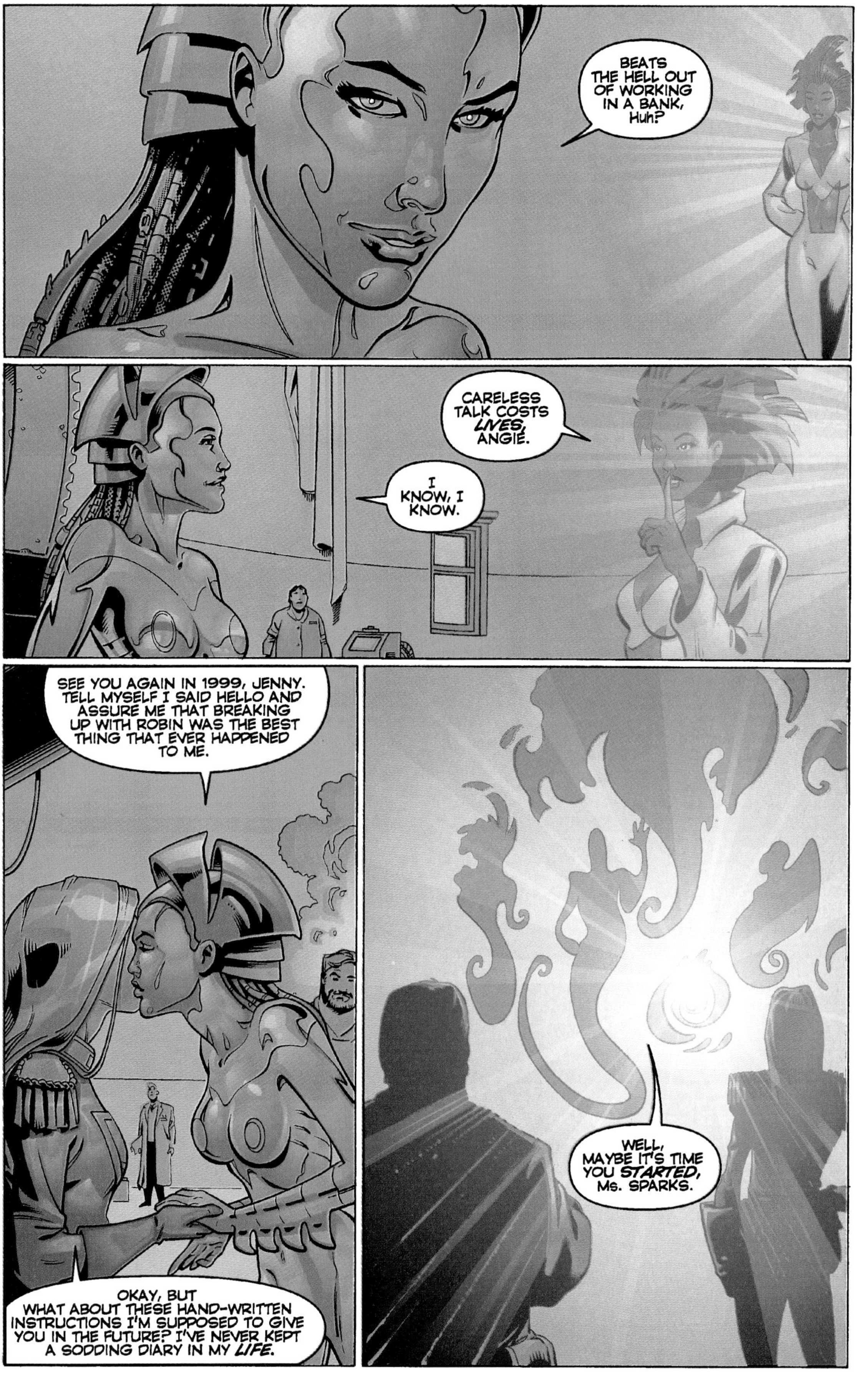
BEATS THE HELL OUT OF WORKING IN A BANK, Huh?
CARELESS TALK COSTS *LIVES*, ANGIE.
I KNOW, I KNOW.
SEE YOU AGAIN IN 1999, JENNY. TELL MYSELF I SAID HELLO AND ASSURE ME THAT BREAKING UP WITH ROBIN WAS THE BEST THING THAT EVER HAPPENED TO ME.
OKAY, BUT WHAT ABOUT THESE HAND-WRITTEN INSTRUCTIONS I'M SUPPOSED TO GIVE YOU IN THE FUTURE? I'VE NEVER KEPT A SODDING DIARY IN MY *LIFE*.
WELL, MAYBE IT'S TIME YOU *STARTED*, Ms. SPARKS.

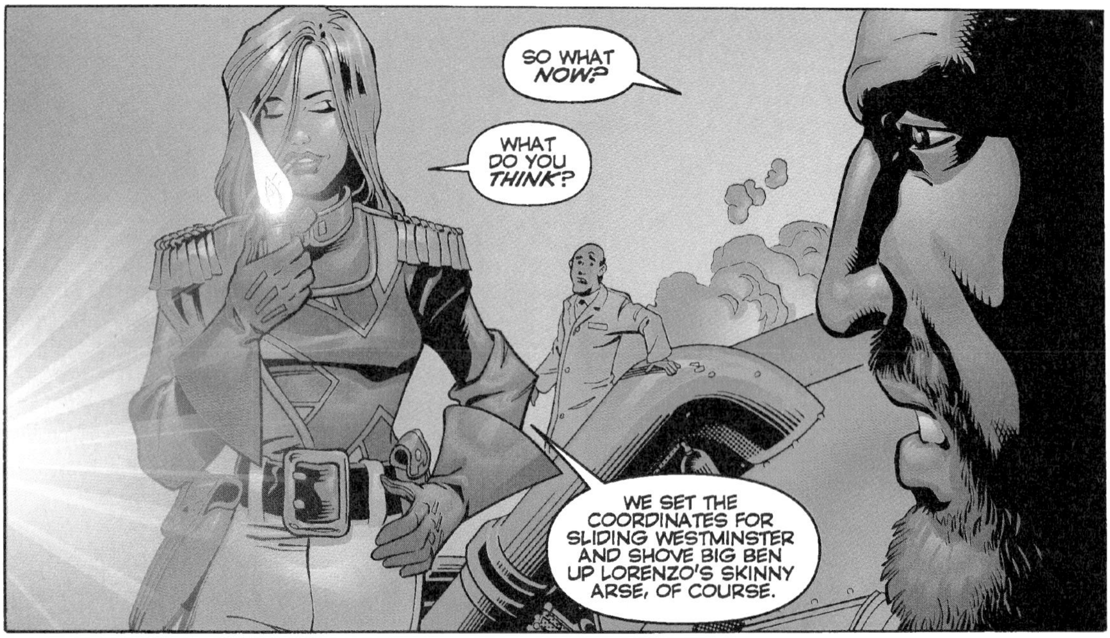
SO WHAT NOW?
WHAT DO YOU THINK?
WE SET THE COORDINATES FOR SLIDING WESTMINSTER AND SHOVE BIG BEN UP LORENZO'S SKINNY ARSE, OF COURSE.

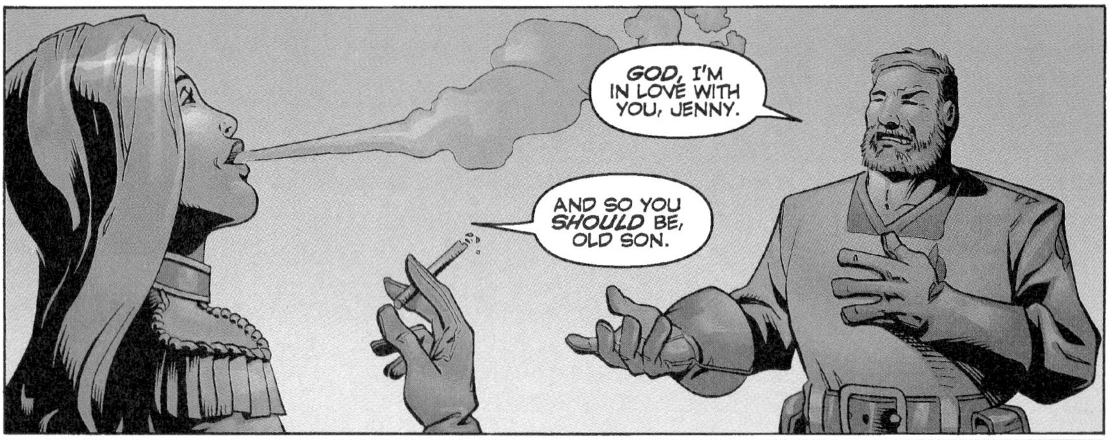
GOD, I'M IN LOVE WITH YOU, JENNY.
AND SO YOU SHOULD BE, OLD SON.

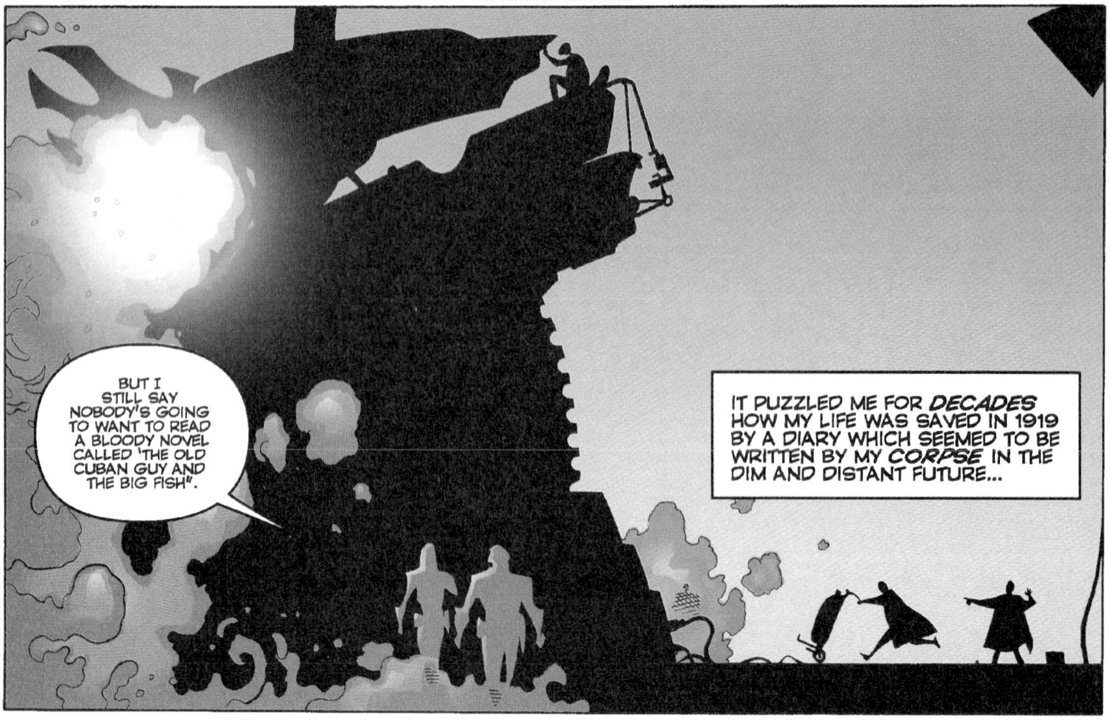
BUT I STILL SAY NOBODY'S GOING TO WANT TO READ A BLOODY NOVEL CALLED "THE OLD CUBAN GUY AND THE BIG FISH".
IT PUZZLED ME FOR DECADES HOW MY LIFE WAS SAVED IN 1919 BY A DIARY WHICH SEEMED TO BE WRITTEN BY MY CORPSE IN THE DIM AND DISTANT FUTURE...

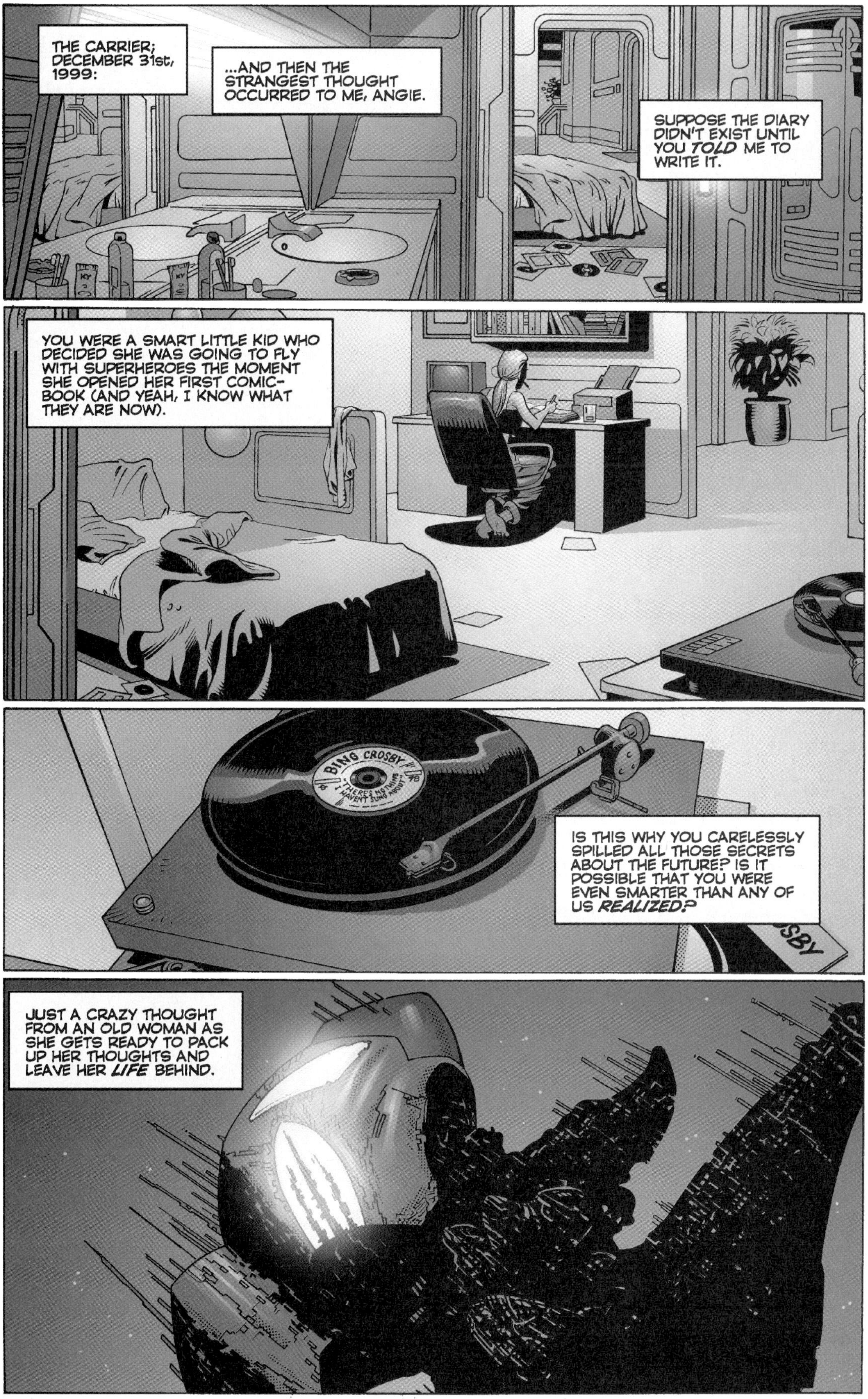
THE CARRIER; DECEMBER 31st, 1999:
...AND THEN THE STRANGEST THOUGHT OCCURRED TO ME, ANGIE.
SUPPOSE THE DIARY DIDN'T EXIST UNTIL YOU *TOLD* ME TO WRITE IT.
YOU WERE A SMART LITTLE KID WHO DECIDED SHE WAS GOING TO FLY WITH SUPERHEROES THE MOMENT SHE OPENED HER FIRST COMIC-BOOK (AND YEAH, I KNOW WHAT THEY ARE NOW).
BING CROSBY
IS THIS WHY YOU CARELESSLY SPILLED ALL THOSE SECRETS ABOUT THE FUTURE? IS IT POSSIBLE THAT YOU WERE EVEN SMARTER THAN ANY OF US *REALIZED?*
JUST A CRAZY THOUGHT FROM AN OLD WOMAN AS SHE GETS READY TO PACK UP HER THOUGHTS AND LEAVE HER *LIFE* BEHIND.

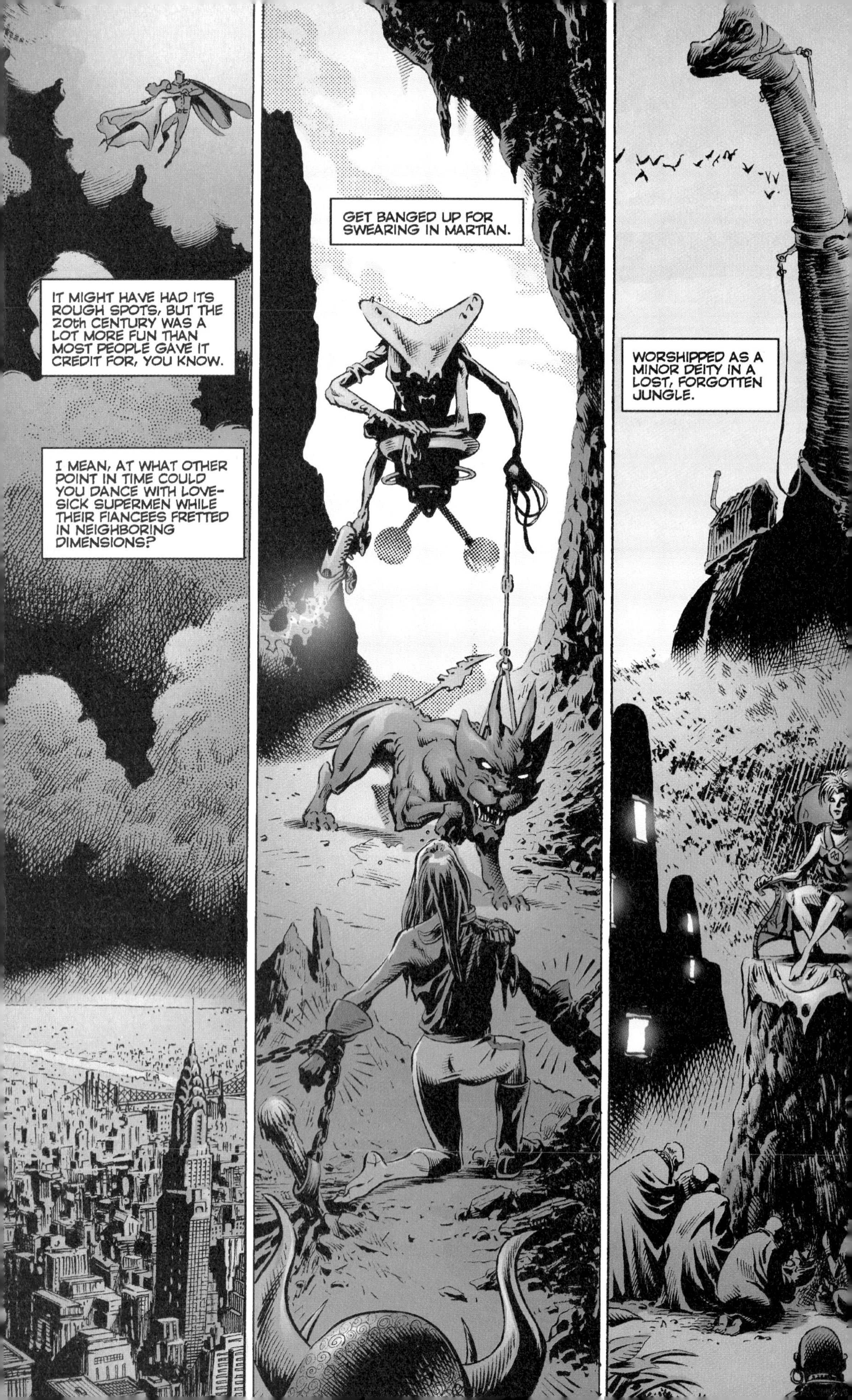
IT MIGHT HAVE HAD ITS ROUGH SPOTS, BUT THE 20th CENTURY WAS A LOT MORE FUN THAN MOST PEOPLE GAVE IT CREDIT FOR, YOU KNOW.
I MEAN, AT WHAT OTHER POINT IN TIME COULD YOU DANCE WITH LOVE-SICK SUPERMEN WHILE THEIR FIANCEES FRETTED IN NEIGHBORING DIMENSIONS?
GET BANGED UP FOR SWEARING IN MARTIAN.
WORSHIPPED AS A MINOR DEITY IN A LOST, FORGOTTEN JUNGLE.

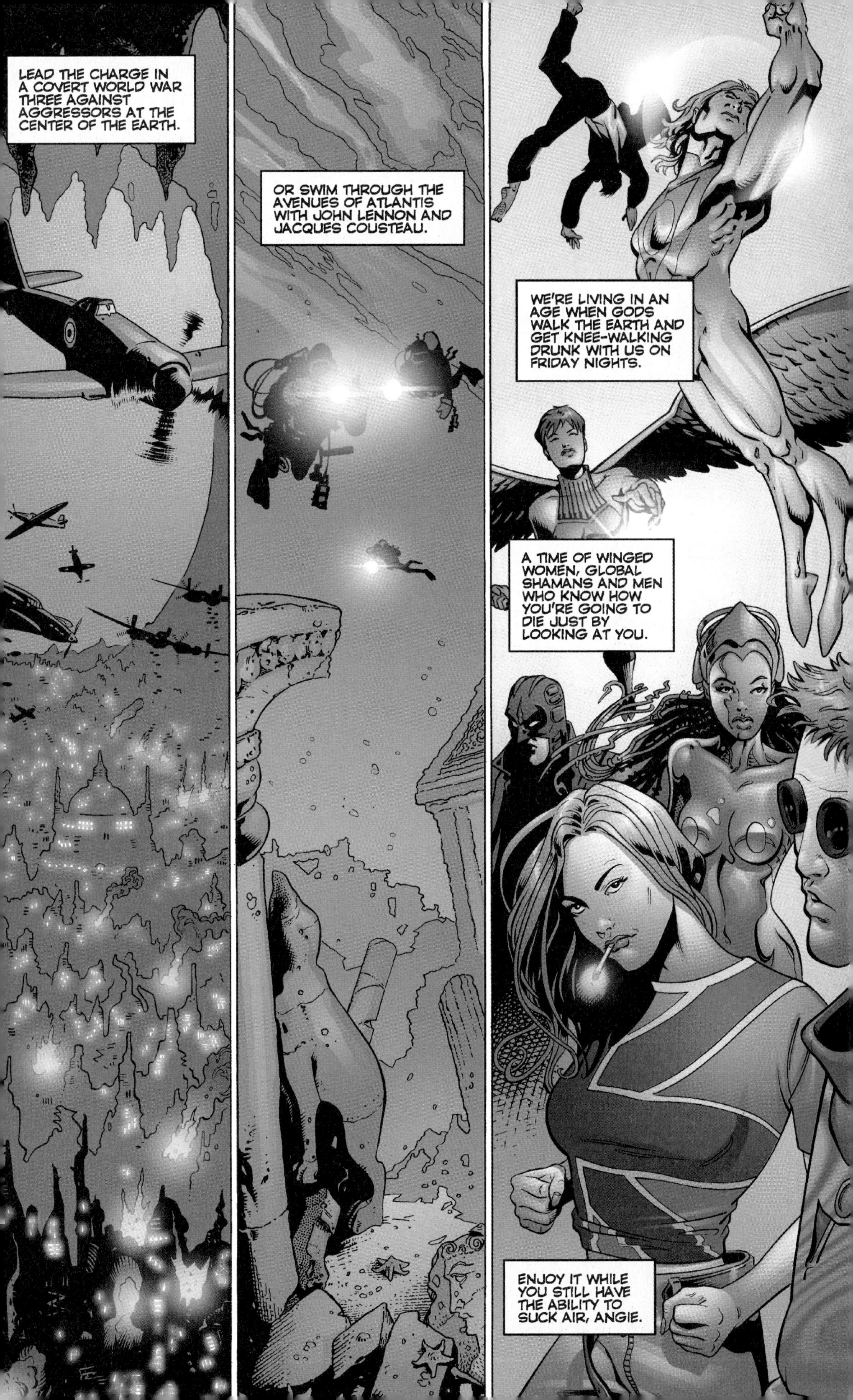
LEAD THE CHARGE IN A COVERT WORLD WAR THREE AGAINST AGGRESSORS AT THE CENTER OF THE EARTH.
OR SWIM THROUGH THE AVENUES OF ATLANTIS WITH JOHN LENNON AND JACQUES COUSTEAU.
WE'RE LIVING IN AN AGE WHEN GODS WALK THE EARTH AND GET KNEE-WALKING DRUNK WITH US ON FRIDAY NIGHTS.
A TIME OF WINGED WOMEN, GLOBAL SHAMANS AND MEN WHO KNOW HOW YOU'RE GOING TO DIE JUST BY LOOKING AT YOU.
ENJOY IT WHILE YOU STILL HAVE THE ABILITY TO SUCK AIR, ANGIE.

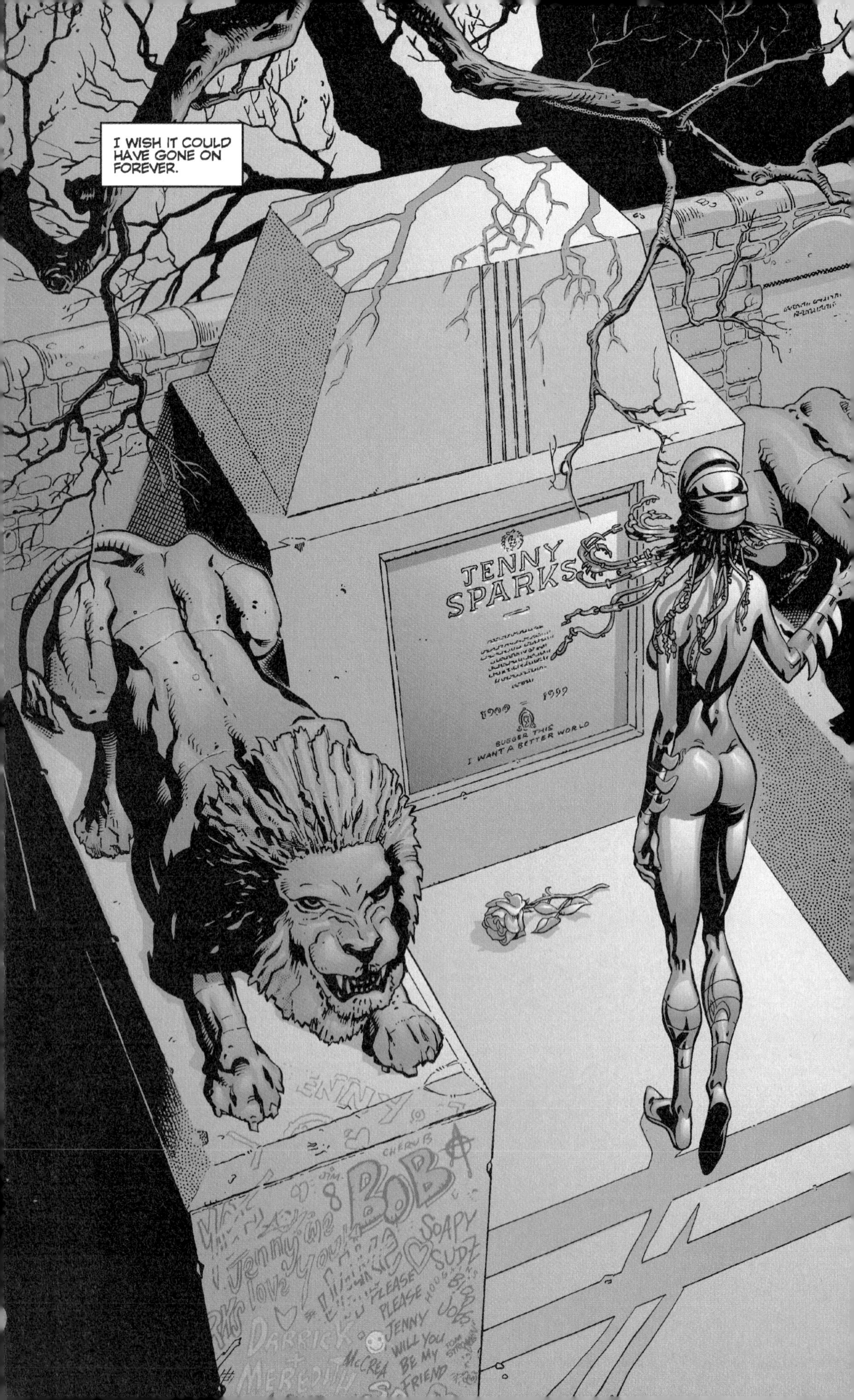
I WISH IT COULD HAVE GONE ON FOREVER.
JENNY SPARKS
1900 – 1999
BUGGER THIS I WANT A BETTER WORLD
CHERUBS
BOB
Jenny we love you!
SOAPY SUDZ
PLEASE PLEASE JENNY WILL YOU BE MY FRIEND

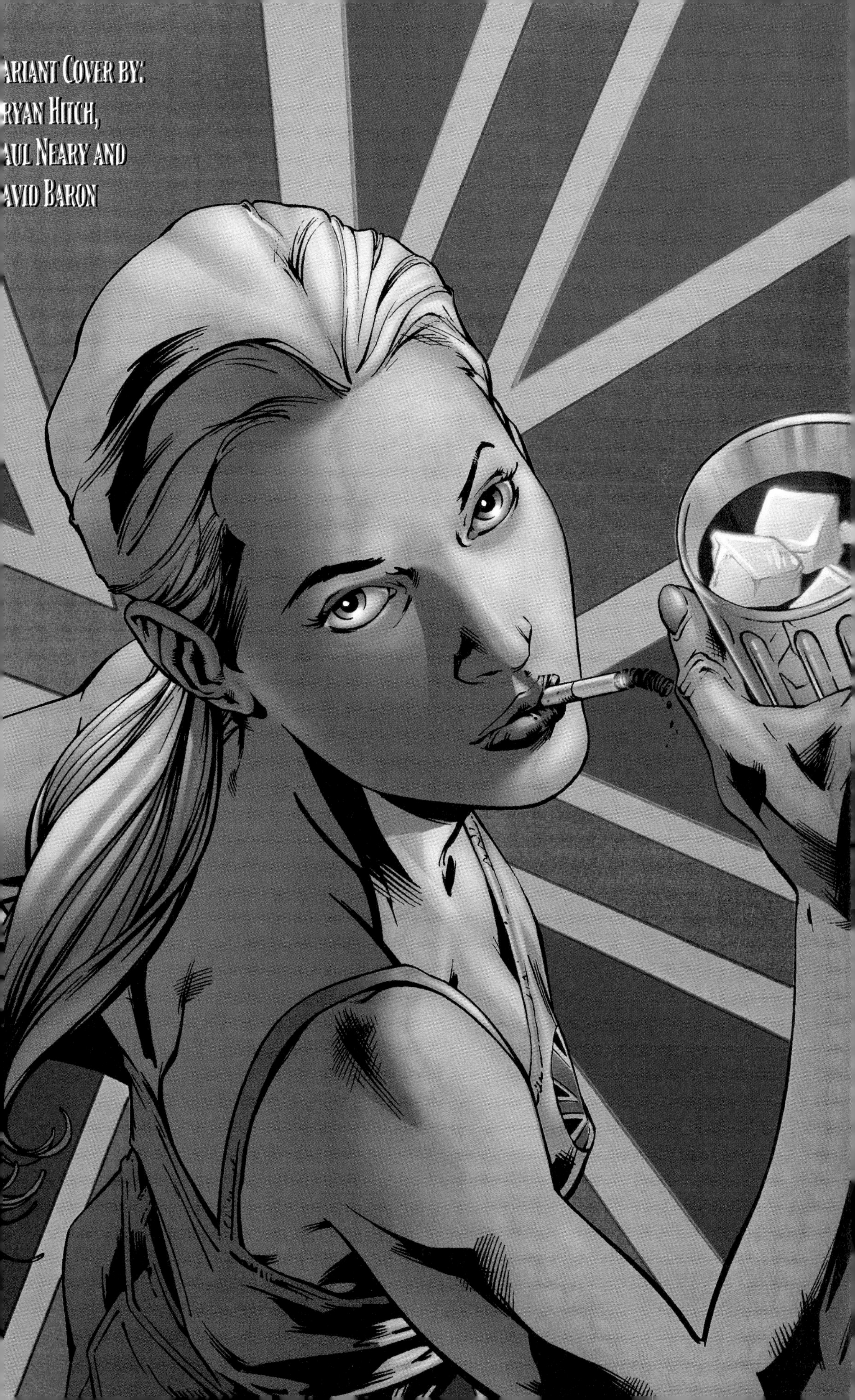
ARIANT COVER BY:
RYAN HITCH,
AUL NEARY AND
AVID BARON

WILDSTORM COLLECTIONS

The Authority: Relentless
Ellis/Hitch/Neary

**The Authority:
Under New Management**
Ellis/Millar/Hitch/
Quitely/Neary/Scott

Crimson: Loyalty & Loss
Augustyn/Ramos/Hope

**Crimson:
Heaven & Earth**
Augustyn/Ramos/Hope

**Crimson:
Earth Angel**
Augustyn/Ramos/Hope

**Deathblow:
Sinners and Saints**
Choi/Lee/Sale/Scott

**Danger Girl:
The Dangerous
Collection #1-3**
Hartnell/Campbell/Garner

**Divine Right:
Collected Edition #1-3**
Lee/Williams

Gen¹³
Choi/Lee/Campbell/Garner

Gen¹³: #13 ABC
Choi/Lee/Campbell/Garner

Gen¹³: Bootleg Vol. 1
Various writers and
artists

Gen¹³: Grunge the Movie
Warren

Gen¹³: I Love New York
Arcudi/Frank/Smith

Gen¹³: Interactive Plus
Various writers and
artists

Gen¹³: Starting Over
Choi/Lee/Campbell/Garner

**Gen¹³:
We'll Take Manhattan**
Lobdell/Benes/Sibal

**Kurt Busiek's Astro City:
Life in the Big City**
Busiek/Anderson

**Kurt Busiek's Astro City:
Confession**
Busiek/Anderson/Blyberg

**Kurt Busiek's Astro City:
Family Album**
Busiek/Anderson/Blyberg

**Kurt Busiek's Astro City:
Tarnished Angel**
Busiek/Anderson/Blyberg

**Leave It to Chance:
Shaman's Rain**
Robinson/Smith

**Leave It to Chance:
Trick or Threat**
Robinson/Smith/Freeman

Wetworks: Rebirth
Portacio/Choi/Williams

**Planetary/Authority:
Ruling the World**
Ellis/Jimenez/Lanning

**Planetary:
All Over the world
and Other Stories**
Ellis/Cassaday

**Planetary:
The Fourth Man**
Ellis/Cassaday

**StormWatch:
Force of Nature**
Ellis/Raney/Elliott

**StormWatch:
Lightning Strikes**
Ellis/Raney/Lee/
Elliott/Williams

**StormWatch:
Change or Die**
Ellis/Raney/Jimenez

**StormWatch:
A Finer World**
Ellis/Hitch/Neary

WildC.A.T.s: Gang War
Moore/Various

**WildC.A.T.s:
Gathering of Eagles**
Claremont/Lee/Williams

**WildC.A.T.s:
Homecoming**
Moore/Various

WildC.A.T.s/X-Men
Various writers and
artists

**Wildcats:
Street Smart**
Lobdell/Charest/Friend

**Wildcats:
Vicious Circles**
Casey/Phillips

WildStorm Rising
Windsor-Smith/Various

OTHER COLLECTIONS
OF INTEREST

**The Batman Adventures:
Mad Love**
Dini/Timm

**Batman:
The Dark Knight Returns**
Miller/Janson/Varley

Batman:Faces
Wagner

**Batman:
The Killing Joke**
Moore/Bolland/Higgins

Batman:Year One
Miller/Mazzucchelli/Lewis

Camelot 3000
Barr/Bolland/Various

The Golden Age
Robinson/Smith

Kingdom Come
Waid/Ross

Ronin
Miller

Watchmen
Moore/Gibbons

For the nearest comics
shop carrying collected
editions and monthly
titles from DC Comics,
call 1-888-COMIC BOOK.